BOUGHT. APRIL 1997.

For Ian.

D. J. Sweeney. 15.7.97.

GW00630757

A LANCASHIRE TRIANGLE

PART ONE

A History of the London & North Western's Railways
in and around the South Lancashire Coalfields

By

DENNIS SWEENEY

TRIANGLE PUBLISHING

Copyright © D. J. Sweeney 1996
First published 1996 by Triangle Publishing.
British Library Cataloguing in Publication Data.
Sweeney D. J.
A Lancashire Triangle Part One
ISBN 0-952-9333-06
Printed in Great Britain by
The Amadeus Press Limited, Huddersfield.
Text by D. J. Sweeney.
Maps by Alan Palmer.
Compiled by Alan Price.
Train movement tables by Brian Kaye.

Cover Photo:

Working from Speakmans Sidings, Leigh, to Sandersons Sidings, Worsley, Stanier 2-8-0 No 48324, banked by another member of the same class, heads a long coal train through Tyldesley in 1965. At Sandersons the train will be split for onward transportation by NCB locomotives, via the colliery railway, to Sandhole Colliery for washing.

Photo, J.R. Carter

Plate 1. Tyldesley lost its railway in 1969 but lives on in the form of the Authors Model Railway.

CONTENTS

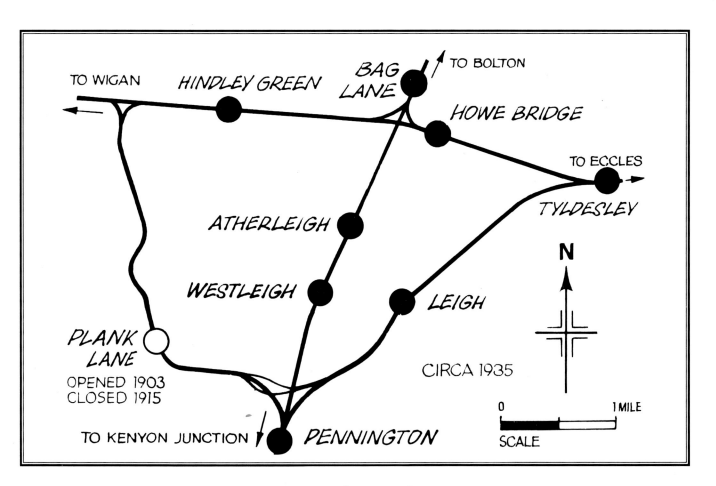

A Lancashire Triangle.

INTRODUCTION

IT has been my primary objective to deal with those railways of the Leigh, Tyldesley and Atherton areas of South Lancashire, bounded by the London & North Westerns Railway lines from Springs Branch Junction to Eccles Junction via Tyldesley, from Tyldesley to Kenyon Junction via Leigh, and Pennington Junction to Bickershaw Junction via Abram. Thus have devoted my efforts to this end. I cannot however, completely neglect other routes and connecting lines that are essential to illustrate the workings of the overall railway scene within this "Lancashire Triangle". Similarly, some attention must be paid to the proliferation of industrial lines built to serve the coalfields of the district. These were, in the first instance, the catalyst for the beginnings of the railways, not only of South Lancashire, but the country as a whole.

There had, by the turn of the nineteenth century, been colliery tramways or plateways for many years in various parts of the country, often linking colliery to a navigable river or canal. All of these were either horse drawn or worked by gravity, which with a few exceptions served only their immediate locality. None were for public use.

A proposal in 1801 by the Surrey Iron Railway Company for a horse drawn railway of some six miles between Wandsworth and Croydon, for goods only, became the country's first Public Railway Act to be passed by Parliament. The first fare paying passengers were carried on the Swansea & Mumbles Railway in 1807, again another horse drawn railway in isolation.

Richard Trevithick, a Cornishman and generally accepted as the inventor of the steam locomotive, had in 1805, taken a locomotive to Newcastle where, he felt his revolutionary ideas would be more readily accepted than they had apparently been elsewhere. This was the first of a number of visits to the north-east by Trevithick, where he met and inspired the young George Stephenson and other engineers who were busy with the stationary steam engines there.

A number of engineers began to investigate the locomotive and its possibilities. In 1812 Blenkinson & Murrays rack and pinnion locomotives trundled along the Leeds and Middleton Colliery Railway. At the same time Robert Daglish built his "Walking Horse" to Blenkinsops pattern on the Orrell Colliery Railway and in 1814 Stephenson built his first locomotive "*Blucher*" in the north-east. He recognised the failings of these early locomotives and encouraged by his employers set about trying to improve performance.

Between 1819 and 1821 Stephenson built the Hetton Colliery Railway near Sunderland, eight miles in length and using no less than five of his locomotives. In 1821 Stephenson, now of independent means, approached Edward Pease the promoter of the Stockton & Darlington Railway and persuaded him to use locomotives on the railway. Subsequently the relevant Parliamentary Act was amended to allow locomotive use. Stephenson was appointed engineer on the Stockton & Darlington and on its opening day, 27th September 1825, drove his new "*Locomotion No. 1*" hauling the directors coach and no less than 33 loaded wagons to tumultuous applause. Although a colliery line and in part worked by stationary engines using rope haulage, in the early years of its life a single vehicle for passenger use was horse drawn at little more than walking pace.

Plans for the Liverpool & Manchester Railway first emerged in 1822, the subsequent history of which is well documented. Some years before Stephenson had said "I will do something in coming time which will astonish all England", he certainly would and did!

South Lancashire is an area that can most certainly lay claim to have been present at the birth of the worlds mainline railways.

Situated between the expanding cities of Liverpool and Manchester lay quiet towns and villages that were soon to become the centre stage for a world revolution in transport. Existing "roads" alternated between quagmires in winter and rutted ways in summer and were incapable of meeting the expanding demands of industry and commerce.

The recently built canals offered a much better prospect for the transportation of goods and materials, providing competition against the pack horse and paying handsome dividends to canal investors of 30% or more, which caused many industrialist to feel they were paying too much for their usage. The canals too were subject to the vagaries of the weather, often frozen up for days on end in winters generally more severe than those of recent decades and in the estuarys tidal flows limited the hours during which traffic could be moved.

It is against this background of inadequate and sometimes expensive modes of carriage that the railways emerged as the prime mover of people and materials, a position in which for the most part they remained unchallenged for a hundred years.

Parliament, conscious of the dividends being paid to canal investors were to place a moratorium on the emerging railways limiting their profits to 10%.

The opening of The Liverpool & Manchester Railway in September 1830 signalled to the world the arrival of railways as a force to be reckoned with, for within, it embodied many of the characteristics of today's modern railway. Double track, locomotives, timetables and stations, all these incorporated together for the first time on George Stephenson's Inter-City precursor. Without doubt George Stephenson can rightfully be regarded as the father of mainline railways. It was he, who had learned his trade on the plateways and in the engine-houses of North-East England who was to persuade others to have a similar faith to his own unshakeable belief in the fledgling steam locomotive. It was by no means assured that the Liverpool-Manchester Railway would use locomotives as against the stationary engine, rope hauled idea, hence the Rainhill Trials. With his determination, he more than any other brought about this transport revolution and in this little corner of Lancashire the foundations of Britain's mainline railway system were firmly laid. The pattern and operation of this new order became the standard which the rest of the world was to observe and follow.

Various railway companies vied for permission to build lines in the area, attracted in many cases by the extensive coal deposits that were to be found in South Lancashire. This in turn led to a rich variety of motive power being used, a situation that lasted well into the 1950's when locomotives built by the London & North Western, Lancashire & Yorkshire, Midland, and Great Central Railways mingled with the later London Midland and British Railways designs, plus a host of industrial locomotives built by numerous private firms.

Looking back it seems hard to believe that so many of our once busy and congested lines are now gone. Miles of track have been closed and lifted leaving whole communities devoid of rail transport. Of course these local closures were just a part in an orgy of destruction that saw 10,000 route miles of track thrown on the scrap heap. The decline of the mining industry in the once mighty Lancashire Coalfield was, at least in part, responsible for the parallel decline of the railways in the area. The rising ascendancy of motor transport and its "convenience factor" which, with continued government support for road building schemes over all else for some 40 years, along with a total lack of any co-ordinated transport policy, merely compounded the problem. Only now is the folly of this beginning to dawn on some of our political leaders, to late however for many of our local lines.

With the opening of the Channel Tunnel a new dimension in rail transport emerges. The connection to the mainline railways of Europe offer tremendous opportunities and could give a much needed boost to rail transport and together with the recognition of the choking environmental consequences that uncontrolled road growth produces, provide the impetus for a change of transport policy. Yet, the rail network this side of the Channel would appear to be under threat from further closures as charges are hiked up, driving more custom from rail to road. At the time of writing the privatisation of the railways is a cause of much anxiety as a result of government ministerial dogma.

Anticipation by a few self-interested parties is outweighed by the acute reservation of the overwhelming majority of railwaymen and rail users who fear that it is merely a Beeching Mk. II in disguise. Only time will tell!

I have set out to deal with the railways of "A Lancashire Triangle" on what is generally a chronological basis, beginning in Part One with the Bolton & Leigh and Kenyon & Leigh Junction Railways together with the early colliery branch railways connected to them within the triangle. The Wigan-Tyldesley-Eccles branch of the London & North Western Railway completes the volume.

Part Two will examine the Tyldesley-Leigh-Pennington, Pennington Loop lines, the Bickershaw Branch from Pennington South to Bickershaw Junction and the Roe Green to Bolton Great Moor Street branch. A look at the colliery lines and the locomotives employed thereon follows and in conclusion a brief summary of proposals that might have been, and an up to date appraisal of future rail prospects for the area.

D. J. Sweeney,
Leigh, 1996.

ACKNOWLEDGEMENTS

THE research and compilation of material that have resulted in these volumes are the culmination of some seven years work which has occupied a great deal of my "spare time," fitted in between my full time occupation as a Joiner and Professional Modelmaker and I would like to express my gratitude to all those who have contributed in any way, shape or form, for without their help it would not have been possible.

First and foremost I must thank Alf Yates, Gerry Bent, Ian Isherwood, Jim Carter, Peter Hampson and Brian Hilton who allowed me access to their complete collections of photographs and in this field particular mention must be given to my good friend W. D. Cooper, now in his ninety third year, who toiled relentlessly in his darkroom to provide me with necessary material for inclusion. Their photographs constitute the majority of views in this work. I hope I have done them justice.

Sadly, Brian Hilton passed away in December 1995. No less than three photographic contributors to this book have passed away in 1996; Alex Mann, Les Smith and Jimmy Jones. Alex had photographed the railway scene around Wigan over many years whilst Les had done valuable research on local Post Office history and the internment of German POW's in Leigh during World War I. Jimmy was a founder member of Tyldesley & District Historical Society, the ex-miner turned poet, widely praised for his efforts. Jimmy first provided me with material in 1980, as an aid in the construction of a model of Tyldesley Station. Over the years any railway material that came Jimmy's way would be passed on to me. He knew I would snap it up. Jimmy, Alex, Les and Brian will all be sadly missed by their many friends.

In matters of signalling operations and locomotive movements the efforts of Bill Paxford, Peter Hampson, Tom Yates and Jim Carter have been substantial and their recollections of a lifetime's work as Professional Railwaymen will also be found in the little anecdotes included in the text.

Frank Talbot, Henry Parkinson and Cyril Golding have provided much of the information regarding the industrial lines of the locality and Harry Townleys snippets of local information, which by co-incidence were contemporary with my own research into the early mineral railways of the district, have come from a lifetime's research into industrial railways covering a much wider area and I thoroughly recommend his and his associates work to readers. The help of Leigh Archive staff, in particular Local Historian Tony Ashcroft, are acknowledged, as is the assistance of Barry King, Wigan Planning Department, for his help in the appraisal of possible future transport infrastructure developments within the Greater Manchester area and Wigan Metropolitan Borough in particular.

Brian Gomm has, over a number of years, provided help and assistance with the publication of photographs in the Leigh, Tyldesley and Atherton Journal, often as a quest for further information. To Brian and all those people who responded to offer information, many of whom I have never met yet have shown a genuine interest in what I was trying to achieve, I sincerely say "Thank You'.

Above all others, to my dear wife Dorothy, whose tolerance and forbearance extend beyond the bounds of all reasonable proportions, for when every corner of the house was occupied by some item of railway or photographic paraphernalia, she would only say, "do we have to have all this rigmarole". God bless her.

A Lancashire Triangle

Railways in the North West in the early British Railways Era

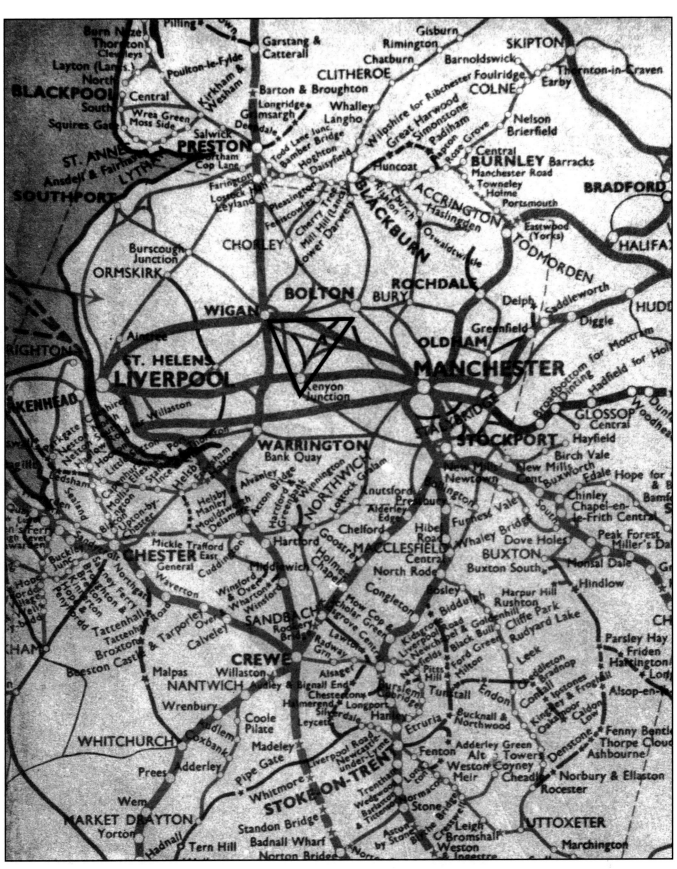

CHAPTER I

THE BOLTON & LEIGH
and
THE KENYON & LEIGH JUNCTION
RAILWAYS

Plate 2. With Fletcher Street Signal Box in the background, a 3F, 0-6-OT *"Jinty"* No. 47378 makes its way from Crook Street Coal Sidings en-route to Lever Street Yard with a morning trip working about 1962. After a spot of shunting at Lever Street dropping off fulls, any empties would be collected prior to working up the line to shunt Plodder Lane Yard and again collecting empties thence returning to Crook Street. Fletcher Street cabin was the only signal box on the Bolton-Kenyon line to have water laid on. *Photo, J. R. Carter.*

THE BOLTON & LEIGH RAILWAY
and
THE KENYON & LEIGH JUNCTION RAILWAY

THE Bolton and Leigh was of course the first public railway in Lancashire, opened for use on 1st August 1828 from its terminus at Derby Street, Bolton, to Wm. Hulton's Collieries at Pendlebury Fold near Chequerbent for the carriage of goods. Stephenson's estimate for the railway was £43,143. 1s. 0d. (£43,143·5) and the Act authorised that £44,000 should be raised before construction began. A further Act of 26th March 1828 authorised an additional £25,000 to be raised in order to complete the railway to its junction with the Leeds-Liverpool Canal at Leigh, the original estimate having been insufficient. The line in its entirety was open for traffic, according to the Manchester Courier, towards the end of March 1830.

That the railway did not cross the canal, but merely went to it, would seem on the one hand an attempt to placate the canal authorities who clearly saw the threat to them that the railway posed, yet on the other a clear indication that they, (the railways) would at some future date wish to make a connection with the Liverpool and Manchester Railway which was under construction, the latter having received Royal Assent in 1826.

The meeting point for these two concerns was to be at Kenyon Junction in 1831, brought about by the construction of The Kenyon and Leigh Junction Railway from Twist Lane, Leigh, where it met the Bolton and Leigh Railway end on, to its junction with the Liverpool & Manchester Railway at Kenyon. The worlds first mainline railway junction between independent railway companies.

The Bolton and Leigh Railway received the Royal Assent on 31st March 1825 and was to run from Lecturers Closes, Bolton, at the foot of Derby Street, to the Leeds-Liverpool Canal at Leigh. George Stephenson was appointed engineer for the projected railway with Hugh Steel as surveyor, ably assisted by Robert Daglish of Orrell Colliery who supervised much of the work, along with Robert Stephenson, George's elder brother. George Stephenson had also been appointed engineer on the Liverpool & Manchester Railway which had suffered a temporary setback with the defeat of its 1824 Bill which occurred on 31st May 1825. Although as a result of this Stephenson was dismissed, he was later re-appointed after a new survey and its guidance through Parliament, by C.B.Vignoles, of the Liverpool & Manchester Railways second Bill. Stephenson's brusk Northumbrian manner and lack of formal education had not stood up well to the canal inspired objections in Committee.

Opening in 1828 the Bolton & Leigh Railway was originally single track throughout, with rope worked inclines using stationary steam engines of 20 horse power (hp) at Daubhill and 50hp at Chequerbent. The opening ceremony took place at Pendlebury Fold were a locomotive, built by the Stephenson's at their Newcastle-on-Tyne works, was "put on the rails" and later, during the journey to Bolton, named the "Lancashire Witch". The complete train consisted of a coach and six wagons reserved for the Hulton family and other notables, plus another seven for Ladies and Gentlemen and the accompanying band.

The Acts for the Bolton & Leigh Railway also authorised branch lines, at the Bolton end, to the Union Foundry on Deansgate (now occupied by the bus station and market hall), Wm Hulton's coal yard at Great Moor Street, and also to the Manchester Bolton & Bury Canal. In the event the latter branch was never built. The branches to Deansgate and Great Moor Street opened in 1829, although the passenger "terminus" at Great Moor Street probably didn't open until through services to Liverpool commenced in 1831.

The "signalling" arrangements at the inclines are in themselves worth a mention. The wagons were attached to the rope at the bottom of the incline and when ready to ascend, the rope was pulled, causing a spanner placed on the rope at the top to fall of. The engine house attendant then put into operation the machinery to haul the train up the incline.

At Bolton the original terminus of the railway was at street level, with the "booking office" little more than a shed. Criticism of facilities led to some improvements being carried out about 1849, the pioneering nature of the Bolton & Leigh Railway and its stations were slowly evolving into a more recognisable form of "user friendly" railway.

As the railway age gathered momentum the general improvement in locomotive performance allowed cable haulage to be discontinued, probably from the late 1840's and consequently the single track became increasingly inadequate to handle the volume of traffic.

An incident on the morning of 28th January

1858 seems to indicate the abandonment of cable haulage, when a locomotive called the "*Redstart*" descending down the incline from Daubhill to Bolton with a freight train ran-away, unceremoniously reducing the Bolton & Leigh station to a pile of rubble, killing an unfortunate platelayer who had hitched a ride from Atherton on the footplate. The locomotives crew had managed to jump clear before the impact.

At the inquiry into the accident the inspector recommended doubling of the track. This however was not carried out for over twenty years when further Acts of 1878 and 1880 authorised deviations at Daubhill and Chequerbent, along with new stations at Daubhill, Chequerbent and Bag Lane.

The original Bolton & Leigh terminus was patched up and continued in use until 28th September 1874 when a new station with four platforms was opened on an adjacent site at Great Moor Street. This also built to cater for Bolton-Manchester traffic via the branch from Roe Green Junction which opened for passenger traffic on 1st April 1875.

Double track between Pennington and Atherton Junctions opened on 31st May 1880 and through Bag Lane on 4th July 1880. The final $4\frac{1}{2}$ miles to Bolton were inspected by Colonel Rich and officially opened to passenger traffic on Sunday 1st February 1885. Kenyon Junction to Pennington South Junction had been doubled in conjunction with the works for the Tyldesley-Leigh-Pennington Branch at a cost of £7,000, authorised by Euston in 1864. A connecting curve from Atherton Junction to the Tyldesley-Wigan line at Howe Bridge West Junction, originally called Chowbent, was also constructed under the 1880 Act and opened in January 1883. Atherton Junction-Howe Bridge East Junction was constructed under the 1861 Eccles-Tyldesley-Wigan Acts.

The Kenyon & Leigh Junction Railway received the Royal Assent on 14th May 1829, to build a railway from Leigh, joining with the Bolton & Leigh Railway at Twist Lane, to Kenyon, thereby connecting with the Liverpool & Manchester Railway now at an advanced stage of construction. This was a full five months before the celebrated Rainhill Trials that were to demonstrate "state of the art" railway locomotives to the world, one of which, namely Timothy Ackworth's "*Sans Pareil*" was purchased by the Bolton & Leigh Railway in 1832 for the sum of £110.00, after a period of "hire" at £15 per month. It continued working on the line until 1844, running two journeys each way between Bolton and Kenyon Junction, a total mileage of about 100 miles per day. Later it found new employment as a pumping engine at Coppull Colliery until 1863. In 1864 it was presented to the Science Museum, Kensington, where it can be seen today.

Through traffic commenced over the Kenyon & Leigh line on 3rd January 1831 when goods services began between Liverpool and Bolton. On 2nd June 1831 a select group of "Gentlemen" were conveyed by special train to Newton Races and on the 13th June 1831 passenger services over the line began, taking 1 hr 40mins for the $28\frac{1}{2}$ mile journey between Bolton and Liverpool. Trains departed Great Moor Street at 6.45am and 2pm, returning from Liverpool at 10am and 5.30pm, with fares at, inside 5s. and outside at 3/6d. The inside accommodation provided by two coaches named "*Elephant*" and "*Castle*", the external accommodation, fully open to the elements, being on wooden seats in open wagons.

Other locomotives owned by the Bolton & Leigh in 1831 were the "*Union*" built by Rothwell, Hick & Co, Bolton in 1830 and two locomotives namely "*Salamander*" and "*Veteran*" built by Crook & Dean, also of Bolton.

The lessee of the Bolton & Leigh and Kenyon & Leigh Junction Railways was John Hargreaves, who by the mid 1830's owned about 200 wagons. He was paying about £9,000 per annum for sole rights to all traffic to Leigh and Bolton and also had contracts with the Liverpool & Manchester Railway. Hargreaves was already well established as a local carrier prior to the arrival of the railway and later, in 1842, joined with Hick at the Soho Foundry, Bolton, becoming Hick, Hargreaves & Co. In August 1845 the Bolton & Leigh and Kenyon & Leigh Junction Railways were absorbed by the Grand Junction Railway who terminated Hargreaves carrier contracts as from 31st December 1845.

The Bolton Great Moor Street Station of 1874 had booking offices at street level, whereas the four new platforms were at an elevated level approached now by way of a bridge over Crook Street. Added accommodation was provided at platform level in the form of General Waiting Rooms, Luggage & Parcels Office, Toilets, Station Master's Office, Foremans Office and a Carriage & Wagon Office.

Great Moor Street Station was controlled from Bolton No. 1 Signal Box. Traffic for the coal drops at Hulton's Coal Yard, which had two roads parallel to the platforms, was drawn out of Crook Street Yard to be worked wrong line and pushed into the sidings. These and also the horse dock at Great Moor Street controlled by Bolton No. 1 cabin.

In the 1940's there was still a good compliment of staff employed here, Station Master, Station Master's Clerk, 2 Platform Foremen, 3 Passenger

Guards, 3 Call Boys and 1 Passenger Shunter. The call boys night duties included lighting fires in the guards brake vans working out of Crook Street and raising the guards as and when required.

Most of the passenger traffic working out of Great Moor Street was push-pull worked. The 6.15am from Warrington however was not, thus requiring the locomotive to run round at Bolton. The platform foreman would contact Bolton No. 1 box for permission to set the coaches back, (towards the signal box) on No. 2 platform. This done the passenger shunter would apply the hand brake in the guards van, hook off the engine which dropped back to the block, set by hand, the cross-over road to No. 1 platform and signal the engine across and re-set the points. When clear, the coaches on No. 2 road would be levered by the shunter allowing gravity and momentum to take its course with the brake again being applied in the guards van, hopefully bringing the coaches to a halt before hitting the stop block. The engine now running out of No. 1 platform and onto its stock in No. 2, ready to work the 8.23 am to Liverpool.

The tradition of special trains for horse racing enthusiasts established in 1831 was continued throughout the life of the Bolton & Leigh Railway with Chester race specials on selected days.

Crook Street Yard handled a great variety of traffic in the exchange sidings, complimented by two large warehouses, one for perishable traffic situated on Chandos Street and a four road ware-house for general merchandise situated between the latter and the main running lines into Great Moor Street Station. On the opposite side of Chandos Street there was a landsale yard for coal traffic, with, alongside Crook Street the stables. The number of private sidings served from Crook Street is impressive by any standard. Hick Hargreaves Ironworks, Townson's Cygnet Joinery Works, Walmsley's Atlas Forge, Bolton Co-op, Magee Marshall's Brewery, and Watson's Steelworks. Also there was regular G.P.O. traffic to deal with and the constant arrivals and shunting of coal traffic that were tripped into Crook Street from Bag Lane or from Patricroft North Yard via Roe Green Junction. With the daily coal trip work-ings out again to Lever Street, Sunnyside Mills and Daubhill Sidings, with smaller amounts going into some of the private sidings mentioned above, Crook Street must have been a very busy place indeed up to the late 1950's.

Most of the freight workings from Crook Street prior to the mid 1950's were in the hands of Plodder Lane crews and their ubiquitous London & North Western 0-8-0 locomotives or 0-6-0 4F's.

Post World War II a working known as the "Day Wigan" train departed Crook Street Yard about

LEIGH
RAILWAY TIME TABLES.

Corrected to January 1st, 1852.

TRAINS FROM LEIGH.

TO LIVERPOOL.			TO MANCESTER.		
7 46A.M.	1st 2d & 3d	cl.	7 46A.M.	1st 2d & 3d	cl.
9 24 „	1st & 2d	„	9 24 „	1st class.	
10 36„	1st & 2d	„	10 36„	1st 2d & 3d	„
1 41P.M.	1st & 2d	„	1 41P.M.	1st 2d & 3d	„
3 36 „	1st & 2d	„	3 36 „	1st 2d & 3d	„
7 3 „	1st 2d & 3d	„	7 3 „	1st 2d & 3d	„

SUNDAYS.

9h. 8m. A.M., and 6h. 48m P.M., both 1st 2d & 3d class.

TO BOLTON:			TO WARRINGTON.*		
8 12A.M.	1st 2d & 3d	cl.	7 46A.M.	1st 2d & 3d	cl.
9 46 „	1st 2d & 3d	„	9 25 „	1st & 2d	„
10 57„	1st 2d & 3d	„	10 36 „	1st & 2d	„
2 32P.M.	1st 2d & 3d	„	3 36P.M.	1st & 2d	„
4 8„	1st 2d & 3d	„	7 3 „	1st 2d & 3d	„
7 48 „	1st 2d & 3d	„			

SUNDAYS.

9 44A.M. 1st 2d & 3d cl.	9 8A.M. 1st 2d & 3d cl.
7 14P.M. 1st 2d & 3d „	6 48P.M. 1st 2d & 3d „

* The Trains to Birmingham and London run at the same time as to Warrington.

TRAINS TO LEIGH.

FROM LIVERPOOL.			FROM MANCESTER.		
6 45A.M.	1st 2d & 3d	cl.	7 16A.M.	1st 2d & 3d	cl.
9 3 „	1st & 2d	„	9 15„	1st class.	
10 0„	1st & 2d	„	10 15„	1st 2d & 3d	„
1 15P.M.	1st & 2d	„	1 20P.M.	1st 2d & 3d	„
3 0„	1st & 2d	„	6 30„	1st 2d & 3d	„
6 15 „	1st 2d & 3d	„	7 0 „	1st & 2d	„

SUNDAYS.

8 40A.M. 1st 2d & 3d cl.	8 45A.M. 1st 2d & 3d cl.
6 0 P.M. 1st 2d & 3d „	6 25P.M. 1st 2d & 3d „

FROM BOLTON:			FROM WARRINGTON.		
7 25A.M.	1st 2d & 3d	cl.	7 40A.M.	1st 2d & 3d	cl.
9 5 „	1st 2d & 3d	„	9 40 „	1st & 2d	„
10 15„	1st 2d & 3d	„	1 25P.M.	1st & 2d	„
1 20P.M.	1st 2d & 3d	„	3 15 „	1st & 2d	„
3 15„	1st 2d & 3d	„	7 0 „	1st 2d & 3d	„
6 40 „	1st 2d & 3d	„			

SUNDAYS.

8 45A.M. 1st 2d & 3d cl.	8 40A.M. 1st 2d & 3d cl.
6 25P.M. 1st 2d & 3d „	6 0P.M. 1st 2d & 3d „

Reproduced from the "Chronicle" Supplement No. 1 of The Leigh Chronicle, dated January 1852.

11.05 am with traffic for Springs Branch via Atherton and Howe Bridge West Junctions. If calling at Bag Lane the train would stop on the main line, shunt any traffic they had for Bag Lane into the sidings, pick any up for Springs Branch, back onto the train and right away to Howe Bridge West Sidings, calling here also to drop empties and pick up fulls. Departure from Howe Bridge West would be about 12.25pm to work via Platt Bridge and Fir Tree House Junctions to Springs Branch, Ince Moss Sidings. On arrival at Ince Moss the locomotive would shunt its own train as required for the return working to Bolton. The engine would then be turned to work out of Bamfurlong North End or Pemberton Corner via Golborne Junction and Kenyon, sometimes calling at Kenyon to pick up Bag Lane or Bolton traffic. It was the duty of the Yard Foreman to notify Kenyon No. 1 signalman that the "Day Wigan" was required to stop. The signalman then set the road, working the train into the loop, thereby keeping the main line clear. After departing Kenyon the train would continue to Bag Lane Up Sidings where the freight would be broken up into a single engine load for working up Chequerbent Bank to Chequerbent Yard and Hulton Sidings. If Hulton Sidings had any traffic for Crook Street the "Day Wigan" would pick this up then right away to Crook Street. Arrival at Crook Street was the end of shift for the train crew, this turn usually being accomplished in six hours or so.

A direct working into Crook Street were vans of bananas, Ex Garston to Ince Moss Sidings and again a London & North Western 0-8-0 utilised for this, a Springs Branch turn, perhaps once a week. The train usually collected 8 or 9 vans at Ince Moss and worked un-assisted to Crook Street via Fir Tree House, Platt Bridge, Howe Bridge West and Atherton Junctions.

Deliveries of Burton water to Magee's Brewery Siding was a much favoured trip from Crook Street, usually each day, the railway personnel being allowed one free drink per delivery. The necessary utensil needed for this purpose was chained to the wall with the barrel positioned above.

All the workings in and out of Crook Street Yard and also the private sidings were controlled by Fletcher Street Junction signal box.

Crook Street Yard had closed officially on 26th April 1965, although the private sidings continued in use until late October 1967. Lever Street signal box was situated on the Plodder Lane side of Fletcher Street Tunnel, on the branch to Roe Green. This box opened at 7.45 am until 8.30 am, when the signalman would switch it out and attend to his lamping duties at Great Moor Street Station, Bolton No. 1, Fletcher Street and of course

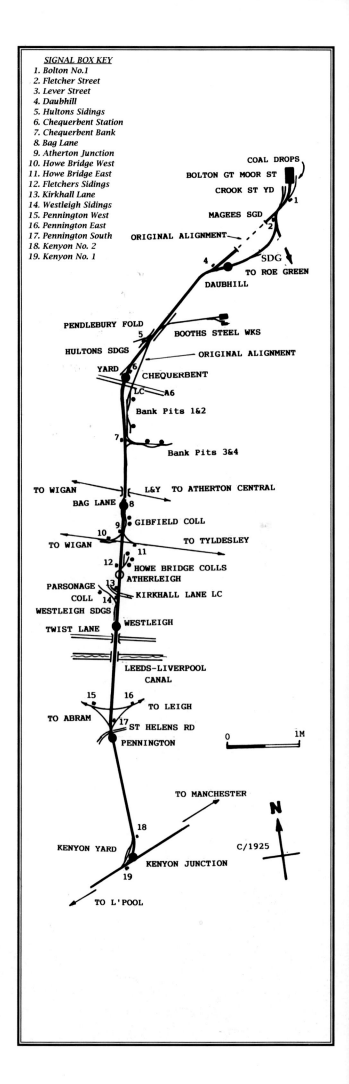

SIGNAL BOX KEY
1. Bolton No.1
2. Fletcher Street
3. Lever Street
4. Daubhill
5. Hultons Sidings
6. Chequerbent Station
7. Chequerbent Bank
8. Bag Lane
9. Atherton Junction
10. Howe Bridge West
11. Howe Bridge East
12. Fletchers Sidings
13. Kirkhall Lane
14. Westleigh Sidings
15. Pennington West
16. Pennington East
17. Pennington South
18. Kenyon No. 2
19. Kenyon No. 1

Lever Street, re-opening the latter at 12 noon to close about 4 pm. By this time the goods yard controlled by Lever Street would have been cleared of traffic.

Withdrawal of passenger services from Bolton Great Moor Street to Manchester and Kenyon had occurred on 29th March 1954, but rather like Lazarus, Great Moor Street was resurrected on an annual basis to cope with Bolton's holiday traffic to North Wales until 1958.

Plate 3. Stanier Class 5 No. 45127 departing Bolton Great Moor Street on 29th June 1957, with a holiday special to North Wales and is seen passing Bolton No. 1 signal box. Most of the stock for these specials had been worked in from Longsight Carriage Sidings but the platforms at Great Moor Street would not hold the full compliment of nine coaches that were usually employed on these trains. As a consequence the train locomotive would be standing on the end of Crook Street bridge with the first couple of coaches off the platform. The last holiday specials from Great Moor Street ran on 28th June 1958 and a total of eight trains carried some 2,800 persons. Bolton No. 1 cabin dates from the period of re-building here in 1874 and was opened for two shifts, 6 am-2 pm and 2 pm-10.30 pm. Very few signal boxes had water laid on and Bolton No. 1 was no exception to this, water having to be carried to the cabin from Great Moor Street each morning by one of the call boys.   *Photo, C.B.Golding.*

Plate 4. Class 5 No. 45231 seen passing Townsons Siding with a mid 1950's Bolton Great Moor Street to North Wales holiday special. Deliveries of building materials to Townson's arrived on a trip working out of Crook Street Yard which, in the post World War II era, was uaually the "Day Wigan".

Photo, P. Hampson

DAUBHILL

DAUBHILL signal box opened at 4.30am to 8.30am for the first trip working from Crook Street Yard with coal traffic into Daubhill Sidings for a number of coal merchants who would begin arriving about 6.30 am to load their lorries. The next task for this early trip was to shunt Tootal's Sunnyside Mills Sidings working coal in and empties out, a job usually completed by about 7am. These sidings held about 20 wagons each. This coal traffic would have been worked into Crook Street from Bag Lane or from Patricroft North Yard via Roe Green Junction a day or two earlier. After switching out Daubhill box the signalman then went "lamping", that is attending to the signal lamps between Fletcher Street distant and Chequerbent.

The original Bolton & Leigh Railway alignment had crossed Daubhill Bar at road level and the first Daubhill Station had been situated adjacent to Sunnyside Mills. The new alignment at Daubhill opened in 1885 and took the railway under St Helens Road. At the lower end of the Daubhill incline part of the line was retained to serve Magee's Brewery and at the top, to access Sunnyside Mills and coal staithes located on the site of the engine house. The rest of the Daubhill embankment was removed and terraced houses were built over the route.

Plate 5. On 9th May 1964 Class 8F No. 48553 seen at the rear of a train of empties, crossing St Helens Road, Daubhill, 8F 48770 is the train engine. The passenger shunter from Great Moor Street was rostered to go to Daubhill and act as hand signalman for these movements across St Helens Road. *Photo, J. G. Holt.*

Plate 6. WD 90147 at Daubhill en-route to Bolton Crook St from Patricroft in early 1964, the more direct route to Bolton via Roe Green Junction from Patricroft having closed in 1961. This is another of driver Jim Carters excellent lineside studys, complete with examples of the paraphernalia of the steam railway in the form of telegraph poles, semaphore signalling, a pipe gantry and typical London & North Western sleeper fencing.

Jim had done the early morning shunt at Tootals Sidings propelling fulls in and drawing empties out. At this late period in the life of the Bolton & Leigh Railway coal traffic was also being worked direct into Tootals from Speakmans Sidings, Leigh, or Chanters Sidings near Howe Bridge.

90147 had emerged from the North British Locomotive works at Glasgow in June 1943 as WD 77160 and immediatley went on loan to the LMS. It was returned to War Department service in February 1945 and later spent some time in France, returning to blighty in 1947. It is seen carrying an 8F, Springs Branch, shedplate from where the locomotive was withdrawn for scrap in April 1964.

Plate 7. The first station at Daubhill, on the original alignment, closed on 2nd February 1885, on the opening of the diversionary route. The station on the new route became Rumworth & Daubhill on 24th April 1885, closing on 3rd March 1952. This view, looking towards Bolton, dates from 1950.
Photo, Stations U.K.

13

HULTON SIDINGS

HULTON Sidings, named after Wm. Hulton who had been an ardent supporter, and later became Chairman of the Bolton & Leigh Railway. He had also been responsible for persuading George Stephenson to take up the position as engineer on the project. Wm. Hulton was already mining in this area prior to the arrival of the railway and had a number of mines that were sited on both east and west sides of the proposed Bolton & Leigh Railway. These were served by branch lines from the outset and it was from this location at the nearby Pendlebury Fold, that the ensemble hauled by "*Lancashire Witch*" commenced on that historic day in August 1828.

Early in the 20th century John Booths Steel Fabrication Works had been established in this locality, served by a branch line from Hulton Sidings. All traffic for Booths, mainly steel, was worked into Hulton Sidings and shunted into Booths between 8am-10am, six days per week *c.*1950's by a trip locomotive, which after departing Booths usually worked to Bag Lane Yard to shunt and take a light load to Crook Street.

With the post-war boom in building and civil engineering a concrete works was built at Pendlebury Fold, on the site of the former Hulton Collieries brickworks. This received regular deliveries of materials by rail right up until closure of the railway.

Plate 8. An early 1960's shot at Booths Sidings. 8F No. 48771 had worked to Booths with empty bolster wagons from Bag Lane and is seen shunting girders from Booths onto the rest of its train on the Loop Road before returning to Bag Lane and Patricroft. The bridge girders are of considerable length necessitating the addition of a "weltrol" at each end. This shot also gives a good view of the nearby concrete plant at Pendlebury Fold, built on the site of the former Hulton Collieries Brickworks. Behind the locomotive are Hulton Sidings and the similarly named signal cabin. The Guard in the foreground is thought to be Len Fogg, one of a number working out of Crook Street. Others were Tommy Leah, Stan Edwards, Sam Twigley, Robert McKenzie and Billy Nixon, the latter nicknamed the "Flying Flea" on account of his workrate in attending to his train.

Photo, J. R. Carter.

Plate 9. Ex -WD 2-8-0 No. 90371 waits to re-join the main line at Hulton Sidings in the early 1960's after depositing a load of stone at Pendlebury Fold Concrete Works. Behind the locomotive are a couple of empty bogie "well" wagons either for Booths Works or Crook Street Yard. This former War Department locomotive was built by The North British Locomotive Company at their Hyde Park Works, Glasgow in September 1944 as No. 78561, going on loan to the LNER in March 1947 and to BR at nationalisation but not purchased by the latter until December 1948. After a spell in the Edinburgh area the locomotive was transferred to Rose Grove, Burnley, eventually finding its way to Patricroft shed from where it was withdrawn in April 1964.

Photo, J. R. Carter.

Plate 10. On 28th December 1967, Stanier 8F No. 48749 is seen in the Pendlebury Fold Siding after shunting a couple of stone hoppers into the works yard. The photograph is taken from the guards van, shunted with the rest of the train into Hulton Sidings.

Photo, G. Bent.

15

Plate 11. Ex War Department 2-8-0 No. 90686 receives banking assistance on the Up Main with a coal train from Bag Lane and is seen near the connection to Wm. Booths Steel Fabrication Works in the early 1960's as plate layers attend to the track. Appropriately this locomotive was built at Vulcan Foundry Newton-Le-Willows, the history of which goes back to the very beginings of the railway age. The locomotive emerged from Vulcan works as WD No. 79225 in December of 1944, and was loaned to the Great Western Railway in April 1947, being purchased by British Railways in December 1948, but not in fact receiving its BR number until December 1951. The last shed of this locomotive was Springs Branch from where it was withdrawn for scrap in 1965.

Photo, J. R. Carter.

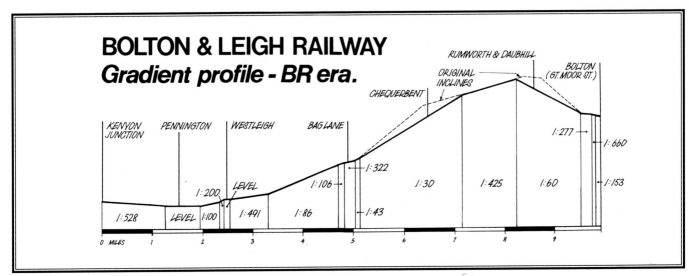

CHEQUERBENT

THE original Chequerbent Station, more appropriately described as a convenient "Halt" for the Hulton family, had been sited south of the A6 road, near to the engine winding house. From about 1840 there had also been an engine shed at this location, later found to be unsuitable as there were no water facilities for locomotives here. The London & North Western Board discussed alternative locations where water was more readily available and accommodation seems to have been provided at Leigh in the late 1860's, near the Leeds-Liverpool Canal. Ordnance Survey maps for the period do show an engine shed at this location.

There had been a single mine shaft at Chequerbent, alongside the Bolton & Leigh Railway, in the 1830's. In the 1890's other shafts were sunk there with Bank Pits 1 and 2 again being sunk alongside the original line south of the Manchester-Chorley (A6) road. Also sited south of the A6, but further to the east and served by a new line of colliery railway branching from the original alignment were Bank Pits 3 and 4. The latter came to be known locally as "Pretoria Pit", a name forever etched into the annals of mining on account of a disaster which occurred there on 21st December 1910, when 344 men and boys died as a result of an underground gas explosion.

The Chequerbent deviation as opened in 1885 passed under the A6 road with the new Chequerbent Station sited in a cutting on the north side of the road-over bridge, complimented by a new Station Masters house built alongside and a number of railway cottages fronting the A6.

The new alignment diverged from the old alignment near Pendlebury Fold, to a point some 600 yards south of the A6. However, the old track continued to be used by Hulton Collieries to access their mines, from the northern end only, worked by their own locomotives which continued to cross the A6 on the level. In the early years of the present century a triangular junction was installed south of Chequerbent, linking up with colliery lines from Pretoria and Bank Pits 1 & 2. The last of Hulton Collieries mines, which ironically was Pretoria, closed in 1934.

Chequerbent Goods Yard was situated alongside the Up line adjacent to Chequerbent Station. Here were reception sidings for Norris's steel traffic which, c.1940's could be quite considerable and also for coal to be bagged and distributed by local merchants, including for example Wm. Foreshaws of Westhoughton. These sidings were

Plate 12. Chequerbent Bank signal box on an unknown date. This cabin was sited alongside the Up line, 1,387 yards from Bag Lane and closed shortly after mining operations ceased at Hulton's Collieries. The Signalman is believed to be Charlie "Digger" Rigby.
Photo, Heyday Publishing.

controlled by Chequerbent Station signal box which was sited about 50 yards from the Bolton end of the Down platform, almost directly opposite the cattle dock.

In later years, a site adjacent to Norris's was taken over by J. K. Holt, a scrap metal dealer and a number of colliery locomotives were cut up by Holt, some at the site of purchase, others here at Chequerbent. For years, after withdrawal from service, Ex WD 0-6-0 Austerity "Harry" resided amongst the debris until sold to the Shropshire Locomotive Society in 1992.

Chequerbent Goods Yard closed on 27th February 1965 and today presents a forlorn spectacle. Some of the redundant facilities were taken over by local coal merchants as deliveries continued by road for some years after rail traffic ceased. The whole area is now derelict and in a sorry state; yet it is worth wandering on the adjacent embankment of Stephenson's original alignment where a few rail chairs from the late

Plate 13. North of the A6 at the top of Chequerbent Bank, as Ex works Stanier Class 5, No. 45258 gets ready to depart for Bolton after dropping off coal wagons in the yard here and re-marshalling its train on 4th June 1962. Today, this is one of the few locations were the former railway trackbed and also the remnants of the coal yard are still discernible and are in fact visible from the M61 Motorway which passes just a short distance north of this location. To the right of the locomotive the connecting approach road from the A6 to the M61 would later be built.

Photo, J. R. Carter.

Plate 14. A viewpoint similar to Jim Carter's 1962 photograph on ***Plate 13***, shows creeping vegetation obscuring all but the former Norris's works. *Photo, Author.*

Plate 15. The original alignment of the Bolton & Leigh Railway which crossed the Manchester-Chorley road on the level, better known today as the A6, is marked by the bus shelter and on the opposite side of the road the crossing keepers house dating from 1829, now has a more modern look. *Photo, Author.*

nineteenth century can be found amidst the vegetation and rotting sleepers.

Should the proposed A5225, Wigan, Hindley and Westhoughton by-pass come to fruition it will pass through the site of Chequerbent Yard and destroy what little does remain here of Stephenson's original alignment. It ought not to happen. Is it beyond the realms of possibility that this historic length of railway embankment, complete still with immaculately laid masonry, be preserved for posterity. The first Public Railway in Lancashire deserves better treatment.

Plate 16. Chequerbent Goods Yard Weighbridge in June 1995 presents a scene of dereliction. Note the check rail still in situ, last used by rail vehicles some 30 years ago. In the background the M61 motorway now carries the freight traffic that once filled yards like these. *Photo, Author.*

Plate 17. One of the rail chairs still in situ on Stephensons original alignment adjacent to Chequerbent Yard, this example dating from 1895 and in all probability cast locally for Hultons Collieries. This section of railway was retained and used as a connection to Hultons Collieries after the Chequerbent deviation came into use. *Photo, Author.*

Plate 18. Chequerbent Station Signal Box as seen about 1954. Directly opposite the signal box was the cattle dock, and cattle arriving here for local farms would be driven down the A6 to their destination. Note the embankment of Stephenson's original alignment to the rear, much of which is still in situ today (1996).

Photo, P. Hampson.

Plate 19. Chequerbent Station looking south towards Atherton about 1954. Although the waiting rooms appear rather spartan, the platforms and covered way were a considerable improvement on previous facilities at this location. The platforms have, at some period in LMS days, been re-built with pre-cast concrete panels, a method of construction continued in the BR era.

Photo, P. Hampson.

Plate 20. A view northward towards the A6 from the trackbed of Stephenson's original alignment, clearly marked by the darker vegetation. Here may be found stone sleepers, remarkable survivors of Stephenson's 1828 alignment. On the extreme left the 1885 diversion is rapidly succumbing to nature.

Photo, Author.

Plate 21. Super power on Chequerbent Bank in the early 1960's as WD Austerity 2-8-0 No. 90371 heads a load of twelve sand hoppers for Pendlebury Fold, banked by a Stanier 2-8-0. The train is seen approaching the A6 road at the top of the incline. *Photo, J. R. Carter.*

Plate 22. Chequerbent Bank was one of the steepest inclines on mainline railways in Great Britain, officially having a gradient of 1 in 30, but in places made much worse by mining subsidence.

A load of nine hoppers of sand would be handled competently by lesser rated motive power on other parts of the system. Here the severity of the gradient is dramatically emphasised, not only have we BR Standard Class 7 Britannia, No. 70012 *"John of Gaunt"* up front but also Ex-LMS Class 8F, BR No. 48214, working from Bag Lane, giving assistance at the rear. The load of sand is bound for the concrete works at Pendlebury Fold, near to Hulton Sidings and the date is 29th October 1967. *Photo, G. Bent.*

Plate 23. Chequerbent Bank on 14th July 1956 as an un-identified Hughes "Crab" 2-6-0 receives banking assistance from a Class 5 locomotive at the rear of a returning holiday special to Bolton Great Moor St from North Wales. On the Down line another Class 5 returns light engine to Bag Lane. Note the subsidence in the track to the rear of the train, giving a gradient here of approximately 1 in 18.

Most of these holiday specials on this day were observed to have Ex LMS Class 5 locomotives in charge hauling nine coaches. The exceptions being this seven coach train as seen, and one other hauled by a BR Standard Class 5.

Plate 24. In the going away shot the former trackbed of the original alignment of the Bolton & Leigh Railway is just discernable to the right of the train locomotive. Also on the right are the dirt tips of the former Hultons Collieries, Chequerbent and Bank Pits Nos. 1 and 2.　　　　　　　　　　　　　　　　　　　　　　　　　　　*Photos, C. B. Golding.*

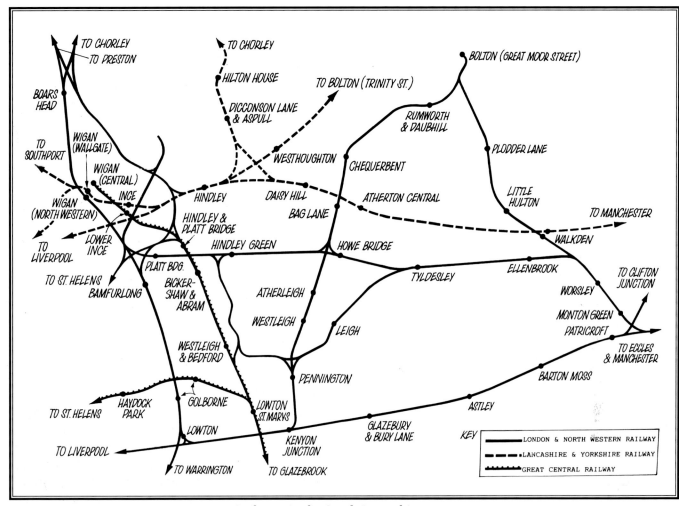

Railways in the South Lancashire area.

Plate 25. Not an exact reproduction of C. B. Golding's photograph at Chequerbent (**Plate 24**), for the over-bridge from which it was taken no longer exist and the 1885 route on the left now abounds with trees. Nevertheless, a similar northward view affords a pleasant landscape, transformed into meadowland. On the right, atop the hill, were it not for a nearby warning, sign indicating the presence of old (Chequerbent) mine shafts, the small area of woodland belies its former past. Adjacent to it, on the left, (**see Plate 20**) some 170 years of history may be seen in the shape of Bolton & Leigh Railway stone sleepers, remnants of the first Public Railway in Lancashire. *Photo, Author.*

BAG LANE

Bag Lane had been re-named Atherton prior to 1847, becoming Atherton (Bag Lane) on 2nd June 1924, to distinguish it from the Lancashire & Yorkshire Railways Atherton Central. Bag Lane Station closed on 29th March 1954, with the Goods Yard officially closing on 7th October 1963. However, shunting operations to private sidings continued almost until final closure of the line in 1969. The Howe Bridge West to Atherton Junction chord closed on 18th January 1965, being dismantled in November 1965. At the same time Atherton Junction signal box was abolished.

An unusual feature of shunting operations at Bag Lane was that instructions for all point movements to the Signalman were given by hand whistle, each point having a different code, the Yard Foreman giving the necessary signal. Locomotives would shunt their own trains and re-marshall as required. "Souths", that is all traffic for Liverpool or Warrington via Kenyon Yard that had arrived in the Up Sidings, would be shunted across the main running lines into Down Siding No. 1 behind the signal box and into their respective formations.

Bolton traffic was sorted in the Up Sidings and Plodder Lane crews would take at least nine loaded minerals up Chequerbent Bank with a Class 4 locomotive unassisted. If the load for Bolton was considerable, say thirty, three trips up the bank to Hulton Sidings would be needed, the first with a banker, perhaps hauling twelve, with banker, brake van and train engine returning to Bag Lane to repeat the procedure. Any available trip locomotive would be utilised as banker. The final run being a relatively easy one for the experienced Plodder Lane crew having only six on! Some traffic was worked into Bag Lane Up Sidings from Howe Bridge West for forward working to Bolton Crook Street, two trip engines from Springs Branch often assigned to this duty, this in addition to coal dispatches into Bag Lane from Gibfield Colliery.

Gibfield coal traffic was also worked to Fletchers Sidings or to Chanters Sidings by colliery locomotives and crews, including the guard, complete with the collieries own brake van. Running powers over these sections of main line for colliery locomotives had been in existence for many years, probably from the very beginnings of the railway age. Direct Bolton, Crook Street to Warrington trains would also pick up any "Souths" from Bag Lane en-route. Steel traffic for Staveleys also arrived here to be shunted into the latter's own sidings with finished products going

out by rail. Considerable steel traffic for Booths Steelworks and also for Norris's yard at Chequerbent arrived at Bag lane to be tripped worked up the bank.

The closure of Bag Lane and all stations to Kenyon was first mooted in October 1952. Earlier that year, in March, the last trains had called at Chequerbent and Daubhill stations, these being little used. It was said at the time no further closures were being contemplated.

In 1934, 67 trains per day were arriving or departing Great Moor Street, Bolton, by 1952 that number had been reduced to 18. Of these a total of 11 trains per day worked into and out of Great Moor Street over the Bolton & Leigh lines with an extra train on Tuesdays and Thursdays for market days plus additional trains on Saturdays. Cheap fares were advertised after 9.30am, however, the next train to depart Bolton was not until 4.23pm, hardly a service likely to attract passengers away from a regular Leigh-Atherton-Bolton bus service. One concession offered by railway officials in the face of condemnation by local councils to the closure of Bag Lane, Atherleigh, Westleigh and Pennington stations was the offer to open Westleigh specially for rugby league games specials. In the event the line was to see a few passenger trains each year up to 1958 to cope with annual Bolton holiday traffic.

SPECIAL NOTICE

BRITISH RAILWAYS REGRET THAT ON AND FROM

MONDAY 29th MARCH

IT HAS BEEN FOUND NECESSARY TO WITHDRAW
THE REGULAR PASSENGER TRAIN SERVICES BETWEEN

BOLTON AND MANCHESTER
GREAT MOOR STREET   EXCHANGE

AND

BOLTON AND KENYON
GREAT MOOR STREET   JUNCTION

AND THE FOLLOWING STATIONS WILL BE

CLOSED

FOR PASSENGERS, PARCELS AND PASSENGER
TRAIN MERCHANDISE TRAFFIC

BOLTON   ATHERTON
GREAT MOOR STREET   BAG LANE

PLODDER LANE   ATHERLEIGH
LITTLE HULTON   WESTLEIGH
WALKDEN   PENNINGTON
LOW LEVEL

BRITISH RAILWAYS

The Kenyon-Bolton line closed like many others, in sections. The first to go was Atherton Junction to Pennington South Junction on 17th June 1963, followed on 16th October 1967 by the Bolton to Hulton Sidings section. Next was Hulton Sidings to Howe Bridge East Junction on 6th January 1969 and finally the remaining stretch from Pennington South Junction to Kenyon Junction on 5th May, 1969.

Plate 26. Working tender first 8F No. 48700 descends past Staveleys Siding, Bag Lane, with empty hoppers from Hultons Sidings, on 22nd December1967. *Photo, G. Bent.*

"Railway Extension at Atherton. (Bag Lane)

"The remaining portion of single line between Atherton and Pennington on the Bolton-Leigh-Kenyon line has been doubled and on Monday 5 July was opened for traffic. The new station at Atherton is not yet complete, but is in use. The platforms are approached by a spacious under-ground passage, the booking office being below, so that passengers will have no occasion to cross the line." *Leigh Journal,* 10th July 1880.

The new station at Bag Lane replaced the original spartan accommodation and was approached on a new road alignment, Railway Street, so constructed as to pass under the recently inaugurated double track arrangement, thereby making the level crossing on Bag Lane redundant. A public house and a row of cottages had been demolished to make way for the new works. During 1970, after closure of the line the road was re-laid over its original path and in 1993 Railway Street over-bridge was demolished.

Also in 1880 the level crossing at Lovers Lane was abolished and a new bridge built to carry the railway over the lowered road level.

In June of 1861 Bag Lane had become the first station in the district to acquire a telegraph office, courtesy of the Electric & International Telegraph Company, open for public use 8am-8pm.

Plate 27. In this view of Bag Lane taken on 9th September 1971. considerable effort is required to interpret the above contemporary description. The demolition men have been and gone, leaving only the now overgrown platform edge to remind us that once there was a station here. *Photo, Ian Isherwood.*

Plate 28. A summers morning on 1st April 1965 as a pair of Stanier Class 8F locomotives Nos. 48770 & 48181 double head a mixed freight train up Chequerbent Bank and are seen crossing the Lancashire & Yorkshire line north of Bag Lane Station, the latter hidden from view by the morning mist. Visible to the rear of the train is Staveleys Works, rail connected and also manufacturers of specialist rail tank wagons. The train will split at Hulton Sidings, one locomotive to shunt there and the other locomotive continuing to Daubhill Coal Yard. The fireman leaning out of the cab is Mike Childs, now a BR Inspector.   *Photo, J. R. Carter.*

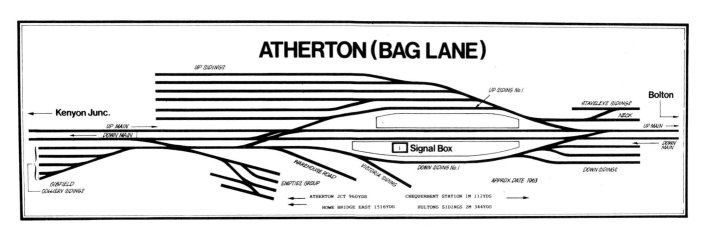

Plate 29. After being tripped worked from Fletchers Sidings, Howe Bridge on 14th September 1957, colliery loco-motive *"1861"* formerly *"Ellesmere"*, HE/244/61, is seen in Bag Lane Goods Yard five days later awaiting onward trans-portation to Scotland.
Photo, B. Roberts, courtesy Jim Peden.

NOTICE.—When seated, please to hold this ticket in readiness till called for, *as no person will be per-mitted to proceed without producing a ticket.*

No gratuity allowed to be taken by any Guard, Porter, or other Railway Servant. Smoking is strictly prohibited.

NOTICE.—When seated, please to hold this ticket in readiness till called for, *as no person will be per-mitted to proceed without producing a ticket.*

No gratuity allowed to be taken by any Guard, Porter, or other Railway Servant. Smoking is strictly prohibited.

NOTICE.—When seated please to hold this ticket in readiness till called for, *as no person will be per-mitted to proceed without producing a ticket.*

No gratuity allowed to be taken by any Guard, Porter, or other Railway Servant. Smoking is strictly prohibited.

NOTICE.—When seated, please to hold this ticket in readiness till called for, *as no person will be per-mitted to proceed without producing a ticket.*

No gratuity allowed to be taken by any Guard, Porter, or other Railway Servant Smoking is strictly prohibited

BOLTON AND LEIGH RAILWAY.

FROM BAG-LANE TO

Provided there be room in the Carriages on their arrival.

At   o'clock,   184

No.   Paid   Entered

(Turn over.)

BOLTON AND LEIGH RAILWAY.

FROM BAG-LANE TO

Provided there be room in the Carriages on their arrival.

At   o'clock,   184

No.   Paid   Entered

(Turn over.)

BOLTON AND LEIGH RAILWAY.

FROM BAG-LANE TO

Provided there be room in the Carriages on their arrival.

At   o'clock,   184

No.   Paid   Entered

(Turn over.)

BOLTON AND LEIGH RAILWAY.

FROM BAG-LANE TO

Provided there be room in the Carriages on their arrival.

At   o'clock,   184

No.   Paid   Entered

(Turn over.)

Reverse.   Obverse.

A sheet of tickets from the 1840's. Details would be filled in by the booking clerk at the time of purchase.

c. 1934.

A thin line between the hour and minute figures indicates p.m.

KENYON, LEIGH, TYLDESLEY, AND BOLTON (GREAT MOOR STREET.)

22

Week days.	Saturdays only.											From Wigan.		S				S	S	From Wigan.		SO	S	SO		
Liverpool (L.St.) dep.				5 45				7 53			9 0				10t 5				11 0		11S 0	11 0	12 0	12 10		
Warrington ,,			6 15			7¶ 5		7¶40	8 30		9¶ 8		9S32			10 35			11¶0		11S 0	11 55	12 15	12 44		
Earlestown ,,			6 25	6 35		7¶15		8 8	8 38		9 25		9S40		10 12	10 50			11 35		11S35	12 14	12 50	1 8		
Newton-le-Will'ws ,,			6 33	6 38		7 30		8 23	8 41		9 28		9S43		10 30	10 53			11 38		11S38	12 16	12 54	1 10		
Kenyon Junction dep.			6 42	6 53	7 25	7 36		8 32	8 53		9 34		9 52		10 42	10 58			11 47		11 57	12 23	1 3	1 16		
Pennington			6 46	6 56	7 28	7 38		8 35	8 55		9 37		9 56		10 44	11 2			11 50		12 0	12 26	1 5	1 19		
Leigh arr.				7 1	7 33			8 39			9 42	9 56			10 48				11 55	12 11						
Leigh dep.	5 10	6 5		7 5	7 37		7 50	8 44		9 10	9 43	9 58		10 27	10 49		11 5		11 57	12i13					1 7	
Tyldesley arr.	5 15	6 10		7 10	7 42		7 55	8 49		9 15	9 48	10 3		10 32	10 54		11 10		12 2	12i18					1 12	
Manchester (Ex) arr.		6 42		7 43	8 13		8 38	9 20		9 39	10 14			10 56			11 34			12i39					1 30	
Tyldesley dep.							8 20											11 36								1 30
Howe Bridge							8 24											11 40								1 34
West Leigh			6 51			7 41			8 58				10 0			11 5					12 3	12 29	1 8	1 23		
Atherton (Bag Lane)			6 57			7 47	8 27		9 4				10 6			11 10		11 43			12 9	12 35	1 15	1 29		1 37
Chequerbent for Hulton P.			7 4			7 53	8 33		9 10				10 12			11 16		11 49			12 15	12 41	1 21	1 35		1 43
Rumworth & Daubhill			7 9			7 58	8 38		9 15				10 17			11 21		11 54			12 20	12 46	1 26	1 40		1 48
Bolton (Gt. Moor St.) arr.			7 15			8 4	8 44		9 21				10 23			11 27		12 0			12 26	12 52	1 32	1 46		1 54

Week days—continued.					SO From Wigan.			SO	S				SO From Wigan.	S From Wigan.			SO					SO				
Liverpool (L.St.) dep.	1 5					3 15	4 0									4 50		5 45		6 0			7 0			
Warrington ,,	1 15					3¶10	3 50			4 50						5 27		6¶15		6 42			7 26	7 45		
Earlestown ,,	1B38					3 38	4 5			4 58						5 40		6¶25		6 51			7 35	7 58		
Newton-le-Will'ws ,,	1 48					3 40	4 33			5 2						5 52		6¶28		6 56			7 38	8 1		
Kenyon Junction dep.	1 54		2 15			3 47	4 38			5 12		5 30			5 37	5 58	6 12	6 40		7 2	7 10		7 51	8 15	8 20	
Pennington	1 58		2 18			3 50	4 42			5 16		5 32			5 41	6 0	6 16	6 43		7 5	7 13		7 55	8 18	8 23	
Leigh arr.			2 23		3 28	3 55				5 20			5 31	5 31	5 45		6 20	6 48			7 18		8 0		8 28	
Leigh dep.		1 55	2 28	3 15	3 33	4 5		4 38	4 40	5 25			5 32	5 40	5 50		6 21	6 49			7 22		8 2		8 30	
Tyldesley arr.		2 0	2 33	3 20	3 38	4 10		4 43	4 45	5 30			5 41	5 45	5 57		6 26	6 54			7 27		8 7		8 35	
Manchester (Ex) arr.		2 27	3 9	3 44		5 8			5 12	6 1					6 48		6 54	7C26			8S06		8 46			
Tyldesley dep.				3 27									5 50									7 35				
Howe Bridge				3 31									5 54									7 39				
West Leigh	2 1						4 46					5 35				6 8				7 8				8 21		
Atherton (Bag Lane)	2 7			3 36			4 52					5 41	5 57			6 9				7 14		7 42		8 29		
Chequerbent for Hulton P.	2 13			3 42			4 59					5 47				6 15				7 20		7 48		8 36		
Rumworth & Daubhill	2 18			3 48			5 7					5 52				6 20				7 25				8 41		
Bolton (Gt. Moor St.) arr.	2 24			3 54			5 13					5 58	6 12			6 26				7 31		7 57		8 47		

Week days—continued.				SO					From Wigan.		SO From Liverpool	S	SO From Wigan	SO	SO		Sundays. Through train from Liverpool	Through train from Liverpool		Through train from Liverpool	Through train from Liverpool. Runs on April 19th and 21st, 1935, only.	Through train from Liverpool	
Liverpool (L. St.) dep.					8 40						10 5	10 5		10 35			7 35	2 55		6 35	8 45	9 0	
Warrington ,,					8 55			9 55			10 30	10 30					7 57			6 0	8 27	8 27	
Earlestown ,,					9 21			10 3			10 46	10 46		11 3			8 15	3 36		7 19	9 14	9 41	
Newton-le-Will'ws ,,					9 23			10 20			10 50	10 50		11 5			8 18	3 40		7 22		9 43	
Kenyon Junction dep.		8 45			9 40			10 27			10 57	11 8		11 15	11 25		8 26			7 30			
Pennington		8 48			9 44			10 30			11 1	11 11											
Leigh arr.					9 49				10 40		11 6	11 16	11 16	11 23			8 33	3 53		7 36	9 26	9 54	
Leigh dep.	9 10				9 50	10 20			10 43		11 9	11 18	11 18	11 25			8 45	3 55		7 38	9 27	9 56	
Tyldesley arr.	9 15				9 55	10 25			10 48		11 14	11 25	11 25	11 30			8 50	4 0		7 43	9 32	10 1	
Manchester (Ex.) arr	9 42								11 12		11 39						9 15	4 25		8 8	9 52	10 25	
Tyldesley dep				9 48																			
Howe Bridge				9 52																			
West Leigh		8 51						10 33							11 31								
Atherton (Bag Lane)		8 57		9 55				10 39							11 37								
Chequerbent for Hulton P.		9 3		10 1				10 45							11 43								
Rumworth & Daubhill		9 8						10 50							11 48								
Bolton (Great M. St.) arr.		9 14		10 10				10 56							11 53								

23

Week days.	SO																			S		S			
Bolton (G. Moor St.) dep.		5 55		6 45				7 35				8 22				9 25		10 5	10 30			11 10		12 0	
Rumworth & Daubhill		5 59		6 50				7 39				8 27				9 30		10 9	10 34			11 14		12 4	
Chequerbent for Hulton P.		6 4		6 54				7 43				8 32				9 33		10 13	10 38			11 18		12 8	
Atherton (Bag Lane)		6 10		6 59				7 48				8 39				9 38		10 20	10 43			11 23		12 13	
West Leigh				7 4				7 53				8 43						10 24	10 48			11 27		12 17	
Howe Bridge		6 15														9 40									
Tyldesley arr.		6 20														9 45									
Manchester (Ex) dep.			5 58				7 0				8 0				9 10	9S15				10 10			10 50		
Tyldesley dep.	5 35	6 22	6 37			7 15	7 33			8 10	8 29			9 10	9d35	10 0				10 34			11 25		
Leigh arr.	5 40	6 27	6 42			7 20	7 38			8 15	8 34			9 15	9d40	10 5				10 39			11 30		
Leigh dep.		6 28								8 18				9 16		10 6							11 35		
Pennington		6 31		7 7				7 57		8 22		8 46		9 20		10 9		10 27	10 51			11 30	11 39	12 20	
Kenyon Junction arr.		6 36		7 12				8 2		8 26		8 51		9 24		10 14		10 32	10 56			11 35	11 44	12 25	
Newton le-Will'ws arr.		6 49		7 22				8 30		8 36		8 57		9 32		10 22			11 2				12 6	12 33	
Earlestown ,,		6 53		7¶32				8 32		8 40		9 2		9 35		10g34			11 5				12 9	12 36	
Warrington ,,		7 17		7¶45				8 47		9 1		9 17		10 20		10 54		11j 2	11 34				12SO32	12¶53	
Liverpool (L. St.) ,,		8 7		8 43						9 17		9J39		10 7		10 47			11 57				12e42	1S44	

Week days—continued.	S	SO	SO	S			SO	SO To Wigan.							To Wigan.	SO						SO	S		SO To Wigan.	S	
Bolton (G. Moor St.) dep.			12 35	12 35			1 5		1 50				2 50	3 35			4 20		4SO30	5 5		5 50	5 55				
Rumworth & Daubhill			12 39	12 39			1 9		1 54				2S54	3 39			4 24			5 9		5 54	5 59				
Chequerbent for Hulton P.			12 43	12 43			1 13		1 58				2 58	3 43			4 29		4SO37	5 13		5 58	6 3				
Atherton (Bag Lane)			12 48	12 48			1 18		2 3				3 2	3 48			4 34		4SO42	5 18		6 3	6 8				
West Leigh			12 52						2 8					3 52			4 39			5 22		6 7	6 12				
Howe Bridge				12 50			1 22						3 6						4SO45								
Tyldesley arr.				12 55			1 27						3 11						4SO50								
Manchester (Ex.) dep.		12 20			12n45			1 25		1S30		2 20			3 35			4 10	4S42		5 5			5f40		6 15	
Tyldesley dep.	12 35	12 49			1 18			1 57		1N58		2 46	3S20		4 1	4 15		4 33	5 8		5 45			6f15	6 40	6 41	
Leigh arr.	12 40	12 54			1 23			2 2		2N 3		2 51	3S25		4 6	4 20		4 38	5 13		5 50			6f20	6 45	6 46	
Leigh dep.								2 3		2 18					4 7	4 22		4 46	5 14		5 55			6 25	6 46	6 50	
Pennington			12 55						2 11	2 21				3 55		4 25	4 43	4 50	5 18	5 25	5 58	6 10	6 15	6 29		6 53	
Kenyon Junction arr.			1 0						2 17	2 26				4 2		4 30	4 48	4 55	5 22	5 30	6 3	6 15	6 20	6 33		6 58	
Newton-le-Will'ws arr.			1 10						2 26	2 33				4 11			4 56			5 40	6 15	6 23	6 28	6¶45			
Earlestown ,,			1 12						2 29	2 36				4 14			4 59			5 45	6 18			6¶48			
Warrington ,,			1¶46							2c56				4 25			5 13			6 11				6¶59			
Liverpool (L. St.) ,,			1 45							3 23				5 27			5 40			6 16	6b48			7 51			

Week days—continued.	SO						SO	SO	S	SO				SO		Sundays. Through train to Liverpool. Runs on April 19th and 21st, 1935, only.	Through train to Liverpool.	Through train to Liverpool.	Through train to Liverpool.	Through train to Liverpool.	Through train to Liverpool.	Through train to Warrington		
Bolton (G. Moor St.) dep.	6 30	7 0				8 30		9 5	9 7	9 35			10A45	10 45										
Rumworth & Daubhill		7 4				8 34		9 9	9 11	9 39			10A49											
Chequerbent for Hulton P.	6 37	7 8				8 38		9 13	9 15	9 43			10A54	10 52										
Atherton (Bag Lane)	6 42	7 13				8 43		9 18	9 20	9 48			10A59	10 58										
West Leigh		7 17				8 47			9 24	9 52			11A 3											
Howe Bridge	6 45							9 21						11 2										
Tyldesley arr	6 50							9 26						11 7										
Manchester (Ex.) dep.			6 50	7 40	8 15						9 23	10E15		10 45	11 0	8 50	9 30	12 55	2 45	6 15	8 30	9 30	10 15	
Tyldesley dep.			7 22	8a 7	8 44		9 15				9D57	10E39		11 13	11 28	9 11	9 57	1 17	3 8	6 40	8 55	9 55	10 40	
Leigh arr.			7 28	8a12	8 49		9 20				10D 2	10E44		11 18	11 33	9 16	10 2	1 22	3 13	6 45	9 0	10 0	10 45	
Leigh dep.			7 30	8 22			9 22					10 46		11 20		9 18	10 7	1 24	3 15	6 46	9 1	10 1		
Pennington		7 20	7 34	8 26		8 50	9 25		9 27	9 55		10 49	11A 6											
Kenyon Junction arr.		7 25	7 38	8 30		8 55	9 30		9 32	10 0		10 54	11A11	11 26			10 14			6 53				
Newton-le-Will'ws arr.			7 50			9 1	9 43		9 43			11 9	11S18	11 34		9 28	10 21		3 28	7 0	9 15	10 13		
Earlestown ,,			7 53			9 5	9 50		9 50			11 12	11S23	11 37		9 31	10 25	1 36	3 30	7 4	9 17	10 17		
Warrington ,,			8 2			9¶30	9 55		9 55					11 56		10 19	10 47	3 7		7 33		10 26		
Liverpool (L. St.) ,,			8 49			9 46	10 35		10 35			11 50				10 2	11 15	2 6	4 10	8 19	9 57			

¶—One class only. **A**—5 minutes later on Saturdays
a—On Sats. leaves Tyldesley 8.15 p.m. arr. Leigh 8.20p.m.
B—On Saturdays leaves Earlestown 1.34 p.m.
b—On Saturdays arrives Liverpool 7.17 p.m.
c—On Saturdays arrives Warrington 3.7 p.m.
D—On Sats. leaves Tyldesley 10.5, arr. Leigh 10.10 p.m.
d—On Sats. dep. Tyldesley 9.37, arrive Leigh 9.42 a.m.

E—On Friday, December 21st. 1934, leaves Manchester 10.10p.m., Tyldesley 10.34p.m., Leigh arr, 10.39p.m.
e—Arrive Liverpool 12,45 p.m. on Saturdays.
f—On Sats. leaves Manchester (Ex.) 5.45 p.m., Tyldesley at 6.17 p.m. & arr. Leigh at 6.22 p.m.
G—On Saturdays arrives Manchester 7.28 p.m.
g—On Saturdays arrives Earlestown 10.25 a.m.
i—On Saturdays leaves Leigh 12.20 p.m., arr. Tyldesley 12.25 p.m., Manchester (Ex.) 12.56 p.m.

J—On Saturdays arrives Liverpool 9.46 a.m.
j—Applies on December 22nd, 1934 and April 18th, 1935, only.
N—On Saturdays leaves Tyldesley 2.12 p.m., and arrives Leigh 2.17 p.m. **n**—On Saturdays leaves Manchester (Ex.) 12.48 p.m. **S**—Sats. excepted. **SO**—Sats only.
t—Leaves Liverpool at 9.30 a.m. on Saturdays.
Y—One class only except on Saturdays.

For complete service between Leigh and Manchester, and between Tyldesley and Howe Bridge, see pages 16 – 19

TRAIN MOVEMENTS THROUGH ATHERTON BAG LANE 1955

am/pm	Time Arr.	Dept.	Train No.	Except	Class	From	To
						UP LINE	
am	5.58			MX	G LE	Springs Branch	Bag Lane
am		6.29	138		G LE	Springs Branch	Bolton
am	7.29				K	Fletchers Sidings	Bag Lane NCB Loco
am	7.49		111	MX	K	Tyldesley	Bag Lane
am	7.36	8.08		MO	F	Warrington	Bolton
am	9.41				K	Chanters Sidings	Bag Lane NCB Loco
am		10.15	138		K	Bag Lane	Bolton
am		10.35	292		K	Bag Lane	Bolton
am	11.00		139	SO	G LE	Springs Branch	Bag Lane
pm	1.04				K	Chanters Sidings	Bag Lane NCB Loco
pm	1.07			MSX	K	Liverpool Edge Hill	Bag Lane
pm		1.50	288	SX	G LE	Warrington Dallam Sidings	Bolton
pm	3.10		138		K	Bamfurlong Sidings	Bag Lane
pm		3.30	138	SO	K	Bag Lane	Chanters Sidings
pm	4.00		293	SX	K	Fletchers Sidings	Bag Lane
pm	4.35	4.50	138	SO	K	Chanters Sidings	Bolton
pm	3.45	5.15	293	SO	J	Kenyon Junction	Bolton
pm	5.22		139	SX	K	Chanters Sidings	Bag Lane
pm	5.26		293	SX	K	Fletchers Sidings	Bag Lane
pm		6.00	138	SX	K	Bag Lane	Bolton
pm	6.25		139	SX	K	Howe Bridge West	Bolton
pm	7.00	7.00		SX	G LE	Kenyon Junction	Bag Lane
pm	7.06	7.36	293	SX	K	Kenyon Junction	Hultons Sidings
pm	8.14	8.14	140	SX	J	Bamfurlong Sidings	Bag Lane
pm		8.21	293	SX	K	Bag Lane	Bolton
pm	8.30	8.55	120	SX	K	Kenyon Junction	Bolton
						DOWN LINE	
am		6.25		MX	H	Bag Lane	Liverpool Edge Hill
am	7.40		138		K	Bolton	Bag Lane
am		8.05			J	Bag Lane NCB Loco	Chanters Sidings
am		8.20	111	MX	K	Bag Lane	Ellenbrook Sidings
am	9.10		292	MX	K	Hultons Sidings	Bag Lane
am	9.30		292	MO	K	Hultons Sidings	Bag Lane
am	11.28	11.43	138		J	Bolton	Bamfurlong Sidings
pm	12.00		293	SO	G LE	Patricroft Loco	Bag Lane
pm		12.15	293	SO	J	Bag Lane	Kenyon Junction
pm		12.24			J	Bag Lane NCB Loco	Fletchers Sidings
pm		1.10			K	Bag Lane NCB Loco	Fletchers Sidings
pm		1.38		MX	G LE	Bag Lane	Springs Branch Loco
pm	2.00		291	SX	G LE	Patricroft Loco	Bag Lane
pm		3.25	293	SX	K	Plodder Lane	Fletchers Sidings
pm		4.08	120	SX	K	Bolton	Tyldesley
pm		4.50	293		K	Bag Lane	Fletchers Sidings
pm		5.12	139	SO	G LE	Bag Lane	Springs Branch Loco
pm		5.48	293	SX	K	Bag Lane	Kenyon Junction
pm		5.51	139	SX	K	Bag Lane	Howe Bridge West
pm	5.58	6.05		SX	F	Bolton	Warrington via Tyldesley
pm	6.25	6.35	138	SO	K	Bolton	Ince Moss Junction
pm		7.15		SX	K	Bag Lane	Weaste Junction Sidings
pm	7.35		138	SX	K	Bolton	Bag Lane
pm		7.50	138	SX	G LE	Bag Lane	Springs Branch Loco
pm	8.06		293	SX	K	Hultons Sidings	Bag Lane
pm		8.18	139	SX	G LE	Bolton	Springs Branch Loco
pm		9.15	140	SX	K	Bag Lane	Wigan Engine Shed Siding
pm	9.03	9.21		SX	H	Bolton	Winwick Quay

Plate 30. Bag Lane on 27th March 1954, as BR Standard 2-6-4T No. 84004, one of a Class first introduced in 1953 calls with the Bolton Great Moor Street-Kenyon service, which was to be withdrawn two days later on the 29th March.

Photo, D. Chatfield.

Plate 31. On the same day, Ivatt LMS taper boiler designed 2-6-0 No. 43026, seen here in its re-built form with single chimney, calls at Bag Lane with the 08.23am Great Moor Street to Liverpool Lime Street service, this the only working at this period to have three coaches allocated, having arrived officially in Great Moor Street at 07.12am, Ex 06.15am from Warrington Bank Quay. This turn was worked by a Dallam, (Warrington) crew with a Bank Quay guard. It was regarded as something of an achievement if this early train made it to the top of Chequerbent Bank without slipping to a halt. Often liberal applications of sand or trackside ash were applied to the rails to give some traction. Sometimes this had the desired effect but failure to get the train moving again would necessitate the guard having to walk back to Bag Lane Station and request assistance under "Regulation 20 clause I", so required to permit a banking engine to enter a section already occupied under the absolute block system. The guard would then in effect act as pilot on the banker. Usually the locomotive called to assist was shunting at Bag Lane prior working the rostered 06.25 Atherton Bag Lane to Edge Hill freight. Needless to say the 06.15 Warrington to Great Moor Street rarely arrived at its destination on time.

Photo, B. K. B. Green.

Plate 32. 8F No. 48749 shunting in Bag Lane Up Sidings and photographed from the trains brake van in an adjacent road on 28th December 1967.

Photo, G. Bent.

Plate 33. 28th December 1967 as Stanier 8F No. 48749 begins the climb towards Chequerbent Bank having shunted Bag Lane Yard now seen departing with freight for Hulton Sidings. *Photo, G. Bent.*

GIBFIELD

GIBFIELD Colliery dates from the late 1820's and would have been operational by the time the Bolton & Leigh line opened in 1829. It would therefore have been connected by rail to the Bolton & Leigh from the outset given Lord Lilford's known association with this pioneering venture, thus making the transport of coal to Stock Platt Staithe, near the present Platt Street, Leigh, a simple matter.

The lessees of Lord Lilford's Atherton Collieries, of which Gibfield at this period was the largest, were the Fletcher's who originated from Bolton, later being known as John Fletcher and Others from 1840. Whilst there is no evidence to suggest that Fletcher's owned any locomotives at this time, it is probable however that coals from Gibfield were hauled by John Hargreaves, the lessee of the Bolton & Leigh, either to the Stock Platt Branch, which deviated from the Bolton & Leigh line at Atherleigh, or to Fletcher's yard at Bolton. Contemporary writers record colliery engines running along the Bolton & Leigh in the 1830's without much hindrance and a loop line at Gibfield would have facilitated loading arrangements. As it turned out this arrangement for working the Stock Platt Branch were not to be permanent and lasted only for 15-20 years, more of which anon.

In 1831 the Bolton Chronicle describes an accident on the Bolton & Leigh, "at the turn of the road" Bag Lane, leading to Colonel Fletcher's Collieries. A locomotive named the "*Liverpool*" hauling five wagons from Liverpool to Bolton had overturned, killing both driver and fireman. The cause of the accident was said to be the large wheels of the locomotive, some six feet in diameter. This locomotive had been built by Edward Bury of Liverpool and was at this period undertaking trials, supposedly over the Liverpool & Manchester line. George Stephenson was not in favour of such large driving wheels and was against allowing it to run but was persuaded by the Liverpool & Manchester Directors to relent and also to give a report of its progress. Presumably it was Stephenson's report which resulted in this locomotive being prohibited from working passenger trains. It is also an illustration of the close co-operation that existed between these two early mainline railways.

An indication of the importance of Gibfield Colliery in relation to the other mines of Atherton Collieries is the rateable value, set at £750 in 1838, this compares with £208 in total for all their other mines.

Plate 34. About the only feature recognisable in this undated, elevated view south from Gibfield Colliery, is the row of terraced houses, upper right. The bridge which carries Wigan Road (Atherton) over the Bolton and Leigh line is now the junction with Atherleigh Way, opened in 1985. Immediately behind the bridge can be seen an example of London & North Western lower quadrant signals. The triangular area of land in the centre is now occupied by a scrap yard, whilst the plot to the left contains small industrial units. On the opposite side of the road is Gadbury Brick Works built by the colliery owners, for a constant and ready supply of bricks was an essential requirement of the mining industry. The rail connection to Gadbury from Gibfield crossed Wigan Road on the level. *Photo, Authors Collection.*

Plate 35. A quality, opportunist photograph by driver Jim Carter, of Wigan Coal & Iron Company locomotive "*Crawford*" of 1883 vintage seen in reverse gear alongside the main lines at Gibfield Colliery in the early 1960's and shot from the footplate of a passing WD locomotive working light back to Patricroft.

Plate 36. Hawthorn Leslie HL/340/1867 "*Atherton*" at Gibfield in 1905. Note the detail differences between this locomotive and the earlier "*Ellesmere*" of 1861. (*see plate 46*).

Photo, courtesy of Lancashire Mining Museum.

34

Plate 37. Gibfield Colliery *c.* 1935, as seen from alongside the main London & North Western running lines looking north. As to be expected Manchester Collieries wagons are prominent. The locomotive is thought to be Hunslet built 0-6-0 "*Lilford*" works No. 561 of 1892, purchased from the New Hemsworth Colliery, being scrapped in 1938 and unlike its predecessor of the same name too big to traverse the Wharf Tunnel to Leigh.

Photo, Lancashire Mining Museum.

Plate 38. An elevated northward view at Gibfield Colliery from about 1930. Coal Pit Lane is on the extreme right. Over on the left between the chimneys, the main line to Bolton can be seen with, on the horizon, Hulton's Bank Pits at Chequerbent and their associate slag heaps.

Photo, courtesy Jim Peden.

ATHERTON JUNCTION

ATHERTON Junction cabin controlled the route to Howe Bridge Junctions and also the southern exit from Gibfield Colliery Sidings, where a fireman's call box was situated, for use by the colliery locomotive crews when requiring mainline running to Fletchers Sidings or Chanters Sidings. The basic shape of "A Lancashire Triangle" was formed by the construction of the Wigan-Tyldesley branch, opened in 1864. At this period, the railway that formed the western side of the triangle, except that is for a short portion at its northern junction with the Wigan-Tyldesley-Eccles route, was owned by Ackers Whitley & Company who were mining in the Bickershaw and Abram areas. The northern section was owned by Scowcroft's who were mining in the Hindley Green area.

The Triangle c. 1864.

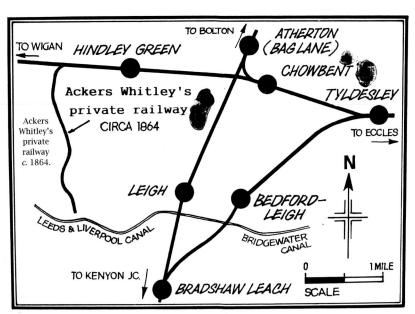

Plate 39. This photograph is taken from the road overbridge on Atherton Road in the mid 1950's with 0-6-0 ST "*Atlas*" receiving some attention from the fireman. On the left is Gadbury brickworks.

Plate 40. An unidentified WD 2-8-0 passing Atherton Junction Signal Box, approaching from Howe Bridge West Junction on 1st January 1965. The lifted section to Pennington, visible at the rear, with the still connected line to Howe Bridge East Junction trailing off to the left.   Photos, Dr. J. G. Blears.

Plate 41. A view from the cab of the leading engine as a pair of Stanier 8F's double head the first train of the day for the Bolton & Leigh line in the early 1960's, having started out from Patricroft North Yard. The location is the curve between Howe Bridge East Junction, the signal box of which is visible on the extreme left, and Atherton Junction. Sometimes it was the practice to work a light engine from Patricroft to Bag Lane early in the morning for duty as banker. However, on this occasion the banker was coupled to the rostered freight. It will detach at Bag Lane where the train would be re-marshalled and then it will perform banking duty over Chequerbent Bank and return light engine to Bag Lane.   *Photo, J. R. Carter.*

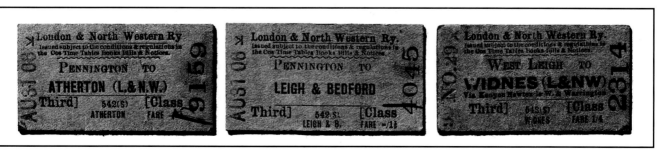

FLETCHERS SIDINGS

FLETCHERS Sidings cabin was sited 803 yards north of Atherleigh Station and controlled the road into Howe Bridge Colliery Sidings and a cross-over situated north of the cabin. Most of the coal traffic from Howe Bridge was worked up to Bag Lane Yard by colliery locomotives, particularly in late LMS days when deliveries to Bedford Wharf ceased. Any traffic for Kenyon would be picked up by a trip locomotive working out of Crook St, usually early morning.

Sinking of the Howe Bridge deep mines date from the late 1840's and eventually comprised three shafts, Victoria, Puffer and Volunteer, plus a drift mine, the Crombrouke Day Eye. All these workings were situated on the eastern side of the Bolton & Leigh Railway and in due course sidings were constructed alongside, and connected with the main running lines. Production at Howe Bridge was to continue for over one hundred years, the last coal being wound in 1959.

Plate 42. A northward view at Fletchers Sidings probably taken in 1964, after closure of the line but before track lifting commenced on 21st September 1964, to be completed by 21st October 1964. Examples of London & North Western Lower Quadrant and London Midland Upper Quadrant pattern signals are in view.

Plate 43. "1861" busy shunting at Howe Bridge Colliery, about 1954.
Photos, Dr. J. G. Blears.

ATHERLEIGH

ATHERLEIGH Station occupied a site on the Bolton & Leigh Railway close to the early Stocks Platt Bridge connection of John Fletcher's Atherton Collieries, not far from Lovers Lane.

From the Bolton & Leigh the branch ran south for a short distance, thence curved to the east, allowing it to cross Leigh Road, at a point just north of Orchard Lane, then continuing south running alongside Leigh Road, past Barn Houses, to terminate at Stock Platt Bridge. (Platt Street) Here a landsale yard, or staithe was built.

Daglish, the eminent engineer of Orrell Colliery fame, carried out geological surveys for Lord Lilford in 1838 and was said to be enthusiastic in his findings regarding coal deposits. He would already have had a familiarity with the area, having been involved with the survey for the Bolton & Leigh Railway in the late 1820's and had met Lord Lilford, over whose land the railway was to pass. He also suggested to Lord Lilford the value of using the Bolton & Leigh line and the canals as a means of transportation for his coal. It is quite possible therefore that Daglish may have engineered this standard gauge branch during the construction of the Bolton & Leigh line. Coal from the early Gibfield Pits, known to be operating in the 1820's, could then have been transported quite easily and directly to Stock Platt. By 1830 the staithe at Stock Platt was open, so presumably the branch line opened at the same time as the Bolton & Leigh Railway, or soon after.

As indicated previously it is likely that the Stock Platt Branch was worked by John Hargreaves on behalf of John Fletcher. However, in July 1845, the Bolton & Leigh Railway was absorbed by the Grand Junction Railway and Hargreaves gave up his carrier business. If this caused problems between Fletcher's and the new owners of the Bolton & Leigh regarding transport of coals to Stock Platt Staithe is not known. In the event, the mainline connection at Atherleigh with the Stock Platt Branch was removed, probably about 1850, with the former standard gauge branch line being converted to 2' 0". gauge using the original alignment and also extended northward running parallel with the Bolton & Leigh line from the rear of Harts Farm to the new deep mines at Howe Bridge and also to one of their earlier mines, the Old Endless Chain Pit at Lovers Lane. Fletcher's had no standard gauge wagons or locomotives of their own at this time so conversion to narrow gauge of the Stock Platt line seems a logical step, enabling Fletcher's to use mine tubs lifted from the pit bottom for direct transport to Stock Platt, albeit now horse drawn. Although the "Gibfield" coals are advertised for sale at Bedford Wharf in 1858, it is uncertain if the narrow gauge railway extended thus far.

Recollections in "Carbon" magazine give the "Old Tram Line" as running from the Endless Chain Pit at Lovers Lane, which was still in operation when the first shafts at Howe Bridge were sunk. The 1864 Tyldesley-Wigan line was said to pass directly over the Endless Chain Pit.

Further information is provided by the Turnpike Surveyors who, in 1856, measured the outside dimensions of the railway crossing at Leigh Road as 2' 2" , thus giving an approximate gauge of 2' 0".*

Evidently the Turnpike Commissioners regarded these railway crossings as a great inconvenience, particularly so at Leigh Road where the crossing was at an acute angle to the road and horse drawn mine tubs would have been slow to cross.

In 1860 the Bolton & St Helens Turnpike Trust obtained Parliamentary powers to regulate the use of level crossings and there are specific references to Fletcher's "railway or tramway". John Fletcher and Others were granted powers to alter the course of their railway so that it crossed the road at an angle of not less than 60 degrees, or alternatively they could build an underbridge. If these alterations were not carried out within two years the Turnpike Trustees had authority to take over Fletcher's railway and dismantle it.

John Fletcher however, had not been idle. In 1857 he and his partners were evidently thinking in terms of standard gauge railways again. The increasing output from Fletcher's Howe Bridge collieries had shown the inadequacy of horse drawn, narrow gauge railways.

Again in the Atherton Collieries magazine "Carbon" of 1921, descriptions are given with reference to the mode of transporting coal from the Lovers Lane and Howe Bridge pits. These are recollections of former Atherton Colls employees, first recounted in 1899: "I used to go and watch a train of full tubs, drawn by horses, going down from Lovers Lane to Leigh. It was very different afterwards when the railway to Bedford Basin was made and wagons of coal were sent, drawn by a colliery engine with a short funnel."

The former is a description of the Stock Platt tramway which was extended in 1857 via Bedford

---

* From information supplied by Mr. C. H. A. Townley.

Tunnel to a new wharf on the Bridgewater canal. The latter refers to the later line of new standard gauge railway opened in 1861 from Howe Bridge deep mines to Bedford Basin.

In early February 1857, "Messrs Fletcher & Lessees of Atherton Collieries, resolve to accept the tender of a contractor of Chorley, (a Mr Saville) for the construction of certain works necessary to an uninterrupted extension of their existing line of coal railway from Stock Platt to the Bridgewater Canal at Bedford".

These works began in April 1857 on the bank of the canal at Bedford, where at an early hour a "large party of labourers had gathered" for the "construction of a new railway of the standard capacity".[1] Many of the local tradesmen were also present and it was suggested by them that the first sod should be cut with some ceremony. This was duly performed by Mr John Redfern, Fletcher's agent at Stock Platt, and was carried out "with suitable vigour", following which the excavations for the works began in "some earnest".

In the evening of that day a party assembled at Mr. Thomas Darwell's "Brown Cow Inn", Leigh, in order to celebrate the event.

The new canal basin was to be 150ft long, 90ft wide and 6ft deep. On the North and South sides loading platforms were to be erected, 8ft wide and 8ft 5 in above water level. A bank was to be formed 12ft 3in wide and 3ft 2in above water level. At the North end of each, embankments were to be laid to provide continuation of the railway from the tunnel to the platforms. The top of these embankments were to be 6ft wide.

As to the Bedford Tunnel, this was 889 ft long. Temporary bridges were erected during its excavation to allow traffic passage over it. In other words a cutting was dug, the tunnel brickwork formed and the whole backfilled again to the previous level.

By september of 1857 the works had been completed and were in use. "Large quantities of coals are now shipped daily at the new pierhead and, in much better condition than by the previous method of carting through Leigh". Evidently this was welcomed by the townspeople for the daily passage of numerous horse drawn carts between Fletcher's collieries and Limerick Basin had been a bone of contention for some time. Limerick Basin was situated on the eastern side of Pennington Bridge, until recently the site used as a builders merchants yard and at this period was the despatch point for canal borne coal from Atherton Collieries.

From February 1858 onwards, Fletcher's were advertising their new wharf:- "by the completion of a direct communication with the canal from their different collieries, John Fletcher and Others

are now delivering their large 6ft, 7ft and Gibfield hand picked coal, subject only to the slight fall necessary to load carts or boats".

The "slight fall" referred to gives an indication attached to the importance of the grading of coal and the price attainable. As a general rule, not withstanding the actual quality of the particular seam of coal, the bigger the coals the better the price.

A court case in 1858, when a number of colliers were accused of "Conspiracy" at Atherton Collieries, resulted in this statement by one of the witnesses; "part of the coals that come up at the pit go by railway and part by canal. Those that go by railway are discharged from buckets at the pit mouth. Those that go by canal go about two miles (on Fletcher's railway) where the buckets are discharged into canal boats". Less transshipment = less breakage = better price.

Unfortunately the point of deviation from the Stock Platt tramway is not shown on any Ordnance Survey map. One clue to its possible location has come to light. In September 1859 a man was arrested for stealing 50lbs of coal from a "tram" on the "wagon road near Barn Houses". Barn Houses was about midway between Orchard Lane and the coal staithe at Stock Platt. It is unlikely that these tubs would have been left in the middle of nowhere when the coal staithes at Stock Platt were only a short distance away. This then was one probable connection from the new tunnel and the tubs deposited there at the end of shift. Another might be the alignment of Henrietta Street, which were it not for the inconvenient location of a silk mill opposite the later Windermere Road, suggest an end on continuation of the tramway from Stock Platt. This would also have necessitated a ninety degree turn to bring the course of the tramway back into alignment with Wharf Tunnel.

In the event the deviation was short lived. With the sinking of the deep mines at Howe Bridge in the 1850's, the increased production had shown the inadequacy of horse drawn transport. The time was now ripe for locomotive haulage.

A report of the Board of Guardians (of the poor) in October 1860 gives details of an application by John Fletcher and Others, to construct a new line of standard gauge railway from Howe Bridge Collieries to Wharf Tunnel, crossing two fields in the occupation of the Guardians. These fields were to the rear of the workhouse, (later Atherleigh Hospital) on its eastern boundary.

This land for the construction of the workhouse had been sold by Lord Lilford to the Guardians in 1850 for £640. Some of the committee members agreed to meet with John Fletcher and his surveyors to find out his "exact intentions". This meeting took place in late October 1860 and certain conditions were agreed upon including, "a wall of close pailing fence five feet high", to the rear of the workhouse, and "a level crossing for carts with a locked gate on each side", on Leigh Rd. No objections were raised at the next meeting of the Board of Guardians to Fletcher's proposals. A price for the land taken had been agreed and apparently the works commenced very rapidly for in mid November the workhouse master had applied to the Guardians for a quantity of lime to mix with soil obtained from Fletcher's new railway.

The new line in its entirety, which met up with the recently built Wharf Tunnel, was opened on 28th May 1861 with much "elat" and "pomp and circumstance". This new enterprise by John Fletcher & Others, had to quote the press report, "brought into total disuse the tram-way by which coals to be shipped on the Bridgewater Canal for Liverpool, Manchester, North Staffordshire and districts were conveyed from the collieries to the flats and barges adapted for this trade."

Two locomotives had been purchased from Messrs Hawthorns & Co, Leith, Scotland and built to S & J Davidsons patent. It was said they were not unlike those at present operating on the Bolton-Kenyon line, but were "duo-in-uno" in character, that is engine and tender being on one set of wheels, and "there is one peculiarity, that the smoke funnels being quite diminutive so as to admit their running through a tunnel which extends under the brick yard between Brown Street and Princess Street and also beneath Queen Street and Chapel Street". These engines were named the "*Lilford*" and the "*Ellesmere*". Their first working throughout the line was about a week before the official opening and caused "quite a sensation" locally.

On the opening day, two trains were formed at Howe Bridge Colliery at about 4pm. The first consisted of the "*Lilford*" and six wagons fitted with seats, in which the Fletcher's and invited guest's took their places, along with the band of the 60'th Atherton Lancashire Rifle Volunteers. The second train with the "*Ellesmere*" in charge was formed of loaded coal wagons. Artillery was employed to fire a salvo announcing the departure of the "*Lilford*" from Howe Bridge. The crowds had gathered in numbers to witness the event and cheered as the train crossed the Bolton & St Helens Turnpike Road (Leigh Rd) and continued past the Union Workhouse. After passing that "delightful portion of the Atherton demesne known as The Avenue" the train came to what had until recently been "a secluded nook" called the "Within Hole where many ancient and strong trees flourish in a dell well watered by the confluence at that point

of two large rivulets" (thought to be the area east of the present Charles St/Holden Rd jct). Many of Fletcher's employees and their families had gathered here. The trees and hedgerows were adorned with "banners, ensigns and decorations".

Passage through the Bedford Tunnel was the next feature along the line. Descriptions of "torrid sensations" and a "likeness to a Turkish Bath" were some of the comments expressed on passing through this tightly gauged tunnel. After arrival at the Canal Wharf the party awaited the coming of the "*Ellesmere*" and its cargo of "black diamonds", whence the ceremony of tipping the first wagon into the barge was gone through.

Shortly after 6pm the return journey to Within Hole commenced "were a collation was held" at this "sylvian location", the caterer being one H Grindrod of the George & Dragon Hotel, Leigh.

The customary speeches were carried out, first by the Fletcher's followed by their colliery managers and other dignitaries. But this was a celebration for all, a carnival atmosphere seems to have been the order of the day for Fletcher's employees and their families, together with many of the local inhabitants alike. Ales were supplied and evidently flowed freely. The band got into its stride and "many honest lads and bonnie lassies tripped most buoyantly on the light fantastic toe". Come the shades of evening the celebrations drew to a close and the last train departed for Howe Bridge with "a heavy load of passengers". Those who lived nearby drifted off for their homes in the dim twilight, treading their way carefully between "innumerable champagne corks and other festival trophies".

The tunnel served Atherton Collieries well for nearly seventy years. In 1929, Fletcher Burrows & Co, as Atherton Collieries had been known since 1874, were amalgamated with Manchester Collieries and the result of this was a reduction in the amount of coal despatched through Bedford Tunnel. During World War II transit of coal by barge from Bedford Wharf ceased altogether and the site became derelict except for the occasional deliveries to the land sales yard there, which continued after World War II for a few years. In 1952 the track of Wharf Tunnel line was lifted as a result of the transference of Atherton Collieries by their new owners as from Jan 1947, the National Coal Board, from the North West Division of N.C.B. to the Wigan area and the resultant re-organisation of coal sales that this produced. However the land sales continued in operation for a period, deliveries being made by road.

The tunnel entrances were bricked up and the shallow cuttings gradually in-filled. A fascinating chapter in Athertons industrial legacy had come to a close. In years to come a whole generation

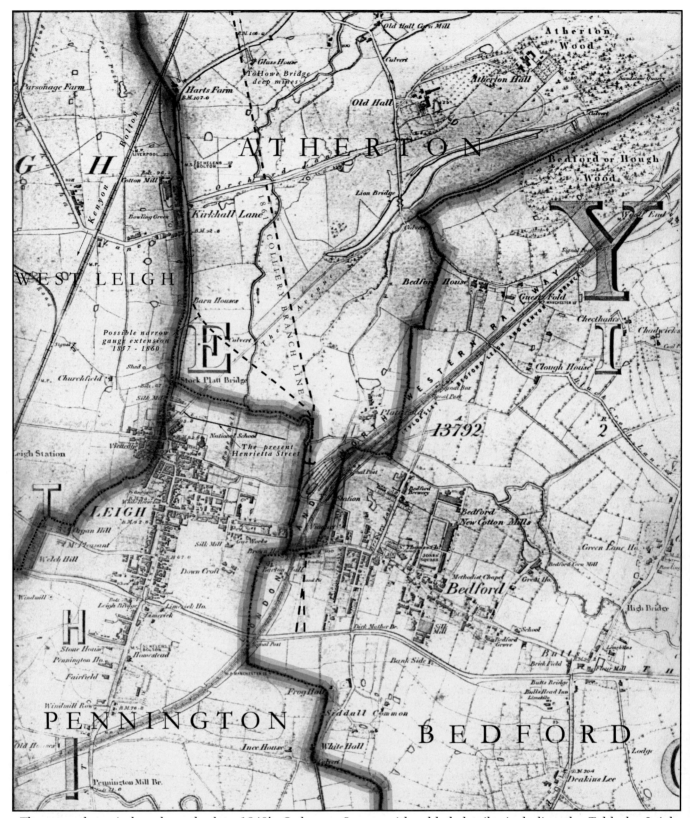

The map above is based on the late 1840's Ordnance Survey with added details, including the Tyldesley-Leigh-Pennington branch of the London & North Western Railway opened in 1864. Unfortunately it is rather misleading as the direct Howe Bridge Colliery-Bedford Wharf standard gauge railway opened in 1861 is not shown, but the by then defunct Stock Platt Branch, showing its early connection with the Bolton & Leigh Railway at top left is. To assist the reader the colliery railway has been indicated, as have the township boundaries, the latter a thorny problem until the 1890's. Also indicated is the probable extension of the short lived horse drawn narrow gauge extension from Barn Houses to Wharf Tunnel.

By use of the Barn Houses deviation Fletchers railway would have remained within the Atherton boundary and not have crossed the Pennington township boundary as the Henrietta Street route would have done, thereby clearing Fletchers of any onus of responsibility regarding a ditch at Stock Platt, referred to as an "open sewer" and the cause of much wrangling between the townships of Pennington, Westleigh and Atherton as to who was causing the mess and who should clear it up.

would grow up ignorant of a tunnel that to this day exists under their very feet and I wonder if, from somewhere in the heavens above, John Fletcher & Others shed a little tear for their forgotten enterprise.

Authors Note. Speculation exist as to why the tunnel had been constructed with limited clearance, 9ft 5" high x 10ft 3" wide. Had it been meant after all purely for horse drawn traffic, or were there engineering limitations imposed by ground levels between Stock Platt and the Bridgewater Canal. I rather think the latter as surveyors bench marks on the 1849 ordnance survey maps indicate little difference in levels between those two points. A horse drawn mine tub would hardly need a tunnel 10ft 3in. wide.

Plate 44. Wharf Street Tunnel as in 1964, bricked up with ventilation courses at the top and the cutting overgrown with vegetation. Note the almost negligible distance from the top of the tunnel arch to the brick wall bordering on Chapel Street directly above. The parapet wall of the Tyldesley-Leigh-Pennington Branch can be seen at the top of the picture.

Photo, Ian Isherwood.

Plate 45. Bedford Basin as viewed from the south bank of the Bridgewater Canal in 1952. On the right hand can be seen coal stacked for landsales, at this period delivered by road. The wheel really had come full circle. The London & North Western Railways viaduct for the Leigh branch line can be seen coming into view on the left and continuing across picture, where, in the centre it bridges Chapel Street and clearly visible below this is the tunnel mouth of Fletchers railway.

Photo, C. H. A. Townley.

Plate 46. After a working life of ninety-six years Hawthorn Leslie 0-4-0 well tank, formerly "*Ellesmere*" 244/1861, is prepared for its journey to Scotland (via Bag Lane) from Howe Bridge Colliery on 14th September 1957 and into preservation. Its original stablemate "*Lilford*" is thought to have been taken out of service about 1898/9. Mitchells, the Bolton machinery firm advertises a locomotive of the same name for sale in 1899. It is thought to have been sold for scrap, but the reason for its withdrawal from Atherton Collieries is unknown.[3] Sister locomotive "*Atherton*" of 1867 was scrapped in 1952. These were the only three locomotives ever to work through the Wharf Tunnel with its restricted clearance, to Bedford Canal Basin.   *Photo, C.A.Appleton courtesy Jim Peden.*

A little imagination is now required to visualise these locomotives running on a line more or less parallel with Charles Street, crossing The Avenue and Holden Road, trundling past the Athletic Sports Ground hauling their trains of loaded, wooden bodied coal wagons bearing the legend "Atherton" to disappear into the tunnel entrance at the end of Gamble Street. This must have been quite a sight for the observer but not so for the driver who had to carry out this task, day in day out, with the tunnel roof just a few inches above his head, deflecting down a deadly cocktail of fumes and smoke being ejected from the locomotives funnel immediately in front of him !

Many people living in Leigh will remember Darlingtons Ironmongery shop on Bradshawgate, the stock for which was kept under one of the railway arches near Leigh Station. Immediately below this particular arch was Wharf Tunnel and over a prolonged period paraffin stored in the arch had been leaking out of its storage tank and seeping into the tunnel, only discovered when fire broke out in the tunnel after the passage of a train.[2]

Two new boilers had been fitted to "1861" during its lifetime and also replacement cylinders. Frames, motion and wheels are original.

---

[1] I quote from the Leigh Chronicle of 11th April 1857, but I think this may have been a case of the reporter jumping the gun. The extension of the Stock Platt Branch would have been to a gauge of 2'-0", but the tunnel was being constructed large enough, just, to take the new standard gauge of railway opened in 1861.

[2] From information supplied by Cyril Golding.

[3] From information supplied by C. H. A. Townley.

Plate 47. Atherleigh station opened rather late in the life of the Bolton and Leigh Railway, on 14th October 1935, to serve local housing estates built after World War I. This view, looking south, dates from the early 1960s. At top left is the iron footbridge over the line at Kirkhall Lane and to the right of that can be seen Hayes Mill on Victoria Street, demolished in mid 1992. *Photo, Dr. J. G. Blears.*

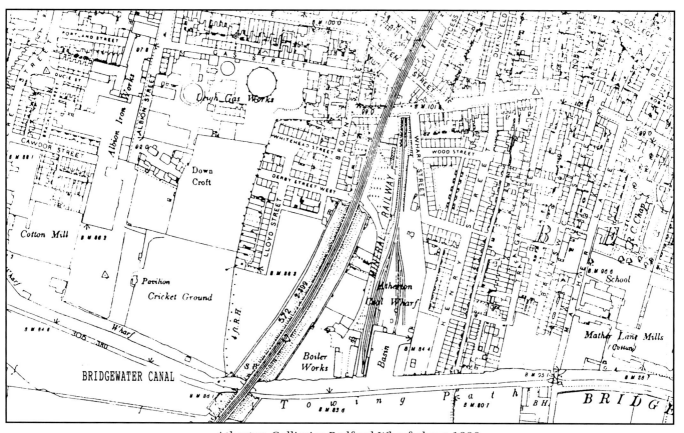

Atherton Collieries Bedford Wharf about 1890

Plate 48. Atherleigh Station, as viewed here from Westbourne Avenue in 1950, gives an impression of being a country location in pleasant rural surroundings where school children thronged the platforms to begin their daily routine, or where perhaps housewives, with shopping baskets at the ready, boarded the market day specials. Whilst Atherleigh was hardly that, the station was usefully sited to serve nearby housing. It was a great pity that the level of passenger services, post World War II did nothing to attract custom. *Photo, Stations U.K.*

Plate 49. Construction of Atherleigh Station underway in 1934 of particular interest is, on the left, two joiners using the platform edge staff for setting out the edge and line of the Up platform. The footbridge gives some of the locals a vantage point for inspection. *Photo, Wigan Heritage Services.*

KIRKHALL LANE CROSSING

A GATE HOUSE constructed at Kirkhall Lane about 1845 was demolished in 1880 when line improvements were being carried out. The existing gates replaced by those of Saxbys patent, interlocked with the signalling. At the same time a footbridge was constructed with a similar structure at Westleigh Station.

The gate house keeper at Kirkhall Lane at this period was one Benjamin Flavell, hence "Bens Brow" a name synonymous with this location even today. Ben had been the only occupant of the gate house and it seems was particularly well liked by the locals. Now aged seventy, Ben had arrived in Leigh in 1830 with a gang of navvies from Dudley to assist in the construction of the Kenyon & Leigh Junction Railway and was at Kenyon on the opening day of the Liverpool & Manchester Railway, keeping the "gazing multitude" off the rails. After completion of the Kenyon & Leigh line he became a platelayer and had assisted in the laying of three types of rails on the Bolton-Kenyon

lines, "fish bellied", "fluted" and "big rails". "Owd Ben" as he came to be known, was on hand when a serious accident occured here in November 1860 involving a goods train. Permanent Way workers were replacing some of the rails near to the crossing and had actually taken out three lengths of rail. Unfortunately they had not given the signalman time to advance the required distance of 1200 yds up the line to warn oncoming trains of the works ahead before doing so. The train was double headed with 57 goods wagons. The train crews saw the signalman running towards them on their approach to the crossing and despite applying the brakes and putting the locomotives into reverse gear could not stop. Both engines overturned upon leaving the rails and the wagons were said to have piled up into a neat pyramid. The footplate staff of the leading engine managed to jump clear, those on the second were killed, despite Bens valliant rescue attempt in dragging one of the footplate men

Plate 50. LMS Stanier designed 2-8-0 No. 48663 running tender first, approaches the level crossing at Kirkhall Lane, Leigh, on 15th June 1963. The occasion is a Locomotive Club of Great Britain (LCGB), brake van special, a day excursion from Bag Lane to Kenyon Junction and return at a fare of 7/6d. This was the last chance to travel over the former pioneering Bolton & Leigh line from Bag Lane to Pennington, closure of that section occuring two days later. The use of brake vans for passenger carrying purposes on main line tours would never be allowed today, but was a common ocurence in those days. The footbridge at Atherleigh (Westbourne Avenue) can be seen on the extreme right. In the centre is Bright Street Methodist Chapel. *Photo, Dr. J. G. Blears.*

whose clothes were on fire, from the overturned engine.

Kirkhall Lane crossing was an important and busy location on the Bolton & Leigh line. Representations had been made by the Leigh District Council in 1895 asking the London & North Western to construct a bridge over the railway line here, which in the event was rejected by the Company. The crossing gates were operated by a wheel in the cabin and only when the gates were closed to road traffic could the gate keeper release the appropriate lever, which in turn allowed the signalman at Fletchers or Westleigh Sidings to operate the signals, thus allowing the approaching train to continue.

Plate 51. A northward view, towards Kirkhall Lane from Westleigh Station, with Hayes Victoria Mill prominent in the centre, and part of the Parsonage Colliery complex which officially closed on 27th March 1992, on the left. The connection to the colliery can be seen just in front of Westleigh Sidings signal box. *Photo, Dr. J. G. Blears.*

Plate 52.

Rugby Specials to Westleigh Station always worked via Kenyon Junction, where, if necessary a pilot would join the train. At Westleigh the engine would be detached from the stock and work light to Atherton Junction to turn in the triangle. Arriving back at Westleigh where, after crossing over, the empty stock would be drawn into Parsonage Colliery Sidings in readiness for the return journey. Previous to the withdrawal of local passenger services over this route in 1954 the 4.20pm from Bolton Great Moor Street was allowed to pass before the returning special worked over into the Westleigh platform. Alternatively if the train was rather long, as in our photograph of the Ex-Whitehaven special and there was not sufficient room between Kirkhall Lane crossing gates and Parsonage Westleigh Sidings access, then the stock would be propelled over the crossing after running round to wait wrong road prior to drawing into Westleigh Station. The signal box at Westleigh Sidings would have to be opened as required for these workings.

During the days of regular passenger workings it was customary practice to open Fletchers Sidings box at 7am, allowing any traffic from Fletchers Sidings to be worked up to Bag Lane by an early morning trip locomotive from Crook Street. The signal box would then be switched out, usually about 8.15am, and the signalman on duty then had to walk to Westleigh Colliery Sidings box in order to open the latter for the passage of the 8.23am Bolton Great Moor Street to Liverpool Lime Street train. By opening Westleigh Sidings box the Liverpool train was allowed to proceed to Westleigh Station and by the time the train had loaded, Pennington South had cleared a Chester to Manchester Exchange via Tyldesley train, thereby allowing the Liverpool bound train to continue without delay, otherwise the train would have been held at Fletchers Sidings. Once the 8.23am was safely on its way Westleigh Sidings box was switched out, the signalman returning to Fletchers Sidings to re-open the box there about 9.15am.

In the 1950's most of the coal traffic from Parsonage Colliery went out via Howe Bridge West Junction on the Tyldesley - Wigan line. However, a small amount left via Westleigh Sidings, usually about 10-15 wagons at any one time, tripped worked to Kenyon Junction Yard for onward destinations. This was the duty of an ex Bolton Crook Street turn, which after shunting Bag Lane for any "south's" would call at Westleigh Sidings to pick up any coal traffic for Kenyon. On arrival at Kenyon the trip workings collected would be shunted as required, the engine then working its way back to Crook Street with freight from Kenyon.

Plate 53. The date is 14th January 1956 as a return Rugby League special from Whitehaven of some considerable length waits on the Up line, having run round in the Atherton triangle. The locomotive is Patriot Class 4-6-0 No. 45549 as built with parallel boiler. The result of the match, a 16-5 win for Leigh.
The second view opposite, showing the train at rest, the locomotive having steam to spare.
Photos, C.B.Golding.

49

Plate 54. Part of the Bolton & Leigh Railway trackbed, from Wigan Road Atherton to Pennington was converted into a by-pass, Atherleigh Way, in 1984/5. A view from the junction of Twist Lane and Atherleigh Way towards the former Westleigh Station site in March 1992. On the extreme right the pedestrian crossing is just visible, this now occupies the former footbridge crossing. The road level was raised here at Twist Lane during construction of the by-pass and the railway bridge which had occupied this site since 1880 was demolished in 1979. The railway embankments at this location were also removed during by-pass work. Hayes Victoria Mill on the extreme right hand and Parsonage Colliery can be identified on Dr J.G.Blears photo on **Plate 51.** Part of the site here is now occupied by a supermarket and further development of the Parsonage site is likely to take place in the near future. *Photo, Author.*

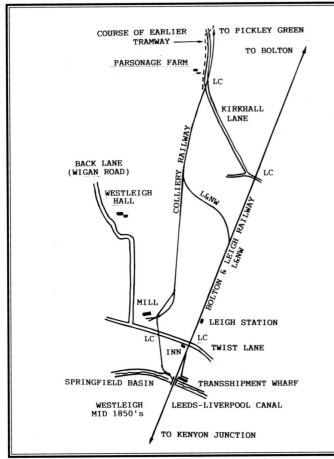

Connections at Westleigh with the Bolton & Leigh Railway in the mid 1850's. The Leigh Station as indicated is that known as the "Shed", sited south of the later Westleigh Station shown in the accompanying photographs. The connecting branch from the main line to the colliery line was owned by the London & North Western, but not it seems the land over which it passed.

In the second decade of the twentieth century, Parsonage Colliery would be sunk in this area. Coal continued to be transported from the Westleigh Coalfield to Springfield Basin on the Leeds-Liverpool Canal until the late 1940's. Westleigh Mill, shown on the 1840's Ordnance Survey, was rail served and a landsale yard had been located here, probably about the time of conversion of the tramway to standard gauge. The colliery railway extended northward to collieries in the Pickley Green area of Westleigh, but deviated from its original course at Parsonage Farm. Further alterations would take place in the 1880's in this area. See area map Chapter II, page 92.

WESTLEIGH

CONNECTIONS had been made here by colliery railways situated on the west side of the main Bolton & Leigh line by 1853, if not before. A report in The Leigh Chronicle gives details of a fatal accident to an employee of the London & North Western Railway in May of that year, during shunting operations between main line and sidings. A further accident occurred near the same location in 1856, involving a train from John Speakman's Broadfield Colliery, which was situated to the north of the yet to be built Tyldesley-Wigan line. However, to trace the origins of this connection we must go back much further.

John Fletcher had come from Bolton, to begin sinking shafts in the Atherton area in 1768 and in 1776 he and Thomas Guest, Yeoman of Bedford, Leigh took a lease for coal mining of 99 years from Robert Vernon Atherton, landowner, of Atherton Hall. By 1803 John Guest, son of Thomas had sold his share to Ralph Fletcher, son of John.

In 1794, The Lancaster Canal Co. had proposed a canal from Aspull to meet up with the Duke of Bridgewaters canal at Worsley. This was strongly objected to by Henrietta Maria Atherton, daughter of R.V.Atherton, deceased. She sent her agent to London and was successful in opposing the scheme. The canal would have passed close to Atherton Hall, cutting across The Avenue and Platt Fold. In 1797 Henrietta married Thomas Powys, who, on the death of his father in 1800, became the second Lord Lilford.

The Duke of Bridgewaters Canal to Leigh from Worsley had received Royal Assent in 1795, the works being completed in 1799. The Leeds Liverpool Canal met this end on at Pennington in 1820. Certainly by this period the opposition that successfully thwarted the Lancaster Canal proposal was regretted.

The early part of the nineteenth century had seen a number of shafts sunk in the Pickley Hey and Pickley Green areas of Westleigh by Ralph Fletcher, in addition to those in the Lovers Lane area. By 1821 Atherton Collieries were working twenty-one pits on land belonging to Atherton Estates. Many of these mines were small operations, employing only a few colliers at each and transport from the individual mine by horse and cart would have been expensive.

Atherton Collieries were using tubs running upon rails fastened to sleepers with "Chowbent" nails in 1800. Dr Lunn in his History of Atherton quotes Taylors Foundry as supplying Fletcher's with 646 yds of iron rails in one year alone. It

seems illogical to assume that these rails were all for underground use, that the Fletcher's had not recognised the value of tramways on the surface, as well as below it. With these points in mind I believe it likely that Fletchers constructed tramways to connect their Lovers Lane, Pickley Green and Pickley Hey Collieries in the early years of the nineteenth century. Part of this system may well have formed the beginnings of another narrow gauge tramway running from Pickley Green to Springfield Basin on the Leeds-Liverpool Canal at Twist Lane. This section of tramway would have opened between 1842 and 1846. The Westleigh Tithe Map of 1846 clearly shows a tramway running from Blackcroft Colliery, Pickley Green, owned by Handley & Co., to Springfield Basin. It is probable that this tramway would have been a 2ft gauge, horse drawn system using mine tubs drawn straight from the pit head to the canal.

Daglish is alleged to have commented in 1838 that Colonel Fletcher worked coal in the Pickley Green area, "but were given up some years ago". This would explain the absence of any tramway between Lovers Lane and Pickley Green on the early 1840's Ordnance Survey maps. The sections around Pickley Green survived because of other developments in the area and are recorded. The abandonment by Fletcher's of their pits in the Pickley Hey and Pickley Green areas would have coincided with the coming of the Bolton & Leigh Railway. This was the impetus for the next stage of railway development by the Atherton Collieries. i.e. the Stock Platt Branch.

As to the other collieries in the area, Springfield, Park, Bankfield, Broadfield and the early West Leigh Lane Collieries, (the latter not to be confused with the Diggles Westleigh Pits) all appear before 1850 with a succession of owners. It is also very likely that conversion to standard gauge of this tramway from Pickley Green to Springfield Basin took place in the period 1850/3 and at the same time connections made near Leigh Station with the Bolton & Leigh line. The point at which the standard gauge colliery line crossed Westleigh Lane was moved to the south of Parsonage Farm, the earlier tramway had run west of and alongside Westleigh Lane to cross at, or near to the present Village Club

Springfield and Blackcroft Collieries were put up for sale in 1857, along with various items of plant & stock. The advert for this sale in the Leigh Chronicle included 38 large railway wagons, 21 other wagons 10 large boats, 7 steam engines 1 locomotive engine, weigh machine, rails etc, and continues "the colliery has access by its railway and pier-head to public canals and railways. The wagon way belonging to the colliery is 2¼ miles long and also produces a considerable and increasing income from the carriage of produce of other neighbouring collieries to the Leeds-Liverpool Canal (at Springfield Basin) and the Bolton-Kenyon Railway." The purchaser was John Speakman, owner of Broadfield.

Further shafts were sunk near to Westleigh Village by Kirkless Hall Coal Co. about 1860, who were advertising coal for sale at 4½d per cwt in 1865 at their yard near Westleigh Mill, off Twist Lane, which was connected by a siding from the colliery railway. These pits were taken over by Wigan Coal & Iron Co. in that same year. Wigan Coal & Iron Co. sank Sovereign Pits in 1876 and had taken over Priestners on the death of its owner John Speakman, in 1873.

In 1882 Wigan Coal & Iron Co. extended the colliery railway to meet the London & North Westerns Eccles-Tyldesley-Wigan line at Howe Bridge West Junction and in 1891 extended it still further to their Eatocks Pits at Daisy Hill, using the former trackbed of John Speakman's Broadfield Colliery line. A connection had already been made by the Wigan Coal & Iron Co. with the Lancashire & Yorkshire Railway west of Daisy Hill Station in 1888 from their Eatocks mine, thereby providing through running from the Wigan Coal & Iron Company's Westleigh coalfield to their Kirkless Iron Works. All the early Westleigh collieries had closed by the mid 1880's, including the original Kirkless Hall Pits.

Wigan Coal & Iron continued to develop their interests here and sank another shaft at Sovereign in 1900. The sinking of Parsonage Pits began in 1914 and marked the final phase of mining operations in this locality. The last of the Sovereign pits closed in 1925, about the same time as Priestners No2. The other Priestners mine continued until 1934 and was the last of the nineteenth century Westleigh Collieries to be dismantled in 1937. Parsonage closed in March 1992, demolition quickly taking place in the Autumn of that year.

For 200 years, probably even more, the winning of coal and all that it entails had been carried out in and around the village of Westleigh, but on that cold November day when Parsonage Colliery chimney hit the dirt, another piece of industrial Lancashire was consigned to history.

Plate 55. Demolition of Parsonage Colliery chimney, 29th November, 1992.   *Photo, Author.*

The original booking office at Leigh, for the Bolton and Leigh Railway is said to have been the Railway Inn, on the diagonally opposite corner to the present similarly named public house built in 1880. One William Rich built the "booking office" Railway Inn in 1833, probably to replace an earlier Inn there. In the 1850's, what is described as a more convenient "shed" was built midway between Twist Lane and the later Westleigh Station.

During holiday week of July 1852 no less than 3,393 tickets were issued at Leigh and special trains were run to Newton Races. In 1859, on three successive days in October, fast excursion trains were run from Bolton Great Moor Street at 6.15am, calling Atherton at 6.32 and Leigh at 6.40, to see Brunels *Great Eastern* Steamship at Holyhead, "to arrive at about 11.15am". "Railway steamboats will convey passengers to and from the pier to the *Great Eastern* free of charge". Fares were :- 1st class, 15/- or 17/6d for two days. or "covered carriages" 10/- and 12/6d for two days. Tourist tickets were available in 1860, valid for one month, to Blackpool, Fleetwood and Lytham, 1st class 8/- 2nd class 6/6d. These early trains to the Fylde Coast would work south to Kenyon Junction and then via Parkside East Junction onto the Wigan Branch Railway and northwards to Preston, which was ironically the route and destination of the last trains from the London & North Western "Bedford-Leigh" station in 1969. From 1861 excursions were being advertised from Atherton and Leigh stations to Bangor and Conway at a fare of 6/-. At this period over 80,000 tickets were being issued annually at Leigh. All this from a "shed".

A goods yard near to the early Leigh Station had closed on 2nd November 1864, on the opening of the goods yard at Bedford Leigh Station.

Where the Bolton & Leigh Railway met the Leeds-Liverpool Canal at Twist Lane, Leigh, a small engine shed is thought to have been built in the late 1860's, probably to replace an 1840's built engine shed at Chequerbent where water supplies were a problem. Since 1832 the canal company had been supplying water for locomotives at Leigh and later editions of the 1849 Ordnance Survey show a "shed" alongside the canal at Twist Lane, in addition to a transshipment wharf.

The Kenyon & Leigh Junction Railway had paid £500 by way of compensation to the Leeds-Liverpool Canal Company for the privilege of being allowed to construct a bridge over their canal at Leigh and an additional £15 per day if navigation was interrupted during its construction.

In 1835 there had been a proposal, not proceeded with, for the construction of a branch line from a point near Twist Lane, to terminate near the Bird-in-th-hand public house, Hindley. On its route connections were to be made with the Ackers Pits at Bickershaw and other nearby collieries in the Hindley Green area. The industrial development of Westleigh and surrounding areas would have been very different had this scheme gone ahead.

Plate 56. Ivatt LMS designed 2-6-2T No. 41212 calls at Westleigh with a Bolton to Kenyon train in the early 1950s.
Photo, John Robinson Collection

Plate 57. This unique view at Westleigh Station, on the Up platform was taken during exercises designed to familiarise the Railway's employees with basic first aid knowledge. Of particular interest is the construction of Parsonage Colliery in the background. Sinking of the shafts at Parsonage had commenced in 1914, suspended in 1917 to re-commence in 1919. It is probable that the photograph dates from 1916, after the railways came under the control of the Railway Executive Committee and the introduction of Ambulance Trains on Britain's railways, necessary because of the appaling number of casualties incurred on the battlefields of France during World War I.

Plate 58. In our second view four of the staff have simulated arm injuries and with their attendants pose for the camera, again on the Up platform. Note the period advertising board on the left which includes pictorial post cards of the London & North Western Railway at a price of 2*d* (lp) per set of six.

Both of these prints were salvaged from Kenyon Junction Station, a few days before demolition took place. One can only wonder what other priceless gems of our railway heritage were lost when such official vandalism occurred at this, and other locations.

Photos, J. Guest,
Courtesy
P. Hampson
Collection.

Plate 59. Westleigh Station *c.* 1950, with the cared for look so lacking at many of today's stations. The footbridge was the vantage point for **Plate 51**, and was a handy short cut for pedestrians going to and from Leigh via the Pit Yard and on to Wigan Road.

The Station buildings as seen here are thought to date from the mid 1860's, replacing the first Leigh Station known as "The Shed", which in turn had replaced the Railway Inn as the Booking Office. The construction of this allegedly spartan building is also unclear but was certainly in existence by the early 1850's. The Station was originally called Leigh, becoming Westleigh on 1st August 1876, closing along with all the other stations on the branch, with the exception of Kenyon Junction, on March 29th 1954 when regular passenger services between Bolton and Kenyon were withdrawn. A few Rugby League Specials used the station until 1958. Again note the concrete platforms which still look new. *Photo, Stations U.K.*

Plate 60. Royalty at Westleigh as H.M. King George V poses for the official photographer at Westleigh Station during his visit to Leigh on 12th July 1913. *Photo, Authors Collection.*

Plate 61. Substantial re-building of "Metal Bridge" which carried the railway over the Leeds-Liverpool Canal near Twist Lane, Leigh, occurred in the mid 1930's. The new works replaced the original construction where the Kenyon & Leigh Junction Railway had connected, end on, with the Bolton & Leigh Railway. This is a view westward taken during re-construction of the bridge. On the far side is Springfield Basin where coals from the collieries in the Westleigh area were transferred to canal barges. In the long ago days of the Bolton & Leigh Railway the transshipment wharf was situated on the extreme right hand, a site later occupied by Engine Shed Row, two up two down housing built about 1880. By this period transfer of goods from railway to canal here had ceased. Springfield Basin however, was to continue in use for many years and four sidings, plus a Loop road which ran alongside the colliery railway and onto a loading jetty here, are shown on the 1929 Ordnance Survey. A new concrete structure was built here in 1984/5 to carry Atherleigh Way over the Leeds-Liverpool Canal.

Plate 62. Flagman James Hampson at work during the re-construction of the railway overbridge at Leigh with Springfield Basin in the background. *Photos, P. Hampson.*

PENNINGTON

THE station here was opened by the Kenyon & Leigh Junction Railway in 1831 and had originally been called Bradshaw Leach, becoming Pennington on 1st February 1877. Pennington became a junction when the branch from Tyldesley via Bedford-Leigh made connections here in 1864.

A proposal was put forward by the London & North Western Railway in 1859 to close Bradshaw Leach, owing it was said to representations made by the Turnpike Road Commissioners who objected to road traffic being delayed at the crossing when trains stopped at the station. This was before the track was doubled from Pennington to Kenyon Junction, in conjunction with the opening of the Tyldesley-Bedford/Leigh-Pennington line and the construction of a road-over bridge here. It was also stated by the London & North Western that receipts from the station did not cover expenses. This met some opposition from the local railway users, one in particular saying he had never seen more than "one conveyance delayed at the crossing", that receipts and usage were more than stated by the railway authorities because "season tickets were often booked at main offices". In the event the railway authorities bowed to public pressure and Bradshaw Leach stayed open.

Plate 63. In this Edwardian view looking north, the line from Tyldesley can be seen trailing in from the right just under the St. Helens Road over bridge at Pennington. This bridge was demolished in 1984 when the Leigh by-pass was under construction. The by-pass itself following the route of the railway line from Pennington to Wigan Road, Atherton. More recently (1994), a further section of trackbed, from Pennington to the A580 East Lancs Road near Kenyon has also undergone the same metamorphosis. *Photo, Authors Collection.*

Plate 64. Pennington South Junction *c.* 1970 with only the Down line remaining. In the background the dismantled bridge of the Pennington Down Loop, at the point where it crossed the Kenyon & Leigh Junction Railway, can be seen. *Photo, J. Eckersley.*

Plate 65. Testimony to the longevity of railway equipment is this 1953 view of a L&NWR lower quadrant gantry at Pennington. Left for Bickershaw, straight on for Bolton and the right hand signal for Leigh & Tyldesley. Note also the advertising hoarding behind the fencing, 1/2*d.* (one shilling and two-pence) i.e. six new pence for the benefit of younger readers, to Bolton, how times change.

Photo, W.S. Garth.

Plate 66. Returning from Kenyon Junction, having run round its train, 48663 calls at Pennington for a photo stop before departing for Bag Lane. Although the section from Pennington South to Atherton Junction closed as from 17th June 1963, a ballast train traversed the branch from Pennington to Westleigh on 9th October 1963, probably on recovery operations.

Photo, Dr J G Blears.

Plate 67. A view of the same signal gantry a couple of years later, taken from St. Helens Road bridge looking south towards Kenyon. The L&NW pattern signals have been replaced by LMS upper quadrant types and with the abolition of Pennington East & West Junction signal boxes the distant arms have disappeared altogether. The signal in the "off" position controlling the line to Leigh, whilst access to the Bickershaw Branch, now operating as a through siding controlled by Pennington South, with the small "calling on" signal giving the train permission to approach Pennington South box for further instructions. *Photo, L. Smith.*

Plate 68. The Kenyon Down Distant remains in situ although the track it served has now been lifted. In the background is the A580 road-over bridge and on the right fog detonator apparatus remains in place next to the plate-layers cabin.

Photo, J. Eckersley.

59

Plate 69. An Edwardian view of Pennington Station complete with some fine examples of period advertising.

Photo, Authors Collection

Plate 70. There must be more "Railway" Inns, Hotels, Taverns, etc. in Gt. Britain than any other genus, this particular one at Pennington depicting a London & North Western Railway 2-2-2 "Problem" Class locomotive of 1859 vintage.

The establishment was more frequently called the "Robin Hood" (the present name), and the railway footbridge seen in the accompanying photographs was also known as "Robin Hood steps". This name arose because of a certain gentleman who lived in a farm close by to the hotel when it opened and who being a frequent figure at the bar, either in manner or appearance (I hesitate to say which), was said to resemble the folklore hero and was therefore nicknamed Robin Hood. Is this a case, perhaps, of truth being stranger than fiction?

Photo, B Hilton.

KENYON JUNCTION

KENYON was sometimes referred to as Bolton Junction Station in the early years and is listed as such in Osbornes guide to The Grand Junction Railway *c.* 1838. The original station here was a source of much criticism in the early years of the railway. Local papers are littered with complainants letters of "poor facilities" and yes, wait for it, "missed connections," when travelling to or from Manchester. The railways did eventually respond to this adverse publicity and a number of timetable alterations appear in print as they attempt to get it right. Waiting rooms as such had again been described as "sheds" offering little shelter, if any, from the elements. The station was officially named Kenyon Junction in July 1843.

In November 1879 the London & North Western had announced their intention to seek powers to make a new railway from the Winwick Branch, south of its crossing by the Liverpool & Manchester Railway, to connect with the Kenyon & Leigh Junction Railway at Kenyon. This was included as part of the plans for the Bolton & Leigh deviations and called "The Winwick and Kenyon Junction Railway". In the event the branch was never built being dropped before the Bill came before Committee.

In late 1882 the contract for the re-construction of the station as seen in the accompanying photographs was let, and by mid 1883 the old station had been demolished, new platforms constructed with the complete re-building of station accommodation on an altogether more grandiose scale taking place. Sidings capacity here was quadrupled to cater for the immense goods and minerals traffic now working via Kenyon. A two road engine shed at this location appears to have been provided about 1840 and was large enough to hold six locomotives. It seems to have closed prior to 1870, possibly when the engine shed at Tyldesley was built in the late 1860's.

Other works undertaken here during the station re-building included the abolition of the level crossing at Wilton Lane, the lane itself being re-routed and carried over the Kenyon & Leigh Railway by a new bridge.

Over the years Kenyon Sidings continued to handle their fair share of goods traffic. Coal from Bag Lane and Westleigh as already mentioned, along with trip workings from Bickershaw & Abram Collieries, Speakmans or Jacksons Sidings. Edge Hill traffic worked via Kenyon Yard, as did traffic from Chester and North Wales. St. Helens Junction to Patricroft trains working via Kenyon called at Leigh and Tyldesley en-route to shunt the goods yards. In addition there were through coal trains from the local collieries, working through to Warrington or Widnes. Sometimes if shunting operations were required at Kenyon and no trip locomotive was available the Yard Foreman would summon a locomotive from Springs Branch.

In the mid 1960's the only coal traffic working via Kenyon was from Jacksons Sidings at Tyldesley. The closure of many of the local collieries and the increasing competition from road transport brought about the closure of Kenyon Goods Yard on 1st. August 1963. The passenger station had closed on 2nd January 1961.

Kenyon No. 1 was a Class 2 signal box situated alongside the Down Liverpool-Manchester line and controlled the junction for the Bolton and Tyldesley routes and the western end of Kenyon Sidings. Kenyon No 1 also employed a Telegraph Lad and because of its important location a telephone concentrator panel had been installed here with lines to Tyldesley, Earlestown, Deal Street (Manchester), the water softening plant situated east of Broseley Lane, Pennington South & Bickershaw Junctions, Barton Moss, Bag Lane, the PW office and the Yard Foreman at Kenyon. Although every signal box was connected to Control, they were not all connected to each other. However, it was possible for some cabins fitted with the appropriate switch apparatus to act as a go between. For example, Springs Branch No. 1 Signalman could, by contacting the Signalman at Howe Bridge West and asking him to turn his switch, speak to the Signalman at Fletcher Street, Bolton, or vice-verca, thus keeping each other informed of any operating problems.

Kenyon No. 2 was a Class 3 cabin sited on the north side of Wilton Lane bridge and had control of the northern end of Kenyon Yard and the Loop, or "Field Road" as the railwaymen called it.

The Station Masters house was situated on the south side of Wilton Lane, between the goods yard access road and the running lines, as were cottages for the Assistant Line Manager and Mechanical Chargemen, who, *c.* 1940's were Bert Bromley and Maurice Griffiths. Platelayer, Arthur Butler and Porter, Tom Foster, employed at Kenyon at the same period, also resided in railway cottages here.

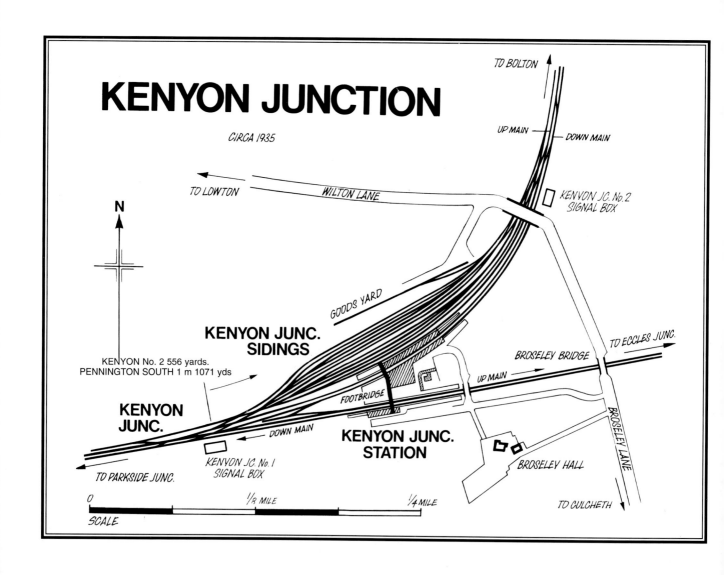

KENYON JUNCTION

CIRCA 1935

TO BOLTON

UP MAIN — DOWN MAIN

TO LOWTON — WILTON LANE

KENYON JC. No.2 SIGNAL BOX

N

GOODS YARD

KENYON JUNC. SIDINGS

KENYON No. 2 556 yards.
PENNINGTON SOUTH 1 m 1071 yds

TO ECCLES JUNC.

BROSELEY BRIDGE

UP MAIN

KENYON JUNC.

FOOTBRIDGE

DOWN MAIN

KENYON JUNC. STATION

BROSELEY HALL

BROSELEY LANE

KENYON JC. No.1 SIGNAL BOX

TO PARKSIDE JUNC.

TO CULCHETH

0 — 1/8 MILE — 1/4 MILE

SCALE

Plate 71. A photograph taken from the road bridge on Wilton Lane looking south about 1954 with the array of lines and sidings reflecting a sight once to be seen all over the railway system having been built up over many years of expansion, soon to show signs of terminal decline. On the extreme left are the main running lines, Down, Up and Loop. The Foreman Shunters cabin is near the signal on the right.

Photo, L. Smith.

Plate 72. Kenyon Junction Station, where, in 1831 the Kenyon & Leigh Junction Railway met the Liverpool & Manchester Railway. This is a view looking east, that is in the Manchester direction. It would seem that an East Junction was contemplated here and the 1849 series Ordnance Survey maps clearly show the earthworks for such a connection. However, no evidence that track was ever laid has come to light. *Photo, W. S. Garth.*

Plate 73. Stanier Class 5 No. 44837 passes Kenyon Goods Yard in the early 1950's with a train of vans from Earlestown Works. *Photo, P. Hampson.*

Plate 74. Departing from Kenyon in April, 1949, with the push-pull service for Bolton, an example of the Ivatt designed 2-6-2 Tank locomotives in the shape of No. 41213 which had been introduced by the LMS in 1946.

Photo, W. D Cooper.

Plate 75. Kenyon Junction Station on 26th March, 1954, as BR Standard 2-6-2T No. 84002 waits at the platform with the push-pull service from Bolton Great Moor Street. These locomotives were introduced in 1953 and were virtually identical to the previous LMS design.   *Photo, D. Chatfield.*

Plate 76. Probably the last remaining structure on the Bolton-Kenyon route is this bridge carrying Wilton Lane over the trackbed, built to replace the level crossing that was situated a few yards to the north and constructed during the 1883 works for the re-building of Kenyon Station and Goods Yard. As can be seen from this 1995 view, it is quite a large bridge with a span of 63 ft. 9 in. and 7 ft deep riveted sides.   *Photo, Author.*

Plate 77. An example of the LMS, Ivatt designed 2-6-0 locomotives first introduced in 1947 with double chimney as seen here. The later engines of this class were built with a single chimney and the early examples subsequently re-built to the same status. In this early BR view No. 43029 pulls away from Kenyon Junction with a Manchester Exchange –Liverpool Lime Street train. The high running plate of these locomotives was, at the time, a very unusual feature for a British locomotive, perpetuated in later BR Standard designs; allowing railway staff easier access to the locomotives working parts.   *Photo, W. D. Cooper.*

Plate 78. A similar viewpoint to the one above taken some forty years later as Class 47 No. 47626 "*Atlas*" passes the site of Kenyon Junction station with a Sundays, Newcastle-Lime Street diversion on 1st April, 1990.

Photo, Author.

Plate 79. A L&NW-designed 19-in. goods engine, as re-built with Belpaire firebox, comes off the Leigh Branch with a troop train in 1939. Note Kenyon No. 1 signal box, minus nameboard thus conforming to wartime regulations.

Photo, P. Hampson.

Plate 80. Railway Cottages at Kenyon, a view in the "Up" direction towards Leigh and photographed about 1965 by contributor Peter Hampson who, at the time, lived in No. 3. The cottages were situated between the running lines and the Goods Yard approach road, off Wilton Lane. One wonders why such imposing properties were demolished only a few years later, irrespective of their no longer being required for railway usage. Wilton Lane overbridge, seen alongside, partly obscures Kenyon No. 2 cabin from view.

Plate 81. May 1969, as an unidentified Type 4 locomotive heads east, seen passing Kenyon No. 1 cabin with a Liverpool Lime Street-Newcastle express. To the rear of the train is the railway over-bridge carrying the Manchester Central-Wigan Central line which had closed to traffic on the opening of the Haydock Branch Junction Chord on 22nd April 1968. *Photo, J. Eckersley.*

Plate 82. Kenyon No. 2 signal box and Wilton Lane bridge about 1964. Before this bridge was constructed during the re-building and exansion of facilities at Kenyon Junction *c.* 1883 there had been a level crossing and gate house here. Kenyon No. 2 worked three shifts, opening at 4.45am Monday and closing at 3am Sunday.

Kenyon No. 2 cabin was abolished on 17th December 1967. Kenyon No. 1 cabin was abolished on 17th September 1972 when track circuit working was instituted, this controlled from the new Warrington Power Box. *Photo, P. Hampson.*

Plate 83. Lights out at Kenyon Junction for the last time as Class 1 Shunter Sid Ball douses the lights on the evening of 30th December 1963 on closure of Kenyon Yard to freight traffic. *Photo, P. Hampson.*

CHAPTER II

WIGAN VIA TYLDESLEY AND ECCLES TO MANCHESTER

PROPOSAL AND CONSTRUCTION

***REPORT FROM THE BOARD OF TRADE
DATED 15TH FEBRUARY 1861.***

Empowers the London and North Western Railway to make:

(1) A railway, length 12 miles 22 chains, from a junction with the company's Liverpool and Manchester Railway, near Eccles (Eccles Junction) to a junction with the North Union Railway, near and to the South of Wigan.

(2) A railway, length 3 miles 39 chains, from a junction with railway (l) at Tyldesley, to a junction with the company's Bolton and Leigh line, at its Bradshaw Leach Station; and

(3) A railway, length 25 chains, to connect railway(l) with the B&L (Bolton & Leigh) at Atherton, in the parish of Leigh, all in the County of Lancaster and to be completed within five years.

And for these purposes to apply the company's funds, and to raise further sums of £350,000 by new ordinary shares and £115,000 by borrowing.

Board of Trade March 1861

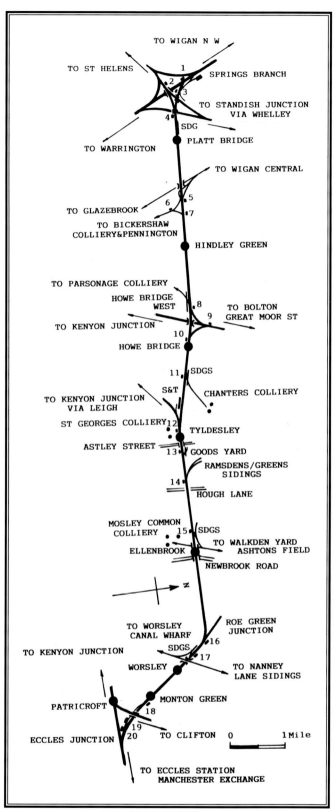

Tyldesley was the premier station on the London & North Westerns branch from Eccles to Springs Branch Junction and the junction for the branch to Pennington. Opened officially on 1st September 1864, with stations at Worsley, Ellenbrook, Tyldesley, Chowbent, Hindley Green and Platt Bridge, with Bedford Leigh on the Pennington Branch. Chowbent became Howe Bridge in April 1901, Bedford Leigh became Leigh & Bedford in 1876 and finally Leigh on 1st July 1914. Bradshaw Leach on the Kenyon & Leigh Line became Pennington on 1st February 1877. Monton Green, between Worsley and Eccles Junction opened in November 1887.

SIGNAL BOX KEY

1	Springs Branch No. 1	11	Chanters Sidings
2	Fir Tree House Junction	12	Tyldesley No. 2
3	Cromptons Sidings	13	Tyldesley No. 1
4	Platt Bridge	14	Hough Lane
5	Bickershaw Junction	15	Ellenbrook
6	Hindley Field Junction	16	Roe Green Junction
7	Scowcrofts Junction	17	Sandersons Sidings
8	Howe Bridge West	18	Monton Green
9	Atherton Junction	19	Patricroft North Yard
10	Howe Bridge East	20	Eccles Junction

News of the proposed Eccles-Tyldesley-Wigan and the Tyldesley-Leigh-Pennington Branch Lines first appear in July 1860 and were well received in the locality.

Not to be outdone however, the Lancashire & Yorkshire Railway again put forward a proposal for a line to the north of the planned London & North Western route. This was to leave the Lancashire & Yorkshire line at Hindley, pass through Atherton, near to the cemetery, thence be routed through the Shakerley Estate to re-join the Lancashire & Yorkshire lines at Pendleton.

At a meeting of the Lancashire & Yorkshire its chairman outlined their proposals saying "this was no new idea, only a fitting opportunity had been awaited". Once again the coal deposits of the area had attracted attention, for the chairman goes on to say, "this field would supply one million tons of coal for four hundred years". No doubt the Lancashire & Yorkshire, acutely conscious of the London & North Western scheme, now regretted not proceeding with one of their earlier proposed lines through or near to Tyldesley. They had clearly missed their chance. Parliament had already indicated that only one of these proposals would be allowed to proceed.

Over the following months various news items appeared in the local press regarding the benefits to the populace that the railway would bring. Nearly all of those referred to and gave favour to the London & North Western plans.

By March 1861 the London & North Western Bill had passed its final reading in the House of Commons and would shortly be submitted to the House of Lords and although their competing Bill had been rejected, the Lancashire & Yorkshire publicly stated their intentions to oppose the London & North Western Bill at every opportunity.

Petitions had already been sent by the inhabitants of Leigh and Bedford to Parliament in favour of the London & North Western proposals and further petitions from Astley and Tyldesley were to follow. Consequently the London & North Western Bill successfully passed through the House of Lords without, as it happens, any hindrance, the Lancashire & Yorkshire withdrawing their opposition to the Bill at the last moment having made a "compromise" after negotiations which terminated in a "Quid-pro-Quo" that it was said, "had no immediate bearings upon the railway accommodations of the district". The Eccles-Tyldesley-Wigan and Tyldesley-Pennington Railway Bill received the Royal Assent on 11th July 1861.

The route of the railway was laid out by Elias Dorning, an engineer with considerable knowledge of the South Lancashire coalfields. Contractors for the line were Messrs Treadwell & Co. The London & North Western engineer was William Baker Esq and the works were to be completed in the spring of 1863 as per the terms of the contract.

The first sod of the railway was cut at Worsley by the Earl of Ellesmere on 11th September 1861. On the appointed day Directors and Officials of the London & North Western Railway and invited guests arrived by rail at Patricroft Station and were then conveyed by cab to Worsley. Others travelled by canal from Manchester. The rendezvous was the Grapes Inn, Worsley, and from there a procession commenced headed by the Earl of Ellesmere's Band. A "select" company of Navvies followed, one bearing aloft a spade of "burnished steel" to be used in the inaugural ceremony, and another pushed a wheelbarrow of Spanish Mahogany, no skimping on timber here!

Following the navvies came the nobility, the Earl and Countess of Ellesmere, the Earls of Powis and Derby, Lord Brackley and others. Directors and Officials of the London & North Western were close behind, including Richard Moon, Messrs Hardman Earl, James Bancroft, Matthew Lyon, J.A.Tinnie, J.P.Westhead, Edward Tootal, T.W.Rathbone and W. Cawkwell, General Manager. The engineer and contractors representatives preceded the M.P. for Wigan the Rt Hon H Woods and the Mayors of Manchester, Oldham and Warrington.

Next came what can only be described as a "whose who" of local commerce and industry and included, Wm Gerrard of Ince Hall Collieries, the Fletchers of Atherton Collieries, Richard Guest, J&E Burton, Caleb Wright, George Green, John Holland, T. T. Hayes, J. Holcroft, James Diggle, H. Jackson of Bedford Lodge, Messrs W. Ramsden, W. Hesketh, J. Gregory of Snapes Colliery, Hindley, W. F. Hulton Esq and many more.

The chosen spot for the ceremony was a "picturesque nook", known as the "Old Factory" on Swinton Road, Worsley. Here stages had been erected for the assembly of guests and a projecting platform from which the cut sods could be dispatched to a deep hollow. The Earl carried out his task in a "workmanlike manner", Mr Moon did likewise and was so followed by several others.

The procession then returned to Worsley Court House, decorated inside and out for the occasion, to a "sumptuous dinner" served at 3pm to 200 guests, at which the obligatory speeches were made. Thomas Part of Wigan gives reference to the Lancashire & Yorkshire powers to build a railway in the same vicinity in 1847, but had allowed them to lapse, and expresses his satisfaction that at last a railway was about to be built.

W. F. Hulton Esq, recollecting back to the beginnings of the railways mentions being introduced to George Stephenson by his father, who he said, had been responsible for persuading Stephenson to leave Newcastle and had "concocted that scheme of railway with him", that is the Bolton & Leigh (to cheers) "which had preceded the Liverpool & Manchester". The contractor, Mr Treadwell stated he could "almost positively" fix the opening date as 1st May 1863.

As the months progress no indication is given in contemporary reports that the construction is anything other than on schedule and would not meet the May 1863 deadline. Work seemed to be proceeding well at various locations along the line. The completion of the bridge over Greens Colliery line at Tyldesley and the operation of locomotives over it bear this out. Press reports are mostly confined to the unusual, for example, the uncovering of the Roman Road at Worsley, or fatalities to workers on the line, the first of which is at Bedford when, in August of 1862, a navvy was killed by some wagons "coming up the line". May of 1863 was a particularly bad month for accidents. A carpenter killed on Leigh Viaduct, a death at Parr Brow Tyldesley in the sandstone cutting there, another navvy killed at Bedford by a "fall of earth" and a "line driver" crushed by spoil wagons at Bradshaw Leach. By this time of course the railway should have been ready to open.

Neither the line to Wigan or the branch through Leigh presented any engineering difficulties. Total length of railway was 16 miles 6 chains. However, there were 88 bridges to construct and the Leigh Viaduct at 350 yds in length consisted of 22 arches, of spans between 23ft and 30ft, with four larger spaces spanned by iron girders.

Late in 1863 the engineers report to the directors states that the works are in "a forward state," 1,400,000 cubic yds of earthwork, out of 1,600,000 have been removed, 81 bridges completed and the viaduct at Leigh "nearly complete". No doubt the sheer number of structures on the lines and an underestimate of the volume of work involved in these was a contributory factor, but the prime reasons for delay would not be revealed until the opening day celebrations. In any event a revised date of spring 1864 was now given for completion.

The viaduct at Leigh was completed by February 1864, but the other bridges are described as only "nearly finished." Of the 36,000 yds of permanent way, 22,000 had been laid and a further 10,000 yds ballasted ready for rails.

What does seem remarkable however, is the fact that the station sites at Worsley, Ellenbrook, Atherton, Hindley Green and Bedford-Leigh had, only now, at this late stage been decided upon.

The site at Hindley Green was fixed after James Diggle secured a personal interview with the directors of the London & North Western. Bedford Leigh station and the goods yard alongside were actually in Atherton; the odd alignment of township boundaries at this location would cause problems in later years with the laying of sewers and making up of roads for no less than three local boards, Pennington, Bedford and Atherton together with the London & North Western Railway, who were held responsible by many for the apparently atrocious state of approach roads to the station, would be involved in setting out and agreeing the proportionate costs to each party.

In February 1864 the Directors of the London & North Western had authorised the allocation of £7,000 in order to double the track between Pennington and Kenyon Junction. Total cost of the railway, excluding land, was £250,000 or £15,625 per mile. The final cost including land purchases and works on the Pennington-Kenyon section was £526,000.

Worsley Station was constructed of white brick with the arched window and door heads in alternate white, red and black brick. There were two first and second class waiting rooms complimented by a "spacious" booking office. Platforms of approximately 300 ft in length were to be paved in red and blue tiles with stone borders and a light glass canopy afforded protection to the passengers. No doubt the more substantial construction of Worsley Station was a concession to the Earl of Ellesmere. For their part the Bridgewater Trustees were to open out approach roads to the station.

All the remaining stations had buildings of timber frame construction, erected by Parnell of Rugby and would have been delivered by rail to the various locations for assembly on site.

Tyldesley had the same arrangements as Worsley, including a glass canopy to afford some protection against the elements and tiled platforms. Tyldesley also had an island platform, on the Down line, reached by an underground subway.

Bedford-Leigh was said to have a "spacious and convenient booking office" under one of the arches, with a waiting room on each platform and separate (wooden) staircases of 43 steps to the Up and Down platforms, also of timber construction.

The platforms at Ellenbrook and Hindley Green were of a more solid nature whilst those at Chowbent were of timber construction. Platt Bridge seems to have been a combination of both (see **Plate 100**). Bradshaw Leach Station at the junction of the new railway and the Kenyon-Bolton line was "re-modelled and improved".

Tyldesley and Bedford Leigh were also provided with Goods "Stations". In all probability the

Plate 84. Construction of the arched viaduct on Queen Street, Leigh, underway in 1863, and the only portion of the structure now remaining. The method of forming a timber arch as a temporary support structure clearly seen here. Note the joiner near the ladder on the right with his 12 inch square and highly polished saw, from usage I might add, not from bulling up. The Gent on the left wearing the topper is obviously of some importance, perhaps Treadwell the main contractor, or the Engineer, Wm. Baker. At this point construction is taking place above Fletchers Bedford Tunnel, built only five years previously. *(Photo, Wigan Heritage Services).*

Tyldesley Goods Station opened on the official opening day, 1st September 1864. Leigh however, did not open for goods until 2nd November 1864, at the same time as the "Old Leigh" goods station on the Bolton & Leigh line was closed.

The works from Kenyon, through Leigh to Tyldesley, were inspected by Colonel Yolland on 17th July 1864, as was the Winwick cut-off line which had been under construction at the same time. On the following day an inspection of the line from Eccles Junction, via Tyldesley, to Wigan took place. Four engines were used to test the bridges. All was well, Colonel Yolland made his report to the Board of Trade and in mid August the opening day was announced.

Wednesday 24th August 1864, apparently a day of bright and glorious weather, a day fit indeed for the ceremonial opening of the new railway, a day well prepared for by the local populace and London & North Western Railway Company alike.

A special train left Manchester, Hunts Bank, at 12.30pm, drawing 18 coaches and one luggage van, each decorated with flags and bright colours. The bells of Salford Churches gave their approval as the train gathered momentum. A stop at Eccles to take on some of the guests, thence to make its way upon the new metals. Small gatherings of people at Worsley and Ellenbrook welcomed the train as brief stops were made there. Tyldesley was reached at 1.09pm. and here was made the greatest effort to celebrate this connection at last with the Railway World.

Every vantage point was occupied. Sunday School Children filled the open fields to the left of Waring St. Triumphal Arches spanned the roads and almost every house had some form of banner or decoration flying in the breeze. The Ellesmere Yeomanry Band provided the musical accompaniment as the train drew into a station overflowing with sight seers and bedecked with colour.

The view from Tyldesley Station was described as "magnificent" with "open country as far as the eye can see" and "fertile landscape relieved by masses of foliage." Richard Moon must surely have been well pleased with the London & North Westerns latest territorial conquest.

Following a brief respite at Tyldesley the train continued to Bradshaw Leach arriving at 1.33pm, where a waiting engine was attached, to depart at 1.38pm, arriving back at Tyldesley at 1.49pm.

A field battery employed nearby, had on returning here, been strengthened by the addition of two mortars, the gunners causing some amusement, retreating hastily after applying the fuse.

Departing from Tyldesley at 1.53pm, the train paused at Chowbent, where flags portrayed the motto "Welcome to Great Britain", a response no doubt by some local wit to a "where the hells Chowbent" remark uttered by some luckless railway official who probably got an earbashing in Lanky dialect into the bargain!

The "grimy faces" of some colliers were to be seen on reaching Hindley Green and after passing Platt Bridge the train continued to Wigan where, at 2.20pm, guests from the North boarded for the return journey to Tyldesley.

On arriving at Tyldesley, the Directors and guests alighted from the train to march in procession headed by the 60th (Atherton) Lancashire Rifle Volunteers Band, 2,100 school children, 800 members of friendly societies, Worsley Yeomanry Band, Tyldesley Drum & Fife Band and the Mosley Band. The procession wound its way through the streets of the town to arrive at the new mill of E&F Burton, where all the children and participants received a "tea" paid for by public subscription, with a donation from the London & North Western.

The dignitaries and invited guests, many of who attended the inaugural sod cutting ceremony at Worsley three years previous, sat down to a more lavish meal, described as a "cold collation" which included an enticing selection of meats; beef, lamb, veal, chicken, lobster or crab and various game, to be followed by entrements and dessert, all washed down with champagne or other wines of quality, available in abundance.

Mr Richard Moon Esq, Chairman of the Board of Directors, presided and proposed the first loyal toasts, to be followed in turn by Mr W.F. Hulton of Hulton Estates, whose family for so long now had been closely involved with the embryo railway system from its very beginnings in the locality.

In his speech to the gathered assembly, Mr W.F. Hulton Esq makes reference to his meeting with George Stephenson in 1825, which he touched upon at Worsley Court House in 1861 and also to the close involvement of Lord Lilford in that "small and old railway from Bolton to Leigh". We also learn from this speech that he had originally given his support in 1861 to the Lancashire & Yorkshire's Bill in preference to that of the London & North Western, for he felt, "his individual interest and a large proportion of those to the North" would be better served by the Lancashire & Yorkshire scheme. He speaks with some regret of having at the time to do this, "for the first time in

his life having to leave his old established friends the London & North Western Company". He thanked the Directors for inviting him and hoped the Chairman and Directors of the London & North Western "would keep their eyes open to that district which lies a little North", for "it would be in their interest to do so, for they would prevent the Lancashire & Yorkshire coming into competition there, by supplying the coal owners with the facilities they wanted". With particular mention to his old friend Mr Hardman Earl and the body of Directors present, he toasted the success of the Eccles-Tyldesley-Wigan line to loud applause.

A number of speakers followed to offer their congratulatory comments on the railway. Eventually it was the turn of Mr Treadwell the contractor, who enlightens us as to the real cause of delay in construction of the line. This it transpires was none other than the British climate, excessively wet in the summers of 1862/3, with suspensions of operations altogether in the intervening winter. Added to this there was "a long time in getting possession of the land". Mr Treadwell added that he hoped the operation of the railway would be more profitable to the London & North Western than the construction of it had been to him.

The Chairman proposed the last toast of the day, "the health and happiness of the navvies." After the National Anthem had been played, many of the guests left about 6.30pm, by special trains for Bedford-Leigh, Wigan and Manchester. Later the celebrations were brought to a close with a firework display.

Tyldesley's railway had arrived in some style and was well received, an association that was to last one hundred and five years. The magnificent uninterrupted view towards the Cheshire Plain would soon be obscured somewhat by continuous mining developments and industrial railways to the South. St Georges Colliery already producing, Nook and Gin Pits to follow; the mines nourished the railways, they would grow, mature and die together. What had been the impetus for the railway would also be its demise, with the mines gone we did not need the railway, so we were told. Ironically the former Lancashire & Yorkshire line on Tyldesley's northern boundary, the advent of which was so long, has survived the rationalisation of the post Beeching era. It has had the last laugh over the "Quid-Pro-Quo" and with not an ounce of those black diamonds in sight continues with its daily duty of transporting an even more valuable commodity, people.....!

WIGAN NORTH WESTERN

WIGAN received its first railway station in 1832 when the Wigan Branch Railway opened its line from Parkside to a terminus at Chapel Lane, Wigan. On 22nd May 1834 the Wigan Branch Railway amalgamated with the Preston & Wigan Railway to become the North Union Railway. In 1838 the North Union opened a new station on the present site when services to Preston commenced. This in turn was replaced by the much larger London & North Western Station built between 1889 and 1894 and which, with the onset of electrification, was substantially remodelled in 1974.

The London & North Westerns Eccles-Tyldesley-Wigan Branch made connections with the North Union Railway at Springs Branch, Manchester Lines Junction, about 1¼ miles south of Wigan, in 1864. Services from Hunts Bank, Manchester, via Tyldesley commenced officially on 1st September 1864 and the North Union Station at Wigan became an important interchange point for connecting services to Preston and the North. In the last quarter of the nineteenth century, services from Liverpool or Crewe often combined at Wigan with Ex Manchester via Tyldesley to Carlisle and Glasgow trains until Preston became the focal point for such operations in the twentieth century.

The North Union Railway was fully absorbed by the London & North Western Railway on 26th July 1889 and the enlarged Wigan North Western Station became the terminus for the Manchester Exchange via Tyldesley local trains. Express passenger services from Manchester Exchange to Windermere, Barrow and Glasgow continued to work via Wigan, making connections at Preston, until the mid 1960's. Recently, from the summer 1994 timetable, it was once again possible to travel directly from Manchester via Wigan North Western to Windermere on the newly inaugurated Manchester Airport via Bolton service.

Plate 85. An early 1960's view as English Electric Type 4 No. D227 pauses at Wigan North Western with an Up express. These locomotives were introduced in 1958, this particular example built locally at Newton-Le-Willows. Given the name "*Parthia*" in June 1963, re-numbered to 40 027 in December 1973, the locomotive was finally withdrawn in April 1983. Note the rake of LMS stock including a period I BCK vehicle immediately behind the locomotive and on the right, Wigan Top Yard full of freight wagons. The latter is now the station car park. *Photo, BR*

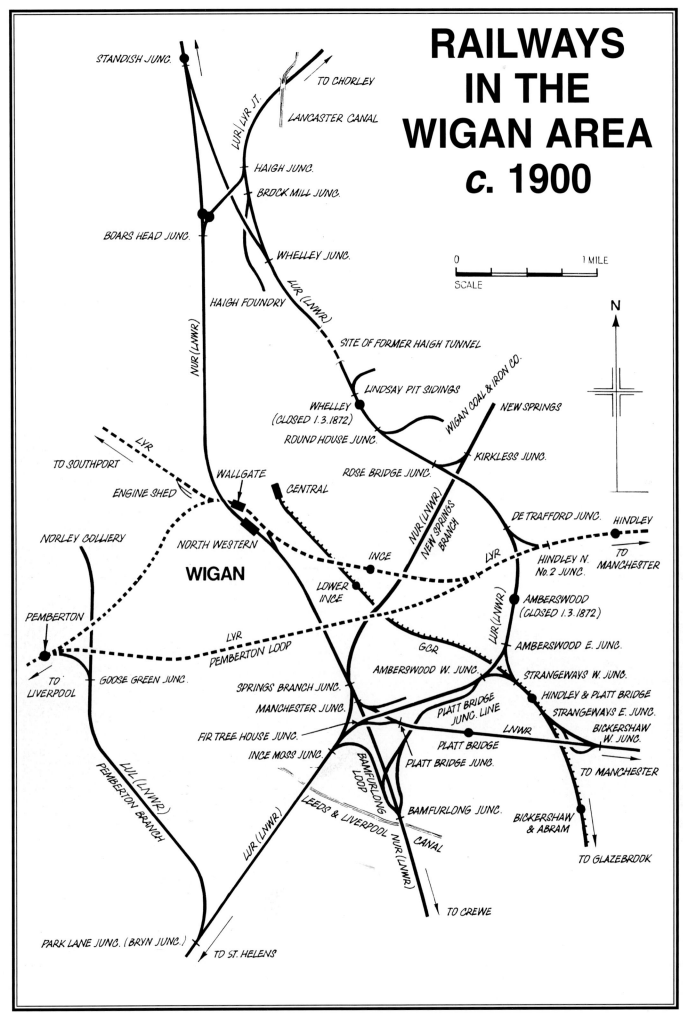

RAILWAYS IN THE WIGAN AREA c. 1900

STANDISH JUNC.

TO CHORLEY

LANCASTER CANAL

LUR/LYR JT.

HAIGH JUNC.

BROCK MILL JUNC.

BOARS HEAD JUNC.

WHELLEY JUNC.

LUR (LNWR)

HAIGH FOUNDRY

NUR (LNWR)

SITE OF FORMER HAIGH TUNNEL

LINDSAY PIT SIDINGS

WHELLEY
(CLOSED 1.3.1872)

WIGAN COAL & IRON CO.

NEW SPRINGS

ROUND HOUSE JUNC.

KIRKLESS JUNC.

LYR

TO SOUTHPORT

ROSE BRIDGE JUNC.

WALLGATE

ENGINE SHED

CENTRAL

NUR (LNWR)

NEW SPRINGS BRANCH

DE TRAFFORD JUNC.

HINDLEY

TO MANCHESTER

NORLEY COLLIERY

NORTH WESTERN

WIGAN

INCE

LYR

HINDLEY N.
No.2 JUNC.

AMBERSWOOD
(CLOSED 1.3.1872)

LOWER
INCE

LUR (LNWR)

PEMBERTON

LYR
PEMBERTON LOOP

GCR

AMBERSWOOD E. JUNC.

TO LIVERPOOL

GOOSE GREEN JUNC.

AMBERSWOOD W. JUNC.

STRANGEWAYS W. JUNC.

SPRINGS BRANCH JUNC.

MANCHESTER JUNC.

PLATT BRIDGE
JUNC. LINE

HINDLEY & PLATT BRIDGE
STRANGEWAYS E. JUNC.

BICKERSHAW
W. JUNC.

FIR TREE HOUSE JUNC.

LNWR

PLATT BRIDGE

INCE MOSS JUNC.

BAMFURLONG LOOP

PLATT BRIDGE JUNC.

TO MANCHESTER

LUL (LNWR)
PEMBERTON BRANCH

LUR (LNWR)

LEEDS & LIVERPOOL CANAL

NUR (LNWR)

BAMFURLONG JUNC.

BICKERSHAW
& ABRAM

TO GLAZEBROOK

TO CREWE

PARK LANE JUNC. (BRYN JUNC.)

TO ST. HELENS

0   1 MILE
SCALE

N

76

Plate 86. A rare visitor to London & North Western metals in the shape of A2 No. 60528 "*Tudor Minstrel*", seen arriving at Wigan North Western on 23rd April 1966 with an Altrincham Society Railtour from Manchester Exchange to Edinburgh via the Waverley route. To the rear is Wigan No. 1 Signal Box with a Stanier Class 5 shunting.

Photo, B Hilton.

Plate 87. London & North Western designed "*Prince of Wales*" Class No. 5770 calls at Wigan North Western with a northbound express during the Easter Holidays in 1926.

Photo, W. D. Cooper.

Plate 88. Shortly after leaving Wigan North Western, Stanier Class 4, 2-6-4T No. 42572 accelerates away with a local train for Manchester Exchange via Tyldesley in June 1960 and is seen on the Up Fast line. This particular two cylinder, taper boiler design was introduced by the LMS in 1935.

Photo, J. R. Carter.

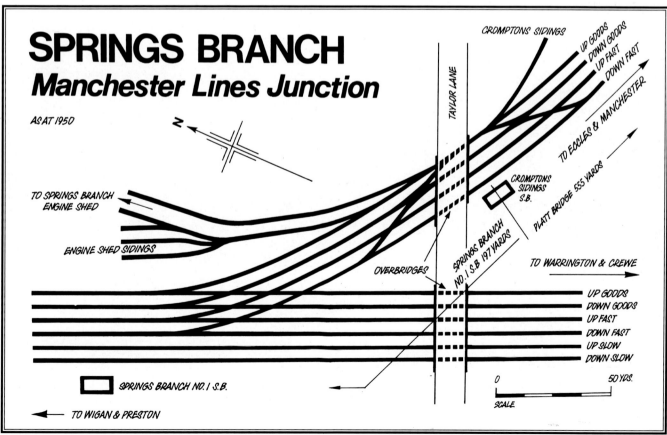

SPRINGS BRANCH
Manchester Lines Junction

AS AT 1950

Z

TO SPRINGS BRANCH
ENGINE SHED

ENGINE SHED SIDINGS

TAYLOR LANE

CROMPTONS SIDINGS

UP GOODS
DOWN GOODS
UP FAST
DOWN FAST

TO ECCLES & MANCHESTER

CROMPTONS
SIDINGS
S.B.

PLATT BRIDGE 555 YARDS

SPRINGS BRANCH
NO. I S.B 197 YARDS

OVERBRIDGES

TO WARRINGTON & CREWE

UP GOODS
DOWN GOODS
UP FAST
DOWN FAST
UP SLOW
DOWN SLOW

☐ SPRINGS BRANCH NO. I S.B.

◀— TO WIGAN & PRESTON

0   50 YDS.

SCALE

Plate 89. Britannia Class No. 70016 "Ariel" heads south on the Up Goods Loop with a parcels train as the Up Fast receives some attention from the P.W. Gang. On the left is Springs Branch Shed and on the right Springs Branch No. 1 signal box, directly opposite of which the Manchester lines diverge,, crossing the Up and Down Goods Loops.

Photo, J. R. Carter.

Plate 90. Class 8F locomotive No. 48257 takes the Up Manchester line at Springs Branch with a Lostock Hall-Bickershaw empties train in February 1968. In the centre is Springs Branch Yard and in the background, engine sheds for the steam and diesel eras.

Photo, Alex Mann.

Plate 91. BR Type 2 No. D7633 at Springs Branch en-route to Howe Bridge West Junction with coal empties for Parsonage Colliery on 16th February 1970. Although closed as a through route via Tyldesley to Eccles Junction only nine months before, track lifting has already taken place here. *Photo, Ian Isherwood.*

Plate 92. Britannia Class No. 70027 *"Rising Star"* (Minus Namplate) reversing off Springs Branch Shed on the Up Goods Line going "Right Away" to Platt Bridge about 1966. *Photo, Alex Mann.*

CROMPTONS SIDINGS

CROMPTONS Sidings signal box controlled all engine movements from Springs Branch Shed worked via the Up and Down Loops, these lines being permissive/wrong line worked, whereas the Up and Down Main lines were absolute block. Cromptons box could not accept a Down Main line train from Platt Bridge unless Springs Branch No 1 box also accepted it, this because of the close proximity of Cromptons to the busy Warrington-Wigan main lines and the falling gradient towards the latter from Platt Bridge. Any failure to bring a train to a halt here could have disastrous consequences as in an incident of a loose coupled coal train approaching Cromptons in the mid 1960's with signals at danger. The weight of the wagons buffering up pushed the engine forward and into a passing car transporter train causing considerable damage. Engines going on/off shed via Cromptons were logged by the Signalman and reported to control; often engines were worked in multiple, making life much easier for the Signalman, having to set the road once rather than a number of times. Even so there were about 100 train movements per shift, three shifts per day. Cromptons box would close at 6am Sunday morning to re-open at 6am Monday morning, although during W.W.II a Sunday turn was worked.

Until the early 1960's the connection to the former Crompton & Shawcross's siding continued in use to a nearby coke plant situated to the east of Warrington Road, the former Fir Tree House Sidings used for this traffic also controlled by Cromptons box. If any mishaps occured which prevented engine movements on/off shed via Cromptons it was possible to come off at Springs Branch No. 1 end "through the yard" working onto the loop lines.

Plate 93. A return working from Howe Bridge West Junction in 1970 as another Type 2 locomotive, No. 5251, minus the "D" prefix but still in the early BR two tone green livery, passing Cromptons Sidings cabin, this particular example a Midland pattern replacement for the original London & North Western cabin. Note also the lifted Up and Down running lines and the slewing over onto the Down Goods. The bridge in the background carried the Fir Tree House Junction to Amberswood West Junction route over the Manchester lines here. *Photo, Alf Yates.*

Plate 94. Some fifteen years later on 13th August 1985, at the same location as *Plate 93,* Type 2 diesel locomotives Nos. 20 104/090 bring up the rear of a return Fiddlers Ferry to Bickershaw Colliery train which on this occasion consists of forty three "Merry-Go-Round" wagons. Out of sight at the head of the train are Nos. 20 018/010.

Photo, Author.

Plate 95. Stanier Class 5 No. 45451 on the Up Goods Loop passing Cromptons Sidings about 1962 to work via Tyldesley with the 08.50 Carlisle-Manchester Ship Canal freight. This working was the duty of Patricroft crews who would travel passenger on a Manchester Exchange to Preston local train making connection with a Glasgow bound express, alighting at Lancaster and connecting with a local passenger train to Carnforth where they would relieve the Carlisle crew. Often time was spent languishing in one of the loops there awaiting the passing of southbound expresses or fast freights prior to departure. On approaching Patricroft it was usual to work into North Yard via the Monton Green Loop, drop off a few wagons there, re-marshall the train, continue to Manchester Ship Canal Sidings and then return light engine to Patricroft Shed.

Springs Branch No. 1 signal box can be seen to the rear of Taylors Lane bridge, the latter being the vantage point for a number of photographs taken here.

Photo, J. R. Carter.

PLATT BRIDGE

ACCESS to the the Tyldesley-Eccles line could also be gained, at the Wigan end, from the west, via Fir Tree House and Platt Bridge Junctions. Alternatively, workings routed south from Standish Junction via the Whelley line used Amberswood East and Bickershaw Junctions to access the Tyldesley route.

In 1863 the Lancashire Union Railway, a group of Wigan coal proprietors, proposed, with the connivance of the London & North Western, a railway to run from St Helens via Ince Moss to Blackburn, deep into Lancashire & Yorkshire territory. Counter proposals from the latter would have resulted in a Blackburn-Chorley-Wigan route. In the event Parliament authorised, in 1864, the construction of the Lancashire & Yorkshire line from its connection at Cherry Tree on the Blackburn-Preston line, to Chorley; the Lancashire Union's line from Adlington to a junction with the North Union at Boars Head, and the Lancashire Union's railway from St. Helens via Ince Moss to Haigh Junction, near Whelley on the north eastern side of Wigan. There it joined with the Boars Head-Adlington line. It was later decided to build the Boars Head-Adlington section as a joint project between the Lancashire & Yorkshire, and Lancashire Union Railways. Included in the Acts for the Lancashire Union Railway was a connecting spur from Fir Tree House Junction, near Ince Moss, to a junction at Platt Bridge with the Wigan-Tyldesley-Eccles line and a junction with the Lancashire & Yorkshire, De Trafford Junction, to Hindley No2 Junction west of Hindley station. The completed Lancashire Union line and the connecting spurs were opened in November and December 1869.

A connection from Standish on the WCML, to a junction with the Lancashire Union Railway at Whelley was opened by the London & North Western on 5th June 1882. The completion of a southern link with the WCML in the form of the London & North Westerns Platt Bridge Junction Railway, opened on 25 October 1886. This connection ran from Bamfurlong to meet with the former Lancashire Union Railway at Amberswood West Junction, thereby providing a much used through route avoiding the ever increasing congested central area around Wigan. Trains using this route were generally referred to as working "Whelley".

Platt Bridge Junction signal box was unusual in that it controlled traffic on two levels, the high level or Manchester lines and the low level or Whelley lines. On the high level were the Up &

Down Goods and Main running lines between Cromptons Sidings and Platt Bridge with, in addition, the route to Fir Tree House Junction. The Goods lines were permissive and also worked wrong line, whereas the Main lines were absolute block. Both the Up and Down lines between Fir Tree House Junction and Platt Bridge Junction were permissive/wrong line worked. Adjacent to the Up Main line was Hindley Green Siding which ran from Platt Bridge Junction towards Platt Bridge Station, this also controlled from Platt Bridge box and for a number of years used to stable the Royal Ordnance Factory (ROF) train stock. On the low level were the Up & Down Goods lines between Bamfurlong and Platt Bridge and the "Up Flying Junction" line from Platt Bridge to Bamfurlong Junction. Any workings signalled on this line would join the Up Fast West Coast Main Line at Bamfurlong Junction, hence the term "Flying".

Platt Bridge Junction box was in continuous operation, working 6am-2pm, 2pm-10pm and 10pm-6am. At weekends the Signalman on at 10pm Saturday evening worked until 8am Sunday morning, with the Signalman who had finished his Saturday shift at 10pm booking on again at 8am Sunday morning until 7pm in the evening, and lastly the poor sod who had worked the first 10pm-8am Sunday shift returned at 7pm and worked through until 6am Monday morning. Those with a mathematical mind will have deduced by now that this allowed one Sunday off in three, in rotation, for each Signalman.

The configuration of lines and sidings at and around this location is in stark contrast to the present day. Gone are the once extensive sidings at Bamfurlong, as have the various connecting junctions emanating from the Whelley route, the latter itself just a distant memory. On the former high level only the redundant single track to Bickershaw remains, terminated at a distance of 2m 39c from Springs Branch, the last remnant of the former Wigan-Tyldesley-Eccles route, now lying silent. On the low level the Up & Down Goods lines run only in the direction of Springs Branch from Bamfurlong Junction, passing en-route, rampant vegetation occupying sites where the hustle and bustle of railway activity was music to the ears of anyone even remotely interested in British Railway practice. The West Coast Main Line itself, this the "Premier Line" in the British Isles, one could today, literally catch a cold waiting to observe a passing train, for a fraction of the traffic that once worked the route now passes, such has been the demise of the railways.

A particular problem associated with loose coupled trains on steep gradients was the possibility of "runaways", that is part of the train breaking loose because of a fractured coupling or, as in the following incident, because of a coupling "jumping".

The train in question was a return empties from Widnes to Bickershaw Colliery, working up the bank from Ince Moss Junction to Platt Bridge Junction in the early 1960's, at approximately 10.30am. After working slow line from Garswood Hall to Ince Moss the train was really getting stuck in to get the wagons over Fir Tree Bank. When the train engine passed Fir Tree House Junction the Driver saw the signals at Platt Bridge Junction set to danger, so he buffered his train up, the result was that twelve wagons and brake van broke from his train and began to roll back towards Ince Moss Junction, gathering speed as they did so. Immediately the Signalman at Fir Tree House Junction gave the Signalman at Ince Moss Junction "vehicles running away wrong line" on the block bell. Now the Signalman at Ince Moss had only a couple of seconds to make up his mind what course of action to take, either let the runaways run off the road into the traps situated on the bank, or to keep it on the road and save the Guard from serious or fatal injury. The latter course of action was taken and the runaways seesawed until coming to a stand. After getting a bank engine to push the rear portion up to the rest of the train, the train went "right away" to Bickershaw.

As emergency regulations had been carried out this incident was reported to the Yard Master at Springs Branch.

Next day, the Block Inspector arrived at Ince Moss Junction Cabin and asked the Signalman why the train had not been run off the road and into the traps provided. The Signalman explained that as no passenger train had been accepted on any adjoining line, he felt it was the right thing to do seeing the Guards life was at stake. However, the Signalman was politely reprimanded and informed if such an occurrence happened again the runaways were to be run off the road and into the traps, thereby protecting the main lines. On his way out of the cabin the Block Inspector gave the Signalman a knowing glance, acknowledging the life saving action of the alert Signalman.

Plate 96. Stanier 8F No. 48509 gets to grips with the climb from Ince Moss to Platt Bridge Junction with coal empties for Bickershaw Colliery about 1966. *Photo, Alex Mann.*

Plate 97. The remaining single track as on 30th October 1994 viewed in the Up direction, that is towards Manchester from the location of Platt Bridge signal box, the remains of which can be seen on the extreme right. This was a BR built cabin which had replaced the earlier L&NW design at the same location. Ike Banks and Bill Brownville were two of the Signalmen to work the box in BR days. The 55 lever frame from this BR cabin is now installed in Warrington Central Signal Box. On the left is the vandalised token box still in situ, lastly used for coal traffic from Bickershaw Colliery.

Photo, Author.

Plate 98. Platt Bridge Junction cabin also controlled the low level, or Whelley lines. Seen on the Up Whelley, low level, on 14th May 1972, is Type 4 diesel No. D220 *"Franconia"* passing Spring View cricket ground with a short freight train having worked south over the Whelley line from Standish Junction. This section is part of the L&NW Platt Bridge Junction Railway. Latterly a section of single track was retained here as a headshunt for sand deliveries to the CWS glass works at Platt Bridge. These deliveries ceased in 1986 and the remaining section of track lifted in 1989. A gas pipeline was laid beneath the trackbed here in 1992 and during 1993 the cricket pitch extended up to the edge of the former trackbed, i.e. the fence on the extreme left.

Photo, Ian Isherwood.

Plate 99. Platt Bridge Junction on 24th April 1968 as Class 8F No. 48115 approaches from Fir Tree House Junction, the signal box at the latter just visible to the left of the locomotive. On the right, two of the Metropolitan Vickers built Type 2 Co-Bo locomotives Nos. 5707 & 5712 approach on the Up Goods line after coming off shed at Springs Branch. Only introduced in 1958 these locomotives were not exactly a success and by September of 1969 all the Class of twenty had been withdrawn for scrap. Between the 8F and the Metrovicks can be seen two of the three tower blocks of flats at Worsley Mesnes which were constructed in the mid 1960's. These, like the Metrovicks were not a success either, demolition taking place in 1991. Built of pre-cast concrete slabs transported over the Pennines by road from Leeds, this type of construction was seen by the powers that be as the answer to the housing problem. They were however, prone to mould growth and damp, and tended to generate "Social Problems". At sixteen storeys high they did offer a superb view of the surrounding area. *Photo, G. Bent.*

Plate 100. Platt Bridge Station *c.* 1951 as viewed in the Wigan direction. At the end of the Up platform on the right is Platt Bridge Siding and in it some of the stock for the Wigan-Chorley ROF works service. Visible in the distance is the L&NW built Platt Bridge signal box which was replaced by a B.R. concrete and brick structure in the early 1960's. Platt Bridge Station closed on 1st May 1961 and the station buildings were later destroyed by fire. *Photo, Stations U.K.*

BICKERSHAW JUNCTION

BICKERSHAW Junction, where the Wigan-Tyldesley line connected with the branch from Pennington, the latter opening as a through route in 1885, and also the junction for connections with Wigan Junction Railway at Hindley & Platt Bridge and through workings onto the Lancashire Union Railways Whelley Branch at Amberswood Junctions.

The Wigan Junction Railways line from Glazebrook to Strangeways Hall Colliery near Hindley had opened in 1879 and was later extended to a passenger terminus at Darlington St, Wigan in 1884. Connections to the Lancashire Union line at Amberswood West Junction from Strangeways West Junction on the Wigan Junction Railway were completed in 1882 and to Amberswood East Junction in the period 1885-6.

In 1883 the London & North Western Railway had applied for powers to construct their own line, The Hindley Junctions Railway, from Amberswood East to Bickershaw Junction. This railway was intended to run alongside, and be independent of, the Wigan Junctions line but the relative Acts as passed by Parliament obliged the London & North Western to meet the Wigan Junction Railway south of Hindley & Platt Bridge Station, at Strangeways East Junction, with running powers being granted to the London & North Western over the Wigan Junctions lines.

The new lines as authorised were a burrowing junction from Bickershaw, passing under the Wigan-Tyldesley line in the Down direction and a south to east curve in the Up direction. These new connections opened on 25th October 1886. It is during the construction of these works that the connection at Amberswood East Junction is thought to have been completed.

The Wigan Junction Railway was absorbed by the Great Central Railway on 1st January 1906.

Through passenger express trains used the Bickershaw-Strangeways East-Amberswood East Junctions route from the summer of 1887 and the route continued to be used for regular passenger workings, particularly the Windermere "Club" Express, until this train began to use the Lancashire & Yorkshire route via Walkden High Level and De Trafford Junction. Holiday specials consistently used this route to by-pass Wigan, latterly from 6th July to 7th September 1968. Great Central holiday specials from Sheffield and Nottingham to the Fylde Coast also worked the "Whelley" via Manchester and Glazebrook.

Plate 101. A view taken in 1954, looking east towards Bickershaw Junction. In the foreground the bridge carries the main running lines over the London & North Westerns Hindley & Platt Bridge Railways Down line connection from Bickershaw Junction to Hindley & Platt Bridge. Examples of London & North Western lower quadrant signals are seen on the left, on the Up line approach from Hindley & Platt Bridge, with London Midland upper quadrant signals for the Up Main to Manchester or the junction for Plank Lane and Pennington in the centre.   *Photo, Authors Collection.*

Plate 102. Also *c.* 1954, this view shows the Hindley Junctions Down single track from Bickershaw Junction, going away to pass under the Tyldesley-Wigan line en-route to Strangeways East Junction, the connection with Great Central metals south of Hindley & Platt Bridge Station.

Plate 103. The bridge abutment as viewed from the Hindley Junctions Down line, looking towards Bickershaw Junction. In the background a line of empty wagons is being shunted from Bickershaw Junction over the connecting spur to Low Hall Collieries on the same date. *Photos, Authors Collection.*

Plate 104. Type 4 diesel locomotive No. D311 at Bickershaw Junction on 21st September 1971 with a coal train for Bickershaw Washery. The trackbed of the Down connection to Hindley & Platt Bridge can be seen on the left, whilst the trackbed of the Up connection follows the line of redundant telegraph poles on the right.

Photo, Ian Isherwood.

Plate 105. This view dates from May 1996, looking east (from the same location as *Plate 101*), with only the single track towards Bickershaw remaining. At a lower level is the trackbed of the former Down Hindley Junctions route, whilst on the far right, on a level plane is the trackbed of the Bickershaw Junction to Low Hall Collieries connection.

Detainees of H.M. pleasure now reside on the far side of the fence.   *Photo, Author.*

Plate 106. Almost at the end of workings from Bickershaw Colliery now as Class 60 locomotive No. 60 073 "*Cairn Gorm*" passes over the trackbed of the former Down Hindley Junctions line with empty Merry-go-Round wagons for Bickershaw Colliery under threatening skies on 12th February 1992. Class 20's Nos. 20 081/016 bring up the rear. The landmark in the background is St. Nathaniel's Church, Platt Bridge.   *Photo, Author.*

Bickershaw Junction Cabin was a Class 4 box and worked three shifts, opening 6am Monday until 6am Sunday. In the late 1940's about 80 trains per shift would pass through section during the morning and afternoon shifts. In March 1952 the locomotive shed at Lower Ince G.C. had closed, their allocation of locomotives for working the Wigan Central to Manchester Central services being transferred to Springs Branch. This necessitated Bickershaw Junction box opening, on Mondays only, at the unearthly hour of 3.30am in order to work light engine movements from Springs Branch to Wigan Central for the early morning workmen's trains to Irlam. Needless to say this was not a popular shift and after a number of complaints to the operating authorities by the signalmen, a Sunday night turn was granted by way of compensation.

Empties for Low Hall Collieries always arrived on the Up Main line, the train stopping with its brake van opposite Bickershaw box to be propelled onto the Hindley & Platt Bridge Down line then via the crossover onto the Low Hall Collieries connection. Outgoing trains would either be drawn out onto the Down Main line or, as often was the case to save blocking the latter, drawn round onto the Bickershaw branch were the locomotive could run round and draw its train directly out onto the main line. The connection from the London & North Western lines to Low Hall was removed in 1966, although in fact no traffic had been worked that way for some years. After closure of Low Hall Colliery a landsale yard continued in use on the site until about 1965 but any traffic worked into it arrived via connections with the former Wigan Junction Railway.

Plate 107. The scene on 21st September 1971, after closure of the through route from Springs Branch via Tyldesley to Manchester. At this period the single track continued only as far as Howe Bridge West Junction Sidings for coal traffic from Parsonage Colliery. Howe Bridge West-Bickershaw Junction closed on 11th February 1975.

After working empties to Howe Bridge, D5257 returned to Bickershaw engine and brake van, and is seen here propelling the van on to the Bickershaw Branch to collect minerals from the exchange sidings at Abram North. *Photo, Ian Isherwood.*

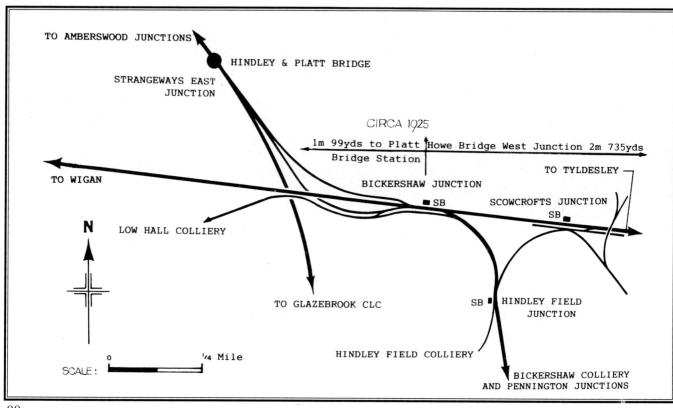

Plate 108. An Ex London & North Western 0-8-0 arrives at Bickershaw Junction with a coal train from Bickershaw Colliery about 1960. At the top of the picture is Scowcrofts Tip, a legacy of earlier mining activity in this area, Scowcrofts being one of the first mining company's to have rail connections here with the London & North Western.

Photo, W.S.Garth.

Plate 109. Stanier designed 2-6-0 No. 42960 approaches Bickershaw Junction with a freight train from Manchester on 24th July 1964, and is signalled to continue on the Down Main as determined by the signal on the far left. Next to this is the signal for trains working via Hindley & Platt Bridge. If, for example, the 7.05pm Manchester, Liverpool Road-Carlisle Goods required a banker the train would stop here for the banker to buffer up, the latter having been waiting at Scowcrofts Sidings. Before departing Manchester, the Liverpool Road Guard would inform Manchester Control that assistance would be required for this train. Manchester Control would inform Wigan Control and a banker would be sent either from Springs Branch or Bamfurlong Sidings. If a banker from Bamfurlong was allocated, this light engine movement would work via Amberswood West Junction and Hindley & Platt Bridge. The London & North Western lower quadrant signals on the right are for workings off the Bickershaw Branch and read, as viewed, left to right, Main line, Hindley & Platt Bridge and Low Hall Colliery.

Photo, Dr J.G.Blears.

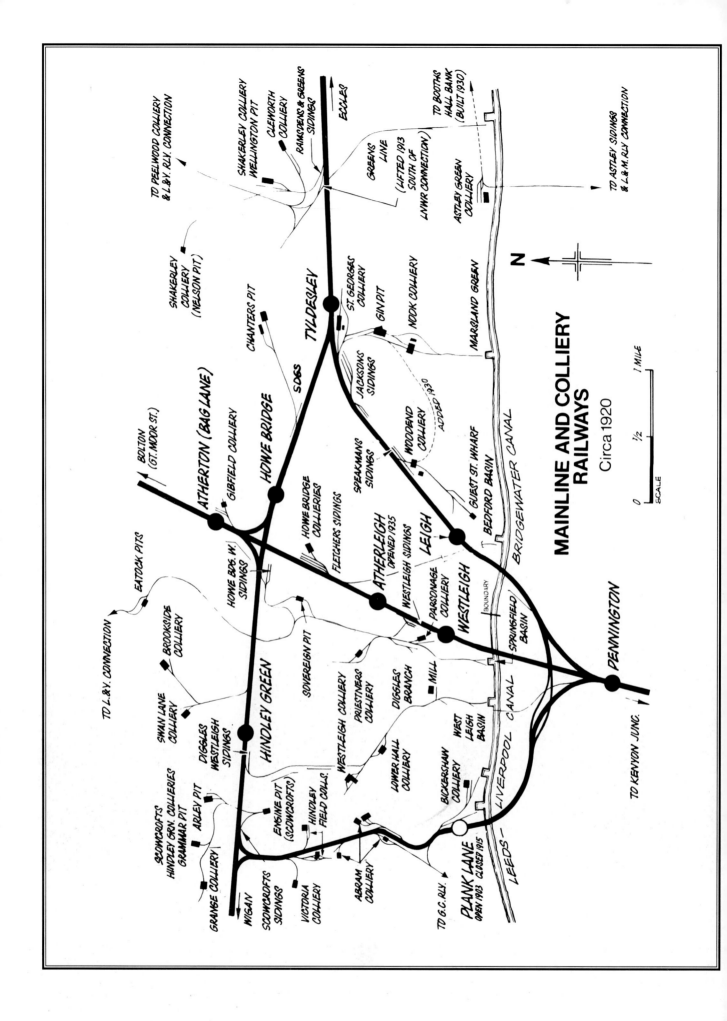

MAINLINE AND COLLIERY RAILWAYS

Circa 1920

N

SCALE

0   ½   1 MILE

SCOWCROFTS JUNCTION

SCOWCROFTS Hindley Green Collieries had been operating in the area from the late 1820's and in 1864 became John Scowcroft & Co Ltd. Scowcrofts were quick off the mark in having a connection from their Engine Pit to the London & North Westerns line here, probably from the opening of the line, certainly by 1865. Shortly afterwards, via an overbridge, their collieries north of the Tyldesley-Wigan main line also received rail connections. It was also possible to work, via Scowcrofts Sidings, onto the Ackers Whitley private railway as far south as Plank Lane. The rundown of Scowcrofts mines began in the 1920's, the last of their collieries, Grange, closed in 1937. Hindley Field Junction to Scowcrofts Junction closed on 27th December 1944.

The sidings here were retained after closure of Scowcrofts Collieries and used for storage of wagons due for repair at Earlestown and also for some traffic from Low Hall. Empties for Low Hall were often deposited in the sidings here on account of Low Hall having only two sidings, reg-ularity overflowing with "fulls". This being the case the Springs Branch trip locomotive would drop the empties at Scowcrofts, work engine and brake van to Low Hall Sidings, draw out the "fulls" onto the Bickershaw curve, run round and right away to Springs Branch, deposit the "fulls" returning engine and brake van to Scowcrofts Sidings to work the empties onto Low Hall. At the latter end of its life, 1940 onwards, Scowcrofts Signalbox was open two turns, 4pm-midnight/midnight-8am, with Saturdays 8am-4pm/4pm-midnight. On Saturdays the last freight working was often the 7.05pm Manchester, Liverpool Road to Carlisle goods, which took a banker from Scowcrofts Sidings to work over the Whelley line via Bickershaw Junction and Hindley & Platt Bridge, to join the West Coast Line at Standish Junction. Once this train was out of section the Signalman would contact control and if no further freight was scheduled, ask for permission to close the box, usually granted. Needless to say this was a much favoured turn.

Plate 110. Bridge 61, between Scowcroft's Junction and Hindley Green, as seen looking in the direction of Scowcroft's in 1954. Just visible at the far side of Bridge 62 is Scowcroft's Home Signal in the "off" position. The photograph is one of a number taken to show the effects of subsidence. *Photo, B.R*

93

HINDLEY GREEN

JAMES DIGGLE of West Leigh Collieries had been instrumental in deciding the site of Hindley Green Station. His personal intervention in meeting with the directors of the London & North Western Railway in 1864 resulted in this location being chosen for its construction. There seems little doubt that it would have been extremely convenient for his personal usage being only a short distance away from his residence at Hindley Green Hall.

Access to the platforms was by footpath from each side of the road-over bridge on Leigh Road, the ticket office being on the "Up" platform, for Manchester trains, as seen in *Plate 112*. Closure occured in 1961. Hindley Green Signalbox, sited at the eastern end of the Up platform, was abolished after the closure of Diggles Westleigh

Collieries *c.*1937/8, but a Lamp Man continued to be employed here for some years after.

To the east of Hindley Green Station there had been a connection to collieries in the Swan Lane and Long Lane areas of Hindley from 1865 which crossed Atherton Road on the level, immediately north of Hindley Green Station. Brookside Colliery opened in the 1870's and was connected to the Swan Lane branch by a short extension. Later, the collieries in the Long Lane area came into possession of the Swan Lane Colliery owners and these also received a rail connection from the Swan Lane branch. These collieries seem to have had a somewhat chequered existence with a number of owners and their fair share of financial difficulties The original Swan Lane Colliery first closed in 1893 to be re-opened in 1910. In the intervening

Plate 111. In early 1992 the road-over bridge at Hindley Green, which for some time had been the subject to a 3 ton weight limit, was demolished at a cost of some £20,000 to enable the Heavy Goods Vehicle to pass unrestricted. This view, in the Wigan direction, dates from 1989 and shows the platforms cleared of vegetation under a manpower services scheme, although the trackbed is somewhat waterlogged. Access to the up platform can be seen to the right of the bridge.

Photo, Author.

period a new shaft had been sunk to the six feet mine, opening in January 1897. The last mine at Swan Lane finally closed in 1928 and the mainline connection dismantled shortly after. In recent times the area has been re-developed with various industrial concerns, a process which is continuing.

A serious accident occured at the Swan Lane Junction on 28th April 1883, when wagons were being fly shunted from the Down Main line, across the Up line and onto the colliery sidings. One of the wagons had been left foul of the Up Main line and an approaching goods train from Preston travelling at speed hit the offending vehicle. Considerable damage ensued, many of the coal wagons were in pieces, others overturned and were scattered about and as the goods train contained cattle wagons many of the animals were said to be badly mutilated. For some time afterwards services had to be diverted via Golborne and Parkside East Junctions.

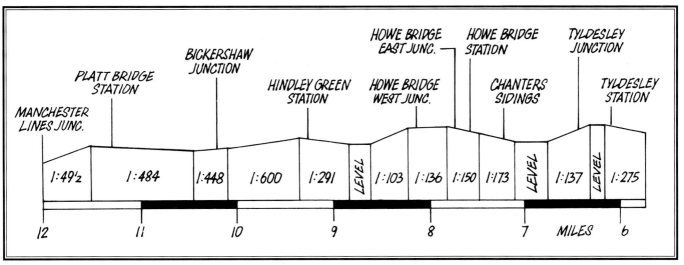

Gradient profile Springs Branch to Tyldesley.

Plate 112. Hindley Green had won the best kept station award in the Liverpool Lime Street District for six years from 1947 on and this photograph from that period illustrates why. Complete with bird boxes and immaculate flower beds it is a credit to those involved. *Photo, Wigan Heritage Services.*

HOWE BRIDGE WEST

THE sidings here had been constructed in conjunction with the Wigan Coal & Iron Company's extension of their colliery railway carried out in 1882, to carry coals from their Sovereign and Priestners Pits at Westleigh to the London & North Western Railway at Chowbent West Junction. During the line alterations to the Bolton & Leigh Railway authorised in 1880, a connecting curve from Chowbent West, later renamed Howe Bridge, was built, to meet with the Bolton & Leigh Railway at Atherton Junction, opening in 1883. The signal box at West Junction also dates from this period.

There had previously been a connection slightly to the west of this new junction to serve Snapes Colliery and a signal box sited near the Westleigh Lane over-bridge near Dangerous Corner controlled this outlet. In the early 1880's, after Snapes connection had been removed, the use of this now redundant signal box as a "new" road-side station was suggested when calls for facilities at Dangerous Corner were first mooted in 1882. A proposal by the Westleigh representatives for a station between Hindley Green and Chowbent resulted in a meeting with a body of London & North Western Board Members at the proposed Westleigh Lane site on 4th November 1882. Little else is heard again of this proposal and in view of developments at Howe Bridge West taking place at the same time it seems reasonable to assume that the London & North Western regarded a station here as a hindrance to lucrative coal traffic.

Snapes colliery had been taken over by the Wigan Coal & Iron Company in 1875 and does not seem to have been connected with the colliery railways in the Westleigh area.

Coal began to be mined from the early 1920's at Parsonage Colliery and a steady flow of traffic to Howe Bridge West Sidings could be seen crossing Westleigh Lane. Some of the coal traffic was worked to Preston or Southport from Howe Bridge and in addition there were numerous trip workings to Bag Lane Sidings. Coking coal went to the Lancashire Steel Corporations Works at Irlam which replaced the ageing Kirkless, Wigan, plant as a centre of production. The latter was demolished in the early 1930's after the formation of Lancashire Steel and the Wigan Coal Corporation from the amalgamation of the Wigan Coal & Iron Company, the Pearson & Knowles Iron Company, the Wigan Junction Collieries and the Moss Hall Coal Company. In the 1940's about 100 wagons per day were dispatched from Howe Bridge West.

Traffic from Howe Bridge West Sidings was, in BR days, either worked to Springs Branch for onward destinations or to Bag Lane Up Sidings. Any traffic for Garston usually went out from Parsonage via Westleigh Sidings and Kenyon Junction. This option was removed with the closure of the former Bolton & Leigh line between Pennington and Atherton Junction in June 1963.

A fire at Parsonage screens about 1964 had resulted in coal being sent to Bickershaw from Howe Bridge Sidings for washing until August 1974, when as a result of new underground connections between Parsonage and Bickershaw Collieries all coal was to be wound at Bickershaw, the colliery railway from Parsonage to Howe Bridge being abandoned. Some coal continued to be wound at Parsonage until May 1976, this being dispatched by road. However, some coal for road despatch continued to be wound at Parsonage until May 1976.

Plate 113. This view of Howe Bridge West Junction is taken from the Smallbrook Lane area, looking towards Atherton Collieries Howe Bridge Pits seen in the background and shows a busy scene with no less than three London & North Western 0-8-0 freight locomotives and what appears to be an Ex Midland Railway 4-4-0 waiting their turn of duty in the early 1950's. *Photos, Dr J.G.Blears.*

HOWE BRIDGE WEST

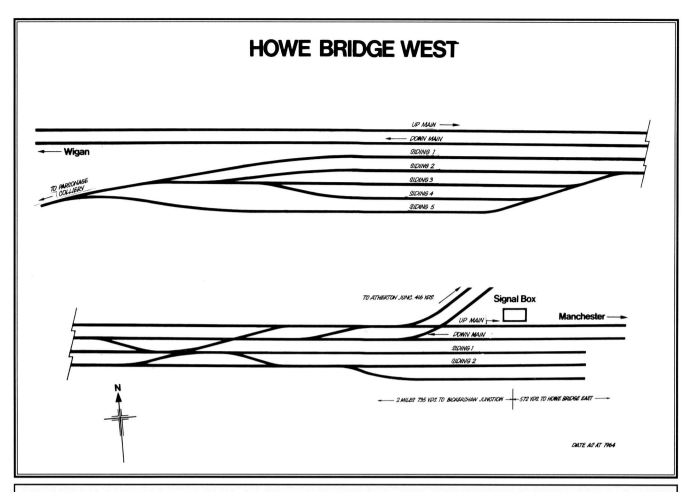

Plate 114. Approaching Dangerous Corner, Westleigh with a coal train from Howe Bridge West Sidings is Type 2 diesel No. D5260 on 5th January 1972. At this period coal from Parsonage Colliery went to Bickershaw for washing.

Photo, Ian Isherwood.

Plate 115. Howe Bridge West Junction on 22nd May 1961, as Britannia Class No. 70015 *"Apollo"* passes with the 4.15pm Manchester Exchange-Glasgow express. The locomotive is one of the Ex-Western Region's with extra hand grips cut in the smoke deflectors, more of which on page 108. *Photo, Dr. J. G. Blears.*

Plate 116. Approaching Howe Bridge West Junction on 24th April 1964 and seen from road level on Lovers Lane, is one of the Capprotti fitted BR Standard Class 5's No. 73127 with a Wigan bound train. Preparations are underway for renewal of the bridge. The second bridge carries the Howe Bridge West Junction to Atherton Junction chord. *Photo Dr. J. G. Blears.*

HOWE BRIDGE

CHOWBENT, or Howe Bridge as it was to become in April 1901, was an all timber structure with access to the Up and Down platforms by a separate flight of steps. The Booking Office was on the Up platform with Waiting Rooms on both Up and Down platforms. Being situated on an embankment, Howe Bridge afforded a good view of the surrounding countryside.

Closure of Howe Bridge occurred on 20th July 1959, but in its heyday had been a busy little station particularly at holiday periods. Even in the late 1940's and early 1950's it was not unknown for 400-500 persons to depart Howe Bridge on the Saturday morning holiday specials and extra staff were drafted in to help out.

Football specials ran from Tyldesley calling at Howe Bridge at 13.30 hrs, $6\frac{1}{2}d$ adults, $3\frac{1}{2}d$ boys,

double headed up Chequerbent Bank plus a banker in the 1930's when Bolton were in the second division!

A regular Manchester Exchange via Tyldesley to Bolton Great Moor Street service operated until May 1942.

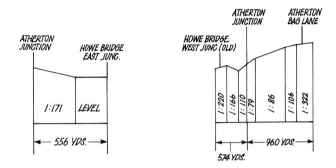

Plate 117. Chowbent Station photographed around the turn of the century showing the Up platform for Manchester trains. *Photo, Wigan Heritage Services.*

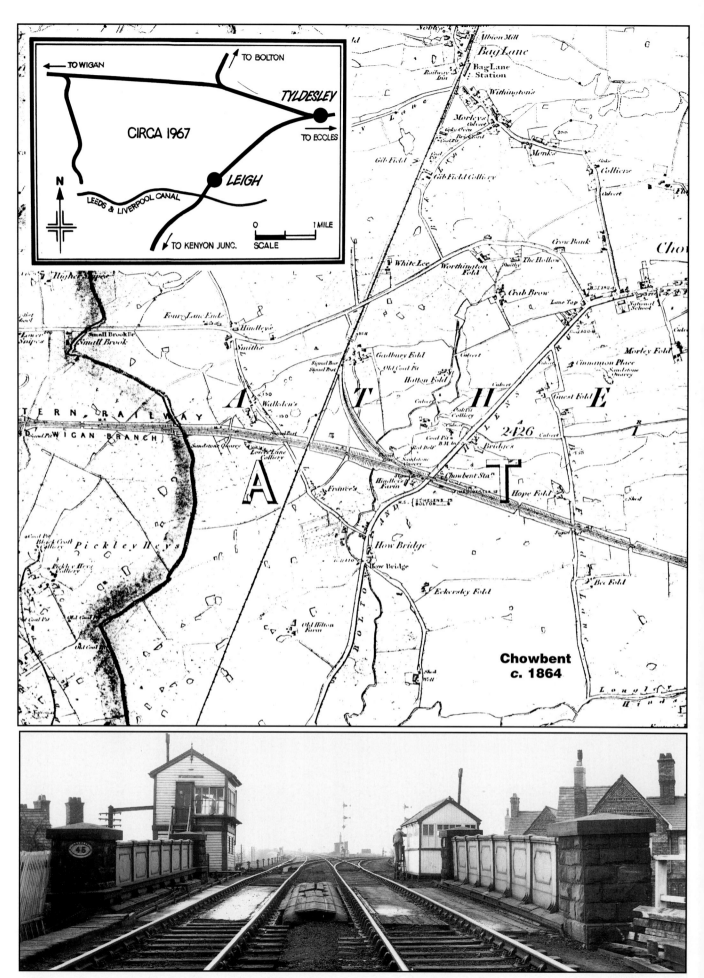

Plate 118. A westward view from Howe Bridge taken on 1st December 1954. The East Junction curve to the Bolton and Leigh line at Atherton Junction is shown, with the main line to Wigan going off to the left. The lamp room on the right seems to be receiving some attention. *Photo, BR.*

Plate 119. A view in the Tyldesley direction also on 1st December 1954. Note the platform edges, waving with the effects of subsidence which has also affected the track further along to a considerable degree. After the line closed in 1969, the bridge was dismantled some time later, like many others for its scrap value. The bridge abutments however were left in place to find further use in the 1980s when opencast workings began off Millers Lane. A Bailey bridge for road transport was erected across Leigh Road to carry the extracted minerals out via the disused trackbed to exit points on Atherton Road, just north of the former Atherton Junction. With the completion of opencast workings all traces of the railway at this location have now disappeared, save for part of the track-bed from East Junction to Atherton Junction. *Photo, BR.*

Plate 120. One of the Stanier Class 4, 2-6-4 tank engines, No. 42571, at Howe Bridge Station about 1960. This one coach train operated for a short time between Tyldesley and Wigan North Western when torrential rain caused flooding in the Worsley area, and the usual Manchester Exchange-Wigan service did not run.

Photo, Dr. J. G. Blears.

***Plate 121.** A* view taken from road level at Howe Bridge in December 1954 which contrast sharply with the present day scene. Not only has the bridge and the railway it carried passed into history but also the trolley buses, once part of an extensive system operated by South Lancashire Transport with their headquarters at Howe Bridge. They too were victims of a very powerful group, the "road lobby" or "oil lobby", call it what you will, but railways, trams and trolley buses all succumbed to this extremely influential and narrow minded group, who still exert an undue amount of influence today. There are many in the Department of Transport who can see no further than a stretch of tarmac!

In this case the advocates of diesel transport had their plans interrupted by the Suez crisis of 1956 and the resulting consternation in Government circles thereafter with regard to oil supplies. Consequently trolley bus operations in the area were given a reprieve from closure until 31st August 1958 when on that day South Lancashire Transport ceased to exist. The order necessary for the company to be liquidated was passed by Act of Parliament on 23rd July 1958. On 1st September 1958 "The Last" trolley bus ran over the system from Atherton to Leigh carrying invited guests.

The houses visible in the photograph form part of Howe Bridge "Model Village" built by Fletcher Burrows for colliery workers and their families.

Photos, Authors Collection.

Plates 122 and 123. After a hundred years or more of deep mining these areas became very prone to mining subsidence, some of it quite serious. These two accompanying photographs of the early 1950's illustrate the efforts needed to prevent movement of structures near Howe Bridge (bridges 41 & 42) the effects of which could have had catastrophic implications on the running of the railway. In these examples concrete shoring has been cast in-situ to prevent further bulging of the bridge abutments.

Removal of these structures and embankments occurred during opencast mining operations in the early 1980's.

Photos, B.R.

CHANTERS SIDINGS

CHANTERS Sidings were situated between Howe Bridge and Tyldesley and connected Chanters Colliery at Hindsford via a short branch line, with the London & North Western line. The branch line was approximately ¾ mile long and had been constructed at the same time as had the main running lines by the contractor Treadwell, and in all probability opened for traffic in 1864.

The colliery dates from 1854 on a much older site. There were two shafts here and both were deepened in the 1890's to reach the Arley Mine at over 1800ft. Chanters was probably the most successful of the Atherton Collieries Pits and continued working, in NCB ownership, until 1966. Later becoming a training school for mining apprentices. Chanters Sidings signal box was built specifically to serve Chanters Colliery workings and had 18 levers, 15 working with 3 spare; in LMS & BR days the box opened two turns, 6am-2pm/2pm-10pm. The ground frame here, situated at the Tyldesley end was controlled from the signal box. There were two sidings, running in a north-easterly direction from the main lines. Usually the colliery locomotive would be on hand to receive the returning empties worked direct from Fleetwood, Wyre Dock, Bolton or Garston Dock, Liverpool, if not the train engine would shunt the empties into the sidings. Some of the coal trains were worked by colliery locomotive working two turns per day with 12/15 wagons, to Bag Lane Up Sidings or, via the Howe Bridge triangle, to Westleigh Colliery Sidings. Others were direct workings, to Wyre Dock for example, whilst some of the traffic went to Springs Branch for northbound destinations. Up to 120 wagons per day was the average dispatch from Chanters Sidings. In BR days Chanters had a contract to supply loco coal to the railways.

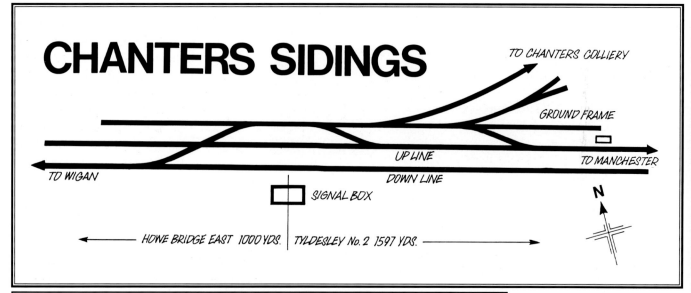

Plate 124. The local collieries had running powers over certain sections of main line, agreements for which with the railway companies, date back to the Bolton & Leigh era. In July 1951, Austerity 0-6-0 *"Humphrey"*, RSH/7293/45, is seen between Chanters Sidings and Howe Bridge with a train of empties, working from Chanters to Gibfield Colliery.
Photo, W. S. Garth.

TYLDESLEY

THE Signal & Telegraph depot (S&T) began to be transferred to Tyldesley from Ordsall Lane, Salford, in the late 1880's and the blacksmiths shop, (*Plate 126*) as seen in the accompanying photographs dates from that period. Previously there had been a locomotive turntable on the site with a connection of the Down Wigan line. A single road engine shed, probably constructed here in the late 1860's, was virtually demolished in November 1878 during a light engine movement through Tyldesley. The engine in question was working to Platt Bridge on the Down Main, and unfortunately the Signalman at Tyldesley No2 box had inadvertently set the points into the shed road. In the shed at the time was a dead engine which, when hit by the misdirected locomotive, was sent crashing through the gable end, down an embankment and ended up in a nearby garden. This was reputed to be the first "Garden Railway" in the area, scale 12"=1 ft. The damage to locomotives and shed were said to be considerable and it is not clear if the engine shed was ever re-built. However, the connection into what became the S&T yard on the same site was re-sited onto the Up Leigh line prior to 1888 and the turntable removed.

Tyldesley Signal & Telegraph staff were responsible for maintaining the signalling apparatus and signal boxes over a wide area, the eastern boundary was, in post World War II days, marked by the A580 road-over bridge at Roe Green. The Roe Green, Sandersons Sidings, Worsley, Monton Green and Eccles Junction installations all coming within the Patricroft area. The southern boundary for the Tyldesley S&T gangs was the Kenyon Up Distant near Parkside East Junction, this an early conversion to colour light controlled from Kenyon No 1 box. From Roe Green, all the equipment on the Eccles-Wigan route as far west as Bickershaw Junction Signal Cabin came under the Tyldesley area, whilst the northern outpost was marked by the Bolton No. 1 and Fletcher Street cabins on the Bolton & Leigh line. On the Roe Green branch, the signalling equipment at Lever Street, Walkden Low Level, Plodder Lane, Little Hulton Junction etc, were again serviced by Patricroft gangs.

On the Bolton & Leigh, Cygnet Ground Frame and Fireman's Call Box (FCB), which gave access to Townsons joinery works were serviced as and when required, as were Magees Siding and Sunnyside Mills Siding. Daubhill, Chequerbent, Hulton Sidings, Bag Lane, Atherton Junction, Fletchers Sidings, Kirkhall Lane, Westleigh and Pennington South Junction signal boxes all came under the auspices of Tyldesley S&T. In the latter years Westleigh box was activated as and when required, the sidings there put to use for stock storage used on holiday specials working out of Great Moor Street, Bolton. Kenyon No 2, situated near Kenyon Yard and Kenyon No. 1 were the southernmost boxes allocated to Tyldesley S&T.

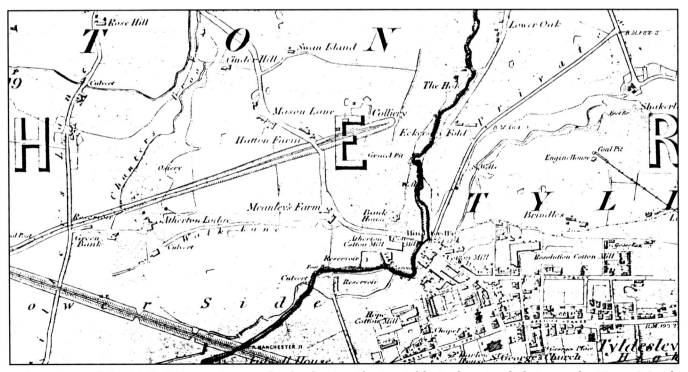

An update of the 1849 Ordnance Survey clearly showing the turntable in the triangle between the Wigan & Leigh lines, where, in the 1880's, the Signal & Telegraph Department was established.

Here though a resident Mechanical Chargeman was always on site, these being extremely busy locations.

The Tyldesley-Leigh-Pennington line with installations at Jacksons Sidings, Speakmans Sidings and Leigh Goods, in addition to the Pennington Loop lines taking in Pennington East & West, the small box at Bickershaw Colliery, the larger signal box at Abram North adjacent to Bolton House Road, and Hindley Field Junction box were all the lot of Tyldesley S&T gangs.

With the run down in traffic via the Pennington Loop and Pennington South Junction to Bickershaw lines in the 1950's the signalling at Pennington South for Bickershaw was reduced in status to "calling on" operation controlled from Pennington South, the ancient London & North Western pattern lower quadrant signals removed, London Midland upper quadrant arms being installed there about 1955. See *Plates 65 & 67* Pennington West Junction box had closed on 25th August 1951 and post World War II was a

Porter/Signalman's job open as and when required. Pennington East Junction box closed on 28th October 1953.

As previously stated, the western boundary for Tyldesley S&T was Bickershaw Junction. At the eastern end of the triangle of lines here was Scowcrofts Sidings and signal box. Scowcrofts mines had ceased production in the 1930's but their sidings remained in use for some years. The Hindley Field Junction to Scowcrofts Sidings curve had closed on 27th December 1944 and Hindley Field signal box abolished. Scowcrofts signal box had been suffering the effects of subsidence and became a problem, eventually being done away with, probably in the early 1950's and the block section extended from Bickershaw Junction to Howe Bridge West.

Howe Bridge West itself was in a precarious state by the late 1950's, gradually slipping down the bank due to subsidence. This posed extreme problems with the mechanical operations of the box and it too was demolished, to be replaced by

Plate 125. Tyldesley Signal and Telegraph Dept., situated in the triangle between the Wigan and Leigh lines with, on the gable end, the time keepers office, complete with geraniums in the windows and staffed by Jack Watson and George Hamp in the 1950's. Next to this was the Telegraph Inspectors Office of one Claude McCutcheon, followed by stores, tinsmiths and at the far end the blacksmiths shop. Note also "Britannia" re-sited on the gable end over the time keepers office. (*See Plate 139*). *Photo, BR.*

Plate 126 (top) and *Plate 127.* Two 1956 views inside the Signal & Telegraph Yard which had a two road siding connection off the Up Leigh line, immediately west of the junction at Tyldesley. A wooden bodied wagon can be seen on one road to the left of the smaller shed. The wooden barrels contained "pots" as used on the telegraph poles and often the subject of target practice by schoolboys. In the foreground are examples of the apparatus used to place detonators on the track.

Photos BR.

a new 1943 standard pattern frame, 40 lever box built inside the triangle of lines at Howe Bridge and brought into use shortly after the new Tyldesley signal box.

The new signal box at Tyldesley, commissioned in 1963, was built on the site of the former cattle dock turntable disused since the early 1950's. This new box, also constructed with a 1943 standard pattern frame had 55 levers and replaced Tyldesley Nos. 1&2 boxes, the London & North Western absolute block system here replaced with track circuits under the Whellwyn block system.

In later years the resulting colliery closures would gradually see off the signal boxes at their relative locations so that by 1968 only Monton Green, Ellenbrook, Tyldesley and Leigh remained on the through Kenyon route. The Tyldesley-Howe Bridge section had closed on 6th January 1969 and at the latter end was used only for through Wigan-Tyldesley-Manchester parcels trains. The Howe Bridge East-Atherton Junction-Hultons Sidings section also closed on this date.

Plans had been drawn up in 1965 to install colour light signalling and track circuits controlled from Tyldesley and Monton Green signal boxes thereby abolishing the intermediate Ellenbrook, Sandersons Sidings and Hough Lane installations. Roe Green cabin had already gone with the closure of the Roe Green Junction to Little Hulton Junction section in 1961. In the event this was never carried out, probably because of the cost involved as the writing was already on the wall regarding closure of this route.

Mosley Common Colliery closed in February 1968 with Ellenbrook signal box being abolished in November of that year and the adjacent sidings isolated, leaving Monton Green as the only intermediate box between Eccles Junction and Tyldesley, a section length, from Monton Green to Tyldesley new box of some 5 miles 665 yards. Now the coal traffic had gone, length of section was not a problem. The distant signals for Tyldesley, at Ellenbrook in the east and Leigh in the west received motorised apparatus, controlled from Tyldesley "new" box.

Lastly installations on the former Lancashire & Yorkshire line, from Crow Nest Junction via Atherton Central to Pendleton Broad Street were also designated the responsibility of Tyldesley S&T Depot, no small area to cover and an extremely busy one in those days.

Plate128. In the summer of 1963 Britannia 4-6-2 Pacific No 70015 "*Apollo*" takes the Wigan line at Tyldesley with the 4.15pm Manchester Exchange to Glasgow train, with Tyldesley Parish Church prominent on the left and St Georges Colliery chimney on the right. In the foreground are the sidings into Tyldesley Signal & Telegraph yard. This train ran non-stop to Wigan North Western arriving at 4.49pm and connected at Preston with through coaches from Liverpool Exchange to depart Preston at 5.35 p.m., giving an arrival in Glasgow at 9.40pm. These Manchester-Glasgow and return trains were rostered for Newton Heath or Polmadie (Glasgow) crews working about turn, i.e. having to "lodge" overnight before working the return trip, a practice now almost forgotten.

Also of interest are the smoke deflectors as fitted here. These are the Western Regions version with no less than six hand grips, complete with brass surrounds. This modification came about after a serious accident at Milton near Didcot on 22nd November 1955, involving another member of the Class, No 70026 "*Polar Star*". At the subsequent inquiry it was suggested that the drivers forward vision had been impaired by the handrails fitted to the deflectors as built, thus those on the Western Region at the time were modified as described, whilst the Eastern Region fitted an additional two grips plus a small horizontal handrail. However, those locomotives originally allocated to the London Midland Region never received any modification at all and eventually with the transference of Britannia's to the north of the country in the early to mid 1960's all three varieties could be observed.   *Photo, J.R.Carter.*

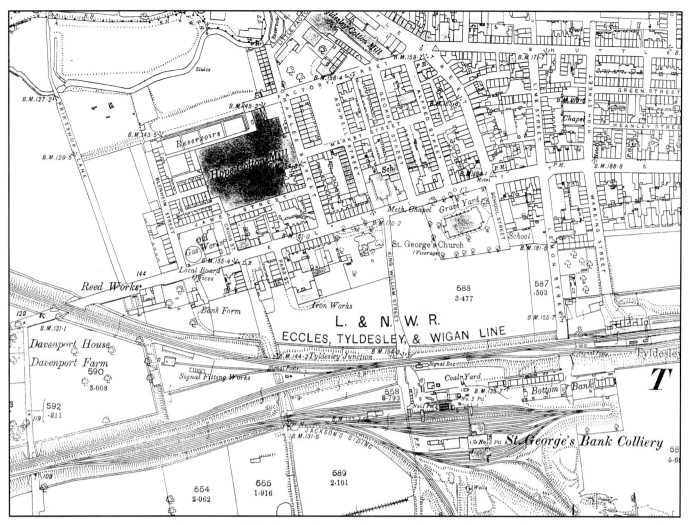

Ordnance Survey maps for the period 1889-90 clearly show the alterations to Tyldesley S&T yard and the expansion at St. Georges (Back-o-th-Church) Colliery.

Plate 129. A Class 5 carrying the "M" prefix to its LMS No. 5114 on the smokebox door and seen approaching Tyldesley off the Up Wigan line and about to cross King William Street Bridge. At nationalisation, on January 1st 1948, 40,000 was added to the LMS Nos. to avoid duplication with locomotives in other regions. The "M" was an extremely rare livery variant, only about forty locomotives are known to have received this prefix as applied here. As it was also a short lived form of numbering in most cases lasting only a few months from when first applied about March 1948, photographs of it are therefore few. However, the LMS lettered tenders and rolling stock lasted well into the mid 1950s. On the left of the approaching train is the road into the Signal & Telegraph Yard. *Photo, W. D. Cooper.*

TYLDESLEY

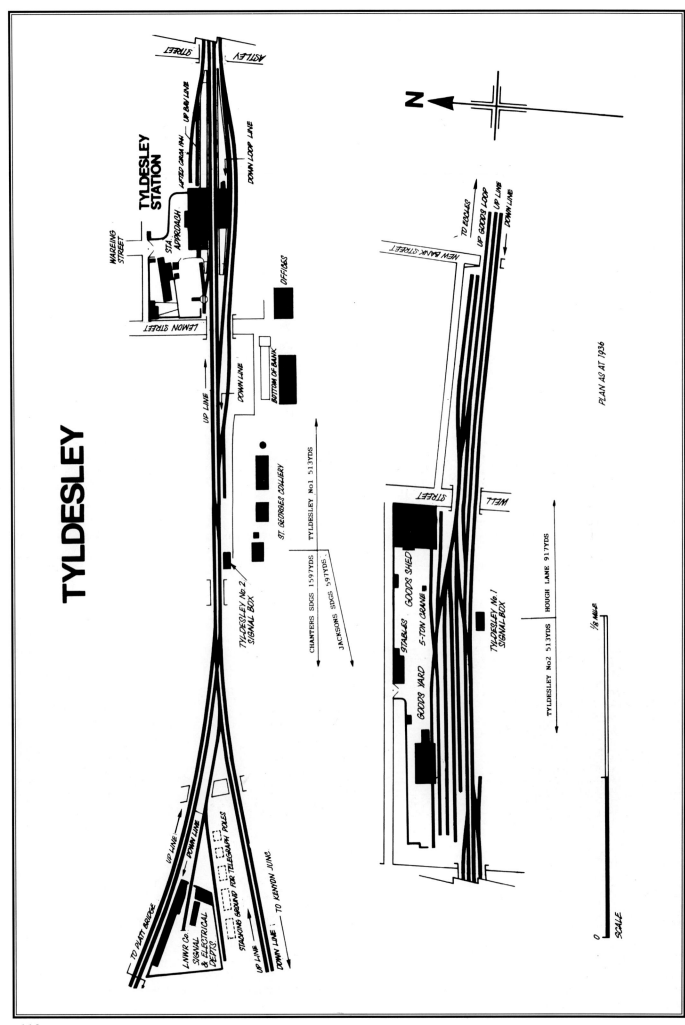

N

TYLDESLEY STATION

ASTLEY STREET

ASTLEY

UP BAY LINE

LIFTED CIRCA 1941

DOWN LOOP LINE

WAREING STREET

STA. APPROACH

LEMON STREET

OFFICES

BOTTOM OF BANK

UP LINE

DOWN LINE

ST. GEORGES COLLIERY

TYLDESLEY No 2 SIGNAL BOX

CHANTERS SDGS 1597YDS

JACKSONS SDGS 597YDS

TYLDESLEY No1 513YDS

UP LINE

DOWN LINE

TO PLATT BRIDGE

L.N.W.R Co. SIGNAL & ELECTRICAL DEPTS

STACKING GROUND FOR TELEGRAPH POLES

UP LINE

DOWN LINE

TO KENYON JUNC.

TO ECCLES

UP GOODS LOOP

UP LINE

DOWN LINE

NEW BANK STREET

STREET

WELL

STABLES

GOODS SHED

GOODS YARD

5-TON CRANE

TYLDESLEY No.1 SIGNAL BOX

TYLDESLEY No2 513YDS

HOUGH LANE 917YDS

PLAN AS AT 1936

⅛ MILE

0

SCALE

110

Plate 130. This west facing view of 27th July 1965 shows the BR built signal box, commissioned in 1963 and built on the site of the wagon turntable, replacing Tyldesley Nos. 1&2 boxes of London & North Western vintage. The lifted track and redundant signals forecast the impending doom for this, as for many other local rail links. *Photo R.J.Essery.*

Plate 131. An example of the L&NWR Company's design of heavy freight engine Class G1/G2, passing Tyldesley No. 2 box in May 1948, with classic examples of pre-war wooden bodied wagons which would themselves disappear with the introduction of the standard 16-ton steel bodied vehicle, soon to be seen in ever increasing numbers. This time the locomotive has quickly received its BR. No. 49324, but sports LMS on the tender. To Carlisle crews, these engines were known as "Wigan Spitfires" *Photo, W. D.Cooper.*

am/pm	Time Arr.	Dept.	Train No.	Except	Class	From	To
am		12.13			K	Ince Moss Junction	Weaste Junction Siding
am		12.34		MO	E	Springs Branch	Liverpool Rd, Manchester
am	1.37	1.37		MX	H	Preston	Patricroft
am		1.47	374	MX	C Fish	Law Junction, Scotland	Oldham Rd, Manchester
am		2.03		MX	E	Carnforth	Liverpool Rd, Manchester
am		2.17	382	MO	C Fish	Wigan NW	Oldham Rd, Manchester
am		2.24		TO	E	Carlisle	Cross Lane
am		5.57	24		A	Wigan NW	Manchester Exchange
am	6.08			SX	B	Wigan NW	Tyldesley
am	6.14	6.15			B	Leigh	Manchester Exchange
am		6.22			D	Carlisle	Liverpool Rd, Manchester
am	6.25		111	MX	K	Kenyon Junction	Tyldesley
am		6.56		SO	D	Carlisle	Liverpool Rd, Manchester
am	7.08			SX	B Motor	Wigan NW	Tyldesley
am		7.15	109	MX	K	Tyldesley	Hough Lane
am	7.14	7.16			B	Kenyon Junction	Manchester Exchange
am	7.27			SX	C ECS	Leigh	Tyldesley
am	7.41	7.42			B	Kenyon Junction	Manchester Exchange
am	7.57			SX	B Motor	Leigh	Tyldesley
am	7.54	8.03			B	Preston	Manchester Exchange
am	8.17		109	MO	K	Kenyon Junction	Tyldesley
am		8.23	352	MX	C Fish	Aberdeen	Manchester Victoria
am	8.15	8.30	111	MX	K	Bag Lane	Ellenbrook Sidings
am	8.52	8.53	188		B	Liverpool Lime Street	Manchester Exchange
am	9.30	9.32			B	Wigan NW	Manchester Exchange
am	9.43	9.55		SX	J	Garston Liverpool	Jacksons Sidings
am		10.14	204		A	Windermere	Manchester Exchange
am	10.23	10.24	40		B	Chester General	Manchester Exchange
am	10.45	10.46		SX	G EB	Jacksons Sidings	Ellenbrook Sidings
am		11.18	336	SO	A	Morecambe E Road	Manchester Exchange
am	11.20		109	SX	K Emt's	Kenyon Junction	Tyldesley
pm	12.05		109	SO	J	Kenyon Junction	Tyldesley
pm		12.06		SX	G LE G	Leigh	Patricroft Loco
pm	12.12			SO	G LE G	Leigh	Tyldesley (1.20/Leigh)
pm		12.09	398	SO	A	Blackpool North	Stoke-on-Trent
pm	12.43	12.46			B	Wigan NW	Manchester Exchange
pm	1.47			SO	C ECS	Leigh	Tyldesley
pm	1.56	1.58	84	SO	A	Windermere	Manchester Exchange
pm		2.07	110	SX	K	Jacksons Sidings	Patricroft N Sidings
pm	2.06	2.09		SO	B	Kenyon Junction	Manchester Exchange
pm		2.18		SO	G LE P	Tyldesley Ex 1.47	Patricroft Loco
pm	1.40	2.22	109	SO	K	Jacksons Sdgs	Patricroft N Sidings
pm		2.55	105	SX	K	Tyldesley	Patricroft
pm	3.03		290	SO	B	Blackpool Central	Tyldesley
pm		3.09		MX	G LE G	Jacksons Sidings	Patricroft Loco
pm		4.05	110	MO	K	Jacksons Sidings	Patricroft N Sidings
pm	4.12				B Motor	Leigh	Tyldesley
pm	4.22		113	SX	G LE G	Leigh	Tyldesley
pm	4.35		292	SX	K	Bolton	Tyldesley
pm	4.41	4.43			B	Wigan NW	Leeds City
pm		5.05	109	SX	K	Jacksons Sidings	Patricroft N Sidings
pm	5.11	5.11		SO	C ECS	Wigan NW	Tyldesley (5.45 K/Jct)
pm	5.34	5.35	C273		A	Blackpool Central	Manchester Exchange
pm		6.00			H	Carlisle	Ordsall Lane
pm	6.02				B Motor	Earlestown	Tyldesley
pm	6.22	6.23			B	Wigan NW	Leeds City
pm	6.12	6.27		SX	F	Bolton	Warrington
pm	7.25			SX	B Motor	Kenyon Junction	Tyldesley
pm	7.55		112	SX	G LE G	Leigh	Tyldesley
pm	7.33	8.15		SX	K	Atherton Bag Lane	Weaste Junction Siding
pm	8.22			SO	G LE P	Wigan NW	Manchester Exchange
pm	8.38	8.43		SX	B	Wigan NW	Manchester Exchange
pm	8.50	9.13	112	SX	K	Jacksons Sidings	Bolton
pm		9.25		SX	D	Garston Liverpool	Oldham Road/Phillips Park
pm	9.23	9.28		SO	B	Wigan NW	Manchester Exchange
pm	9.42	9.45			A	Glasgow Central	Manchester Victoria
pm	9.55			SO	B Motor	Kenyon Junction	Tyldesley
pm	10.29			SO	B	Leigh	Tyldesley
pm		10.40		SO	G LE P	Tyldesley	Patricroft Loco
pm	10.50	10.52		SX	B	Wigan NW	Manchester Exchange
pm	10.52	10.54		SO	B	Wigan NW	Manchester Exchange
pm	11.07	11.15			G LE P	Leigh	Patricroft Loco

SUNDAYS

am/pm	Time Arr.	Dept.	Train No.	Except	Class	From	To
am		1.45	374		C Fish	Carlisle	Oldham Road, Manchester
am		2.14			E	Carnforth	Patricroft N Sidings
am		5.57	24		A	Wigan NW	Manchester Exchange
am		7.14	352		C Fish	Aberdeen	Oldham Road, Manchester
am	8.43	8.50			B	Liverpool Lime Street	Manchester Exchange
am	10.01	10.03			B	Wigan NW	Manchester Exchange
pm	2.16	2.18			B	Wigan NW	Manchester Exchange
pm	4.06	4.08			B	Liverpool Lime Street	Manchester Exchange
pm	7.15	7.17			B	Wigan NW	Manchester Exchange
pm	7.41	7.43	288		B	Liverpool Lime Street	Newcastle-on-Tyne
pm	9.15	9.16			B	Liverpool Lime Street	Manchester Exchange
pm	10.04	10.06	378		B	Liverpool Lime Street	Manchester Exchange

TRAIN MOVEMENTS THROUGH TYLDESLEY MID 1950'S (WEEK DAYS)
DOWN LINE

am/pm	Time Arr.	Dept.	Train No.	Except	Class	From	To
am	12.35			MO	G LE P	Patricroft Loco	Wigan NW
am		1.22	177	MO	A Mails	Leeds City South	Wigan NW
am		1.22			A Mails	Stalybridge	Wigan NW
am		2.24			A News	Manchester Exchange	Wigan NW
am		2.59		MO	H	Ordsall Lane	Preston
am	2.50	3.28		MX	H	Ordsall Lane	Carlisle
am	4.09	4.42		MX	K	Ordsall Lane	Springs Branch
am	5.20	5.23			G LE P	Patricroft Loco	Leigh
am	5.56			SX	G LE P	Patricroft Loco	Tyldesley
am		6.17		SX	B Motor	Tyldesley	Wigan
am	6.26	6.33			B	Manchester Exchange	Preston
am	6.39		109	MX	G LE G	Patricroft Loco	Tyldesley
am		6.45		SX	B	Tyldesley	Leigh
am		7.05	111	MX	K	Tyldesley	Atherton Bag Lane
am		7.12		SX	B Motor	Tyldesley	Leigh
am		7.15		SO	B	Tyldesley	Leigh
am	7.28	7.30			B	Manchester Exchange	Wigan NW
am		7.39	109	MX	K	Hough Lane	Leigh
am		8.00		SX	G LE G	Tyldesley	Leigh (5.57 Ex Leigh)
am	8.23	8.25			B	Manchester Exchange	Kenyon Junction
am		8.30		SX	B	Tyldesley	Wigan NW
am		8.35		SO	B	Tyldesley	Wigan NW
am		8.42	109	MO	G EBV	Tyldesley	Speakmans Sidings
am	8.45	8.47	345	SO	A	Cross Lane	Barrow
am	9.30	9.34	315	SO	A	Cross Lane	Blackpool N via Leigh
am	9.43	9.55		SX	J Emt's	Garston Liverpool	Jacksons Sidings
am	10.45	10.46		SX	G EBV	Jacksons Sidings	Ellenbrook
am	11.24	11.26			B	Manchester Exchange	Wigan NW
am		11.41	110	SO	J Emt's	Patricroft Dn Sidings	Jacksons Sidings
am	11.33	11.44			F Emt's	Ellesmere Port	Chanters Sidings
am		11.48		SX	K	Ellenbrook	Kenyon Junction
am		11.52	293	SO	G LE G	Patricroft Loco	Atherton Bag Lane
pm		12.30	109	SX	G EBV	Tyldesley	Leigh
pm	12.35	12.36		SO	B	Manchester Exchange	Kenyon Junction
pm		12.45	109	SO	K	Tyldesley	Jacksons Sidings
pm	1.03	1.05		SO	B	Manchester Exchange	Wigan NW
pm		1.20		SO	B Motor	Tyldesley	Leigh
pm		1.42	110	SO	K	Tyldesley	Kenyon Junction
pm		1.52	291	SX	G LE G	Patricroft Loco	Atherton Bag Lane
pm	2.09	2.11		SO	B	Manchester Exchange	Wigan NW
pm		2.15	109	SX	G E&2BV	Tyldesley	Jacksons Sidings
pm	2.20		105	SX	K	Ellenbrook	Tyldesley
pm	3.20			SO	G LE P	Patricroft Loco	Tyldesley (3.49 Leigh)
pm		3.21		SO	C ECS	Tyldesley	Springs Branch (Ex 3.03 Up)
pm	3.30	3.30		SX	G LE P	Patricroft Loco	Tyldesley (3.49 Leigh)
pm	3.36	3.40		SO	B	Manchester Exchange	Wigan NW
pm	3.42	3.45		SX	B	Manchester Exchange	Wigan NW
pm		3.49			B Motor	Tyldesley	Leigh
pm	4.17	4.18	37		A	Manchester Exchange	Barrow
pm	4.24			SX	G LE P	Patricroft Loco	Tyldesley (to shunt)
pm		4.25			B Motor	Tyldesley	Earlestown
pm		4.34	39		A	Manchester Exchange	Glasgow
pm		4.43	112	SX	G LE G	Patricroft Loco	Leigh
pm	4.47	4.49			B	Manchester Exchange	Wigan NW
pm		4.50	113	SX	G LE G	Tyldesley	Jacksons Sidings
pm	5.38	5.40			B	Manchester Exchange	Wigan NW
pm		5.45			B	Tyldesley	Kenyon Junction
pm	6.12	6.18		SX	B	Manchester Exchange	Leigh
pm	6.12	6.27		SX	F	Bolton	Warrington (+1BV Tyd)
pm		6.30	292	SX	K	Tyldesley	Kenyon Junction
pm	6.39	6.41			B	Manchester Exchange	Wigan NW
pm		6.45		SX	B Motor	Tyldesley	Leigh
pm		6.45		SX	B Motor	Tyldesley	Kenyon Junction
pm	7.05	7.29		SX	D	Liverpool Road Gds	Carlisle Viaduct Yard
pm	7.32			SO	C ECS	Manchester Exchange	Tyldesley
pm		7.37		SX	G LE G	Tyldesley	Jacksons Sidings
pm	7.24	7.43		SO	E	Liverpool Road Gardens	Carlisle Viaduct Yard
pm		7.49		SX	K	Patricroft Sidings	Garston Liverpool
pm		8.05	112	SX	G EBV	Tyldesley	Jacksons Sidings
pm		8.20		SO	K	Patricroft Sidings	Garston Liverpool
pm	9.46	9.56		SX	B	Manchester Exchange	Wigan NW
pm	9.56	9.59		SO	B	Manchester Exchange	Wigan NW
pm		10.05		SO	B Motor	Tyldesley	Leigh
pm		10.29		SX	E	Liverpool Road Gds	Carnforth
pm	10.43	10.45			B	Manchester Exchange	Leigh
pm		10.59	379	SO	A News	Manchester Exchange	Carlisle
pm	11.08	11.09		SX	B	Manchester Exchange	Wigan NW
pm	11.10	11.12		SO	B Mails	Manchester Exchange	Wigan NW
				SUNDAYS			
AM		1.22			A	Stalybridge	Wigan NW
am		1.41			H	Buxton	Springs Brance N/Sidings
am		2.24	1		C PCLS	Manchester Exchange	Carnforth
am	8.49	8.52			B	Manchester Exchange	Wigan NW
am	9.01	9.52	431		B	Manchester Exchange	Liverpool Lime Street
am	9.54	9.56	448		B	Leeds City	Liverpool Lime Street
pm	3.00	3.02			B	Manchester Exchange	Wigan NW
pm	3.16	3.19	456		B	Manchester Exchange	Liverpool Lime Street
pm	6.49	6.52	387		B	Manchester Exchange	Liverpool Lime Street
pm	7.19	7.22			B	Manchester Exchange	Wigan NW
pm	9.04	9.06	389		B	Manchester Exchange	Liverpool Lime Street
pm		11.27	305		A	Manchester Exchange	Glasgow Central

Tyldesley lost its regular passenger service to Wigan North Western in November 1964, with the last holiday passenger traffic working from Tyldesley to Wigan from 6th July 1968 to 7th September 1968. Tyldesley to Hultons Sidings via Howe Bridge East and Atherton Junctions closed on 6th January 1969. Through goods and parcels traffic ceased to use Howe Bridge East to West Junctions as from 7th October 1968. Passenger services between Liverpool Lime Street via Leigh, Tyldesley and Eccles Junction to Manchester Exchange, continued until 3rd May 1969. The last trains to use the route were returning BICC excursions from Blackpool on that date. Complete closure of the line from Kenyon Junction to Eccles Junction via Tyldesley is officially given as 5th May 1969.

The Minister of Transport agreed to the withdrawal of Wigan N.W.-Manchester Exchange local services in the Autumn of 1964 on condition that there was an increase in the number of trains between Manchester, Tyldesley and Leigh with improved bus services from these stations. This cut right across BR's intended follow-up proposal to withdraw services from Liverpool Lime Street via Kenyon, Leigh and Tyldesley to Manchester and the resultant closure of all intermediate stations. The Minister, it was said, noted this and required that if such a future proposal occured it must be based on a "census" to include "those passengers displaced by withdrawal of the Tyldesley-Wigan locals".

Plate 132. An un-identified 8F approaches Tyldesley in June 1968, working from Howe Bridge West Sidings to Patricroft and photographed from the new signal box adjacent to Lemon Street. In the background is the iron foot bridge, known locally as "Red Bridge" that gave access to Gin Pit Village and Nook Colliery Etc, across what were extensive colliery lines serving the mines here. Nothing remains at this location today to give the casual onlooker any indication that deep mining took place here for over one hundred years, or that express trains passed this way over metals built by the London & North Western Railway. *Photo, Alf Yates.*

It is a well known fact that many of the so called "census" figures were taken during holiday periods when usage would obviously be down and no account was to be taken of special excursions. Many relevant figures supporting retention of services were often deemed inadmissible on the grounds that they did not conform to the criteria as laid down in proposed closure procedures.

 **British Rail**

PASSENGER TRAIN SERVICES

Manchester (Victoria)– Liverpool (Lime St.)

Following the consent given by the Minister of Transport the weekday passenger train service operating between MANCHESTER EXCHANGE and LIVERPOOL LIME ST. (via Tyldesley) will be withdrawn from MONDAY 5th MAY 1969 and the weekday service between MANCHESTER EXCHANGE and LIVERPOOL LIME ST (via Patricroft) will be revised and will operate from and to MANCHESTER VICTORIA STATION.

From the same date the following Stations will be closed: LEIGH, MONTON GREEN, TYLDESLEY, WORSLEY, and subject to authorisation being given by the issue of Road Service Licences by the Traffic Commissioners certain additional non-stop bus services will be introduced between LEIGH & TYLDESLEY and ATHERTON STATION.

This leaflet contains details of the rail and additional or revised bus services operative from 5th May 1969

For some reason it never occured to those presumably well educated individuals responsible for station closures that railway users were hardly likely to continue making their way to the same closed station to board a bus. Consequently these replacement bus services lasted only a short period.

Plate 133. Stanier 8F No. 48491 stands on the Up Main line at Tyldesley awaiting a crew change. The locomotive, which carries a very legible 9H Patricroft, shed plate, had arrived here from Atherton, Bag Lane Sidings after working trip freights over the Bolton & Leigh line. This light engine movement was timed by the Signalman to coincide with the arrival at Tyldesley of a local passenger train from Manchester Exchange, upon which the next crew would arrive "on the cushions" from Monton Green Station having booked on at Patricroft Shed. They would work the engine back to Bag Lane via Howe Bridge East and Atherton Junctions, calling at Chanters Sidings en-route to pick up any fulls, thence to continue trip workings out of Bag Lane Yard.

Driver Jim Carter had climbed the signal gantry at the west end of the platform to take this shot whilst he and his Fireman were waiting for the next booked crew to arrive. Once the locomotive had been passed over they also travelled "on the cushions" back to Monton Green on a local passenger train to book of at Patricroft. However, if time allowed the last "trip" working would be to the Railway on Waring Street for a couple of "scoops".

The photograph probably dates from late spring of 1965 as the Down Loop, on the left, was not lifted before the withdrawal of the Tyldesley-Wigan passenger service which occured in November 1964.

A new staff accommodation block with a flat roof had recently been built in the S&T triangle and is visible in the top left hand corner. Incredibly, on top of this a 4,000 gallon water tank was constructed. It came as no surprise to the staff there that shortly afterwards the roof began to sag and the door wouldn't shut.

Plate 134. BR Standard Class 5, 4-6-0 No. 73127, one of a number of this class fitted with Caprotti valve gear approaching Tyldesley in late 1964 with a short coal train from Speakmans Sidings, Leigh. The train has been marshalled at Speakmans to include an intermediate brake van, enabling the train to be split at Patricroft North Yard for onward destinations. *Photo, J. R. Carter.*

Plate 135. A photograph of the main station buildings on Platform 1, as viewed from Platform 2 on 27th July 1965. Note the timber prop supporting the canopy and the subway leading to the island Platforms 2 & 3 at the far end of the buildings. *Photo, R. J. Essery.*

Plate 136. A very early undated view of Tyldesley taken from allotments that then existed off Wareing Street (the approach road to the station) with what appears to be a London & North Western open top cattle wagon up against the buffer stop near the turntable.

Tyldesley cattle dock handled horses for the Co-op and cattle for Lilleys Farm near Parr Brow, worked direct from Holyhead. There were cattle trains from Penrith, Carlisle and Carnforth, working to Cross Lane, Salford, all calling at Tyldesley. A typical working around the turn of the century was the 6.30am from Penrith, calling at Tyldesley at 12.53pm en-route to Salford and a return working leaving Cross Lane at 3.25pm was allowed five minutes at Tyldesley to collect empty vans. *Photo, Authors Collection.*

Plate 137. A scene from London & North Western days at Tyldesley as passengers, or should I use the current term of "customers" depart from the station about 1920. *Photo, J. Jones.*

Plate 138. Tyldesley Station *c.*1965 as approached from Wareing Street. On the right hand side is the entrance to the cattle yard. The station lost its canopy some time in the early 1960's.   *Photo, R. J. Essery.*

Plate 139. The station frontage c1935 specially adorned for the coronation of King George V complete with "Britannia" over the doorway which was later to find its way decorating the timekeepers gable end (*see **Plate 125***). The young boy in the centre is Tom Yates, later of Tyldesley S&T dept, accompanied by his father and brother Richard. The author readily acknowledges the help and assistance given by Tom in supplying information regarding signalling and telegraph matters and putting names to faces in staff photographs.

Note also the period advertisements," H.P. Sauce" and "Gollyberry Jam" are prominent. Behind the railings on the left is an unidentifiable London & North Western locomotive.   *Photo, T. Yates.*

Plate 140. Presentation to one F. Wilkinson, Station Master since 1953, on his retirement in June 1958. Identified are: L. Alldred, Signalman, Jacksons Sidings; H. Kerfoot. Signalman, Hough Lane; J. Partington, Goods Yard; F. Williams, Inspector, Tyldesley; W. Gore, Platform Inspector, Tyldesley; J. Topp, Porter, Tyldesley; J. Cooper, light duties, Tyldesley; D. Coombes, Station Master, Tyldesley; J. Banks, Booking Clerk, Tyldesley. *Photo, Tillotsons Newspapers*

Plate 141. In this mid-1950's presentation to L. Mills, all personnel have been identified. From left to right: G. Rawlinson, Mechanical Chargeman, Atherton Central; K. Lee, Signal & Telegraph gang, Tyldesley; T. Robinson, Signal & Telegraph gang, Tyldesley; L. Palin, Signal & Telegraph Inspector, Tyldesley; D. Jones, Signal & Telegraph gang foreman, Tyldesley; P. Fletcher, Signal & Telegraph Inspector, Tyldesley; Claude McCutcheon, Chief Telegraph Inspector; and J. Lowe, Signal & Telegraph gang, Tyldesley. *Photo, J. Jones.*

Plate 143. Tyldesley *c.* 1964: Approaching Tyldesley from the Wigan or Leigh directions we would have passed St Georges Colliery on the right hand, just before the station, then passing through towards Manchester, the now defunct Goods Yard on the left. Astley Street runs across picture at the end of the station platforms. The "new" signal box of 1963 stands on the site of the former London & North Western cattle dock turntable. Tyldesley Parish Church occupies lower centre with Elliott Street on the left and George Street on the right. The tennis courts in Tyldesley Park can be clearly seen in the upper part of the picture, alongside Astley St.

Plate 142 (opposite). Continuing out of picture at top left hand we join our second view running past what was Ramsdens/Greens Sidings on the left, the trackbed can be seen to pass under Manchester Road with the now closed Cleworth Hall Colliery on the extreme left. Also at this point on the right is the trackbed of the former "Greens" line coming into the picture at centre and approaching the main lines at an angle. Proceeding eastwards, Hough Lane signal box is seen next to the remains of Tyldesley Gas Works. Hough Lane bridge itself is obscured by cloud shadow, with Tyldesley Cemetery marked by the wooded area also on the right. At this point in history the beginnings of house building projects which will eventually take up all the open aspect to the south of the railway line at this location have begun. The next bridge we meet is one we shall see later in W.D.Coopers study at Chester Road, with the latter running parallel to the railway right up to Parr Brow and the bridge carrying the A577 to Boothstown and Worsley. Ellenbrook Sidings can just be made out on the left of the main line, opposite Mosley Common Colliery, top centre. This was the "super pit", or later the "pit that died" to quote contemporary headlines. The reasons for its demise every bit as controversial as are the methods and reasoning behind recent closures. The last landmark is the A580 East Lancs Road, cutting across the top right hand corner of our picture.

Photo, Aerofilms.

Plate 144. View of Tyldesley Station from Astley Street, dating from 1901. Coal wagons belonging to Astley & Tyldesley Collieries can be seen on the middle left of the photo with London & North Western passenger stock in the station.   *Photo, Authors Collection.*

Plate 145. An example of a local private owner wagon constructed around the turn of the century and pictured at the Well Street end of Tyldesley Goods Yard about 1911, where a wagon repair shop was situated.   *Photo, J. Jones.*

Plate 146. Platforms 2 and 3 at Tyldesley as viewed from Platform 1 with the subway steps in the centre, a mid 1960's photograph.

Photo, R. J. Essery.

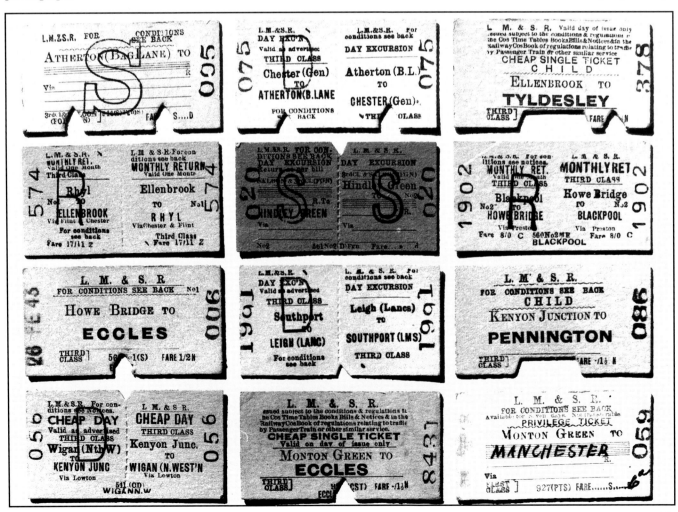

Plate 147. An early BR view of Royal Scot Class No. 46107 *"Argyll and Sutherland Highlander"* seen here approaching Tyldesley Station working the 4.15pm Manchester Exchange to Glasgow Express with five of its six coaches in BR Carmine and Cream livery. The train is seen passing Tyldesley No. 1 signal box and is about to cross Astley Street bridge. Tyldesley Goods Yard is on the extreme left. Tyldesley No. 1 worked three turns, opening 5.45am Monday, and closing at 5.45am Sunday. Tyldesley No. 2 also worked three turns, but was open all hours.

Photo, Authors Collection.

Plate 148. At the same point of approach to Tyldesley as Royal Scot 46107 is an unidentified 8F with a long engineers train in June 1968 for Howe Bridge West Sidings. The adjacent Goods Yard closed on 7th October 1963. Only the through running lines remain, although in preparation for closure, re-ballasting of the track has recently taken place.

Photo, Alf Yates.

Plate 149. Re-built Patriot Class 4-6-0 No. 45531 *"Sir Frederick Harrison"* arriving at Tyldesley on the Down Loop line for platform 4 on 21st October 1963. The train is the 10.50am Manchester Exchange-Wigan North Western local composed of BR Mk. I stock. On the left hand is the tender of Stanier 8F locomotive No. 48770, standing on the Up Main line waiting for the off having just arrived at Tyldesley from Bag Lane after working trip freights into Crook Street. The 8F was being worked to Ellenbrook Sidings for its last trip of the day when signal checked, and ever watch-full for a photograph, railwayman Jim Carter spotted 45531 emerging from under Hough Lane bridge and quickly grabbing his camera made his way from the footplate to take the shot between his firing duties on the 8F. Note the absence of Tyldesley No. 1 signal box in comparison with *Plate 147*.   *Photo, J. R. Carter.*

Plate150. Jubilee Class 4-6-0 No. 45732 *"Sanspareil"*, a name associated with railway locomotives from their inception, approaching Tyldesley Station with the 7.05pm Liverpool Road-Carlisle Goods in the summer of 1964. On the left is the defunct Goods Yard, closed in October 1963, although some private traffic continued to be worked into the sidings. Note the houses on the left known locally as "The Jig", the steepness of the ground or "Banks" on which they stand can be determined by the incline of their ridges.   *Photo, J. R. Carter.*

Plate 151. Astley Street bridge looking south, this photograph taken about the time of closure. Tyldesley Goods Yard was on the left and Tyldesley Station on the right. Note the substantial timber shoreing which had been in place as long as anyone can remember.   *Photo, Authors Collection.*

Plate 152. Signals in the "Up" direction at the end of Platform 2 in BR days. Note the signals on the extreme left, used for working between the bay platform and the Goods Yard. The sign on the main signal post reads "passengers must cross the line by the subway".

Photo, Authors Collection.

Plate 153. Travelling eastwards from Tyldesley, adjacent to the Goods Yard which had been situated on the right, was Well Street bridge (No. 30) seen here in 1982 looking south. The original bridge was substantially rebuilt in the early 1960's with a reinforced concrete deck.

Plate 154. A more recent view at the same location taken in mid 1995. Much of the former trackbed is now walkable.

Photos, Author.

RAMSDENS SIDINGS and GREENS SIDINGS

CONNECTIONS with the London & North Western Railway were made here to serve the collieries of George & William Green's Tyldesley Coal Company and also the Shakerley Collieries of William Ramsden.

Coal had been mined on the Shakerley Estate at Tyldesley from the early 15th century. The sale of Shakerley Estate in 1836 is described as "land of excellent quality, tithe free. Abounding with young timber, inexhaustible coal mines of excellent quality, ready sales would be vastly increased if the projected North Line of Railroad between Liverpool and Manchester be proceeded with". The North Line is a reference to the proposal in 1834 by the Manchester, Bolton & Bury Railway to construct a direct line between Wigan and Manchester, running to the north of Tyldesley, thereby reducing the distance travelled by the circuitous route using the Wigan Branch Railways line to Parkside and thence the Liverpool & Manchester line to Manchester, by some six miles. This proposal was objected to by the Liverpool & Manchester Railway who again recruited C.B.Vignoles to carry out their bidding in opposing the Bill when it came before Parliament. Defeat of the Bill and subsequent events resulted in an extremely long gestation period for a line to the north of Tyldesley, running through the Shakerley Estate. In the event, Shakerley Estate was duly purchased by Jacob Fletcher of Peel Hall, Little Hulton, whose only heiress, a daughter Charlotte Anne, married Robert Wellington 3rd Viscount Combermere in 1866 (later divorced). Therein lie the origins of names given to the Wellington Pit of W Ramsdens Shakerley Collieries and Combermere Colliery of George Greens Tyldesley Coal Company.

George and William Green are reputed to have begun sinking operations under Yew Tree Farm in the mid 1830's, but early information is sketchy. The first edition Ordnance Survey of the mid 1840's indicates a number of shafts on, or in the vicinity of Shakerley Common, including a "Shakerley Colliery" about a half mile to the north of Elliott Street. It seems more likely that coal of any quantity was not produced until the late 1840's from Green's collieries and by 1850/1 their tramway to the Bridgewater Canal at Astley was in operation.

At the Shakerley end, Green's tramway was rather steep so was cable worked. In fact the high ground here was known as the "Banks", a derivative of which, namely "Bongs", became the colloquial name for Tyldesley. Wagons were horse drawn over the remaining section to the Bridgewater Canal and here discharge facilities were built.

In 1864 connections were made with the London & North Western Railway, the main line itself passing over Greens line as the latter descended from the higher ground at this point. The tramway was converted to standard gauge during construction of the main line and sidings were laid for the transfer of traffic, on the lower ground, by the London & North Western. Locomotives were employed by Green's from 1867.

John Holland, who built the first railways in Ireland, joined the Green's whose colliery at Yew Tree became very successful. In fact he went to live at Pear Tree House, on the corner of Mort Lane and Sale Lane, Tyldesley, in 1858.

A new colliery was sunk at Combermere, to the north of Yew Tree in 1867 and the colliery railway extended to it. Combermere Colliery was short lived and closed in the mid 1890's, but on the same site Green's Tyldesley Coal Company established a brick works.

Tyldesley Coal Company's Peel Wood Colliery was a more extensive undertaking, situated alongside the later Lancashire & Yorkshire line on Tyldesley's northern boundary and worked from the early 1880's until 1928. The colliery railway was extended to Peel Wood and in addition connections were made with the Lancashire & Yorkshire Railway in 1888 when the line from Pendleton to Crows Nest Junction, Hindley, opened.

In 1888, colliers of the Tyldesley Coal Company broke through the boundaries of their lease whilst working coal under fields at the bottom of Well Street, Tyldesley, extracting a quantity of coal. The miners had followed the rise of the seam, breaking through into the workings of the Astley & Tyldesley Coal and Salt Company. A long dispute followed resulting in the former having to pay the latter £3,000 by way of damages.

Cleworth Hall Colliery was the most successful of Tyldesley Coal Company's mines, opening about 1874 and continuing in production under NCB ownership until 1963.

Closure of Greens Line, South of the London & North Western connections occured in 1913, when the Tyldesley Coal Company gave notice to the Earl Of Ellesmere, over whose land the railway passed, that the landlease would not be renewed. In the event, some of the track and plant at Astley was sold to the Clifton & Kearsley Coal Company

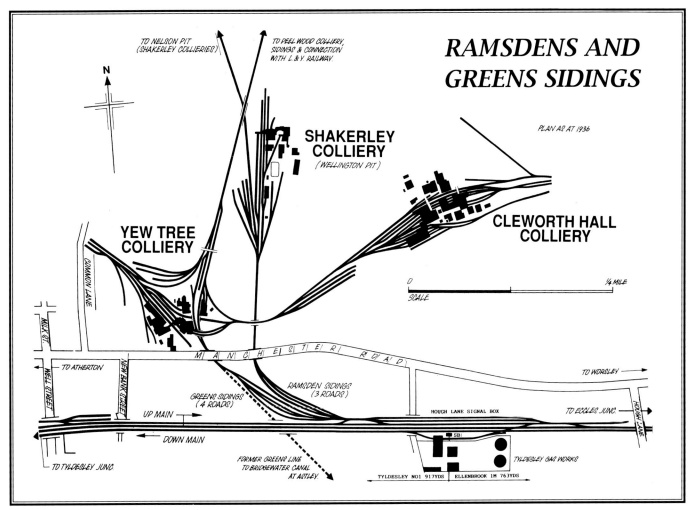

RAMSDENS AND GREENS SIDINGS

PLAN AS AT 1936

TO NELSON PIT (SHAKERLEY COLLIERIES)

TO PEEL WOOD COLLIERY, SIDINGS & CONNECTION WITH L.& Y. RAILWAY.

N

SHAKERLEY COLLIERY
(WELLINGTON PIT)

CLEWORTH HALL COLLIERY

YEW TREE COLLIERY

SCALE

¼ MILE

COMMON LANE

MILK ST.

NELL STREET

NEW BANK STREET

TO ATHERTON

MANCHESTER ROAD

TO WORSLEY

GREENS SIDINGS (4 ROADS)

RAMSDEN SIDINGS (3 ROADS)

HOUGH LANE SIGNAL BOX

TO ECCLES JUNC.

HOUGH LANE

UP MAIN

DOWN MAIN

SB

TO TYLDESLEY JUNC.

FORMER GREENS LINE TO BRIDGEWATER CANAL AT ASTLEY.

TYLDESLEY GAS WORKS

TYLDESLEY NO1 917YDS

ELLENBROOK 1M 763YDS

who were sinking their Astley Green shafts at the time.

In the 1860's there had been three separate accidents on Greens tramway, two of them fatal. All of them happening when wagons returning to the collieries from Astley, were being hauled up the incline.

The latter accident involved one Thomas Leather, who had been in charge of twelve wagons. In some way the haulage rope had slipped, allowing wagons to run backwards. Leather, in attempting to apply the "brakes" had come into contact with a wooden bridge which carried an occupation road over the tramway. The inquest into this accident was held at the Red Lion, on Sale Lane, Tyldesley, and it was requested that this bridge be removed!

August 1862 saw another fatality on the tramway, this time involving loaded wagons descending the incline.

Evidently the London & North western operations in constructing apparently been standing on the tramway, watching a locomotive passing over the newly constructed main line bridge and hearing the shouts of nearby workmen, one immediately jumped clear, the other only turned round and was killed by the descending wagons.

William Ramsden appears to have taken over a "Shakerley Colliery" in 1861 and this particular colliery was, in later years, more commonly known as Nelson Pit. Ramsden's Wellington Pit dates from the late 1860's and was situated about ¼ mile to the north of Tyldesley Coal Company's Yew Tree Pit.

I have not been able to establish an exact date for the connection of Ramsden's Shakerley Collieries with the London & North Western, alongside Greens Sidings. William Ramsden was amongst the invited guest's at the inaugural sod cutting ceremony of the Eccles-Tyldesley Branch at Worsley in 1861. He would undoubtedly have been keen to establish rail connections early on and it seems likely that by the time Wellington Pit opened it was rail served.

The branch to Ramsden's collieries passed beneath Manchester Road, Tyldesley, by a separate underbridge from that of Green's Tyldesley Coal Company, and like the latter, Ramsdens colliery railway ascended the "Banks" on a steeply graded incline. Ramsdens railway passed under the Tyldesley Coal Company's railway before reaching Wellington Pit and beneath it again enroute to Nelson Pit.

Shakerley Collieries were taken over by Manchester Collieries in 1935, when virtually worked out, for their quota of coal. Wellington Pit closed in the same year but Nelson Pit continued in operation until 1938.

Plate 155. Ramsdens and Greens Sidings: This photograph is thought to date from 1935/6 and the sidings are viewed from nearby Nelson Street situated on higher ground. Wagons of Manchester Collieries, who took over Ramsden's Shakerley Collieries in 1935, are seen alongside those of George Green's Tyldesley Coal Company, which in fact remained as an independent concern until nationalisation in 1947. There were seven roads here and as viewed the first three were Ramsdens Sidings and the remaining four Greens Sidings. The industrial loco appears to be either "Edith" or "Shakerley," built for W Ramsden's in 1887 & 1901 respectively by Hunslet & Co. These were 0-6-0 Saddle Tanks with 14" X 18" cylinders and 3ft diameter wheels. In the background a Midland 4-4-0 waits on the Up Loop.

In the last quarter of the 19th century about 100,000 tons of coal per year were dispatched via the London & North Western connection here and additional sidings had been provided by the Company in 1891 at a cost of £500.

Photo, H Gillibrand Collection.

In the mid-1950's opencast operations on the former sites of Shakerley Collieries Nelson Pit and Tyldesley Coal Company's Peel Wood removed any remaining traces of colliery workings. The site at Combermere, which had become a brickworks is still apparent, as is part of the trackbed of the colliery railway that served it, from a point north of the Wellington Pit site. The latter, and what remained of the Yew Tree site, were landscaped in later years after the closure of Cleworth Hall Colliery.

There had been a small signal cabin controlling Greens Sidings and this had been situated alongside the Down line, west of Hough Lane cabin. It was shown on the 1936 Ordnance Survey but probably abolished pre 1940.

An accident took place at Greens Sidings in December 1878 when a Manchester bound passenger train composed of seven vehicles collided with a light engine, the latter crossing from the sidings onto the Down Main whilst going to Tyldesley for water. Although considerable damage to locomotives and stock ensued as a result of the collision, there were no fatalities, but a number of passengers sustained serious injuries.

Colonel Yolland investigated the accident and said it had been caused by the Signalman at Greens Sidings Cabin who had made a mistake as to the signal given from Tyldesley East (No. 1) Cabin. It appears the Signalman at Greens Sidings had thought a train had been signalled, but after some twenty minutes had elapsed and no train had come, he put the appropriate signal for the Manchester train back to danger and opened the points for the light engine to proceed to Tyldesley when the accident occured. Colonel Yolland indicated that train on line signals ought not to be given so long in advance from Telegraph Station to Telegraph Station.

This particular section of line, with Up and Down Main lines parallel to the Up Goods Loop, seems to have been an accident black spot as a number of incidents occured here pre-1890. One involved the Up "Scotch Mail" colliding with a coal train from Springs Branch during shunting movements between the Up Main and Up Goods Loop.

The inquiry into this accident blamed the Signalman at Tyldesley No. 1 Cabin, who it appears, had failed to ascertain that the Up Main was clear before he pulled off the signals for the Mail train, and by the Yard Shunter, who it was said, "ought not to have uncoupled sixteen wagons and left them standing on the Up Main without having received permission of the Signalman to do so". Again there were quite a number of injuries and considerable damage, particularly to the Up Mail locomotive, and to the goods van and wagons of the coal train.

Plate 156. An unidentified Britannia 4-6-2 runs light engine down the bank on the Up line from Tyldesley past the now lifted Greens/Ramsdens Sidings in 1966. The derelict gate on the extreme left was, in years past, closed every New Years Day to preserve the landowners right of way. Note in the far background Nook Colliery. *Photo, A Whalley.*

Plate 157. A returning empty car transporter train from Renthorpe near Wakefield, to Halewood, hauled by a Type 4 diesel locomotive and seen passing the lifted Greens and Ramsdens Sidings in 1967. The train will work via Wigan, Ince Moss, St. Helens, Raven Street, Farnworth, and Widnes No. 8 Deviation Junction to reach its destination.

Photo, A Whalley.

Plates 158 & 159. Two photographs taken from Nelson Street, Tyldesley, about 1963 as viewed looking east, from Greens Sidings.

In *Plate 158 (top)* a Stanier Class 5 descends the bank after passing Greens Sidings and is nearing Upton Lane bridge, seen in the extreme left hand corner of the frame. The working is a local Up trip freight which includes farming machinery from David Browns Leigh, probably en-route to the docks at Manchester for export. In the background is Tyldesley Gas Works, much of it demolished by this period. Also, building work has commenced in the Bodmin Road/Stour Road area, this giving an indication of the date. On the extreme right, above the freight is the trackbed of Greens Line, walkable at the time in its entirety from Greens Sidings to the Bridgewater Canal on Astley Moss. The open aspect of the view has now been smothered by continuous housing programmes, although much of the trackbed of Greens line is still discernable.

For the second view, *Plate 159*, the cameraman has panned to the left and Upton Lane bridge is seen again, this time on the right. Hough Lane signal box is also in view with three LMS built 50ft vans in the Up Siding. An unidentified light engine approaches on the Down line and in the far background is Mosley Common Colliery.

Photographs, H.Gillibrand.

Plate 160. A view of Upton Lane Bridge shortly before demolition took place in 1984. This was the horse and cart road to the gas works. The siding agreement between Tyldesley Gas works and the London & North Western Railway dates from 1880. The Gas Works was new then, the foundation stone being laid, in July 1880, by William Ramsden of Shakerley Collieries, also Chairman of the Gas & Water Committee. Two bottles were deposited in the brickwork cavity, one contained copies of "The Journal", other papers and current coins, whilst the second contained a copy of the works contract.

Photo, Author.

Plate 161. On 23rd September 1964, Stanier 8F No. 48181 is seen working coal empties to Speakmans Sidings, Leigh and Jacksons Sidings, Tyldesley, an afternoon turn from Patricroft North Sidings. On the right is Hough Lane signal box with, behind the guards van, Hough Lane bridge. In the distance, on higher ground, is the bridge spanning the sandstone cutting alongside Chester Road, known locally as "Bomb Bridge" more of which later. On the left is Jubilee Class 4-6-0 No. 45657 *"Tyrwhitt"* upon which photographer Jim Carter had arrived with a P.W. (permanent way) train. The locomotive sports a diagonal yellow stripe signifying that it is banned working south of Crewe due to insufficient overhead clearance on the recently electrified route to Euston. *Photo, J. R Carter.*

Plate 162. A pair of 8F locomotives working tender first haul a freight train down the falling gradient towards Hough Lane and are about to cross the narrow Upton Lane bridge in 1967. Hough Lane signal box is hidden behind the locomotives. *Photo, A. Whalley.*

Plate 163 Also on 23rd September 1964, a good view towards Tyldesley taken from the roof of the guards van which has been shunted into the Up Goods Loop. Immediately behind the locomotive and partially hidden by smoke, had been Ramsdens/Greens Sidings. With the encroaching demise of the steam locomotive, bits and pieces of "Railwayania" began to disappear, hence the missing shed plate from 45657. *Photo, J. R. Carter.*

Plate 164. Our third view at this location, again courtesy of Driver Jim Carter, shows a pair of Stanier 8F's led by No. 48164 with a coal train from Speakmans Sidings, stopped in the Up Loop to allow the passage of a passenger train to Manchester Exchange. Again Tyldesley Parish Church is prominent and also Hough Lane signal box on the left, whilst in the sidings coaches are being stored prior to their use on weekend excursions from local stations. *Photo J. R. Carter.*

Plate 165. Hough Lane Bridge as in 1986, before alterations above road level began. The high point of the footpath, as viewed in the Manchester direction, marks the position of a structure known locally as "Bomb Bridge", demolished in 1984 which will be seen in following photographs and also the extent to which the cutting has been infilled. The original bridge at Hough Lane was found to be unsafe and demolition by explosives took place in 1880, to be replaced by the structure seen here. *Photo, Author.*

Plate 166. Between Hough Lane and Ellenbrook was a cutting through the upper red sandstone, the excavated material from this was used for embankments at Tyldesley and also at Leigh. This same material was used to infill the cutting in 1984 when a reclamation scheme was in progress.

In this 1946 photo, LMS Compound No. 1098 is seen working a Chester to Manchester Exchange train comprising three coaches plus a GWR Siphon Van attached at the rear and is taken approximately half-way along the cutting, the houses on Chester Road overlooking the scene. The bridge under which the train is passing was quite a substantial one, built to carry the horse and cart traffic of an earlier era, consisting of two rivetted girders resting on stone abutments with timber decking and sides on transversely laid timber baulks.

Tyldesley Parish Church is prominent in the background next to, in line of sight, an example of an extremely tall sighting signal, enabling drivers to observe the arm when approaching down the bank from Tyldesley, before beginning to climb again at a point near Hough Lane.

Photo W. D. Cooper

Plates 167 and 168. Photographs taken by the Author of the structure in 1979 when the bridge was still in use. At some stage during the 1960's new timber side panels had been fitted.

Plate 169. With Hough Lane Bridge in the background, Type 2 diesel No. D5076 approaches "Bomb Bridge", seen in W. D. Coopers photograph (***Plate 166***), en-route from Howe Bridge West Sidings to Ellenbrook Sidings. Marshalled behind the diesel is Ex-L&Y ST No. 752, on its way into preservation at the K&WVR, from Parsonage Colliery, Leigh on 24th April 1968.   *Photo, B. Hilton.*

Plate 170. The scene in 1984 from the same viewpoint as demolition of the bridge and infill work takes place. The bridge girders can be seen below awaiting the cutters torch.   *Photo, Author.*

EPITAPH FOR A RAILWAY

(or a train spotters lament)

Silent, this once busy place
that makes me feel so sad,
thinking back to happy days,
when I was just a lad.

To see a Jub or Scot maybe,
or perhaps a brand new Brit,
blasting up the gradient
past the Commin Pit.

Remember the train in gleaming green
carrying its name in red,
Seven Double O Thirty Seven
"Hereward the Wake," it said.

No more will the coal trains rattle
as they did in that distant past,
the 2-8-0's and Super D's
have now all breathed their last.

Nature abounds in places now
where once the Black Fives ran,
all metal to the breaker's yard
into a car, —-or can.

Plate 171. As a boy I spent many happy hours at this and other locations along this section of track, eagerly watching for the tell-tale plume of smoke that signalled the arrival of the next train. In the 1950's the Manchester Exchange via Tyldesley to Barrow & Windermere or Glasgow workings seem to be utilised for running-in turns on ex-works locomotives from Crewe. Both Westinghouse fitted Britannias were observed thus, looking strange beast's indeed with equipment resembling a plumbers nightmare fitted on their smokeboxes. Jubilees, on the Barrow/Windermere and Scots on the Glasgow trains were also regular motive power used on these turns. Another favourite was the 7.05pm Manchester, Liverpool Road-Carlisle Goods, due at Tyldesley about 7.30pm and invariably worked by a Patriot. This working carried products from many of the works in the nearby Trafford Park Industrial Estate.

Plate 172. Infilling of the cutting alongside Chester Road during February 1984.

Photos Author.

Plate 173. Another W.D.Coopers photographs taken about 250 yds. east of ***Plate 166***, giving a better overall view of the cutting and shows one of the Stanier 2-6-4T locomotives, LMS No. 2539, probably with a Wigan N.W. to Manchester Exchange local about 1946 composed of L&NW stock. To give some idea of scale in relation to Model Railways, Chester Road, alongside the cutting is approximately $\frac{1}{4}$ mile in length, or 440 yds, X by 12 (4 mm to 1 ft) =5.280m, or 17ft $3\frac{3}{4}$ in.

Plate 174. A present day view, April 1996.

Photo, Author.

ELLENBROOK

ELLENBROOK Sidings connected the London & North Western with an extensive system of colliery railways here, brought together by Bridgewater Collieries to serve their pits hereabouts and extended to reach its zenith under the ownership of Manchester Collieries Ltd in the 1930's. A volume in itself would be required to fully cover and give justice to the numerous lines and sidings, far beyond the scope of this book. Suffice to say that the Bridgewater Colliery Railways owe their beginnings to the horse drawn tramways and wagonways built to alleviate overcrowding on the unique underground canal system which emerged at Worsley Delph on the Bridgewater Canal.

A horse drawn tramway at this location had been in operation by the mid 1830's and connected a group of pits to the north of Ellenbrook with the Bridgewater Canal at Booths Hall Bank, Boothstown. En-route to the canal the tramway also served pits at Abbots Fold, Boothstown.

The proposal for the London & North Western Railways Eccles-Tyldesley-Wigan line in 1861 convinced the Bridgewater Estates Trustees of the need to work in association with the railways in order to effect a more rapid distribution of their increasing coal production. Therefore the impetus to construct or re-build their internal railways to standard gauge with various mainline connections and sidings, a process which had begun about ten years previously, now continued apace. Eventually these colliery lines were to become part of the Central Railways of Manchester Collieries Ltd in 1929, complete with their own locomotive repair and workshop facilities at Central Workshops, Walkden, which would become the main depot for such activities in NCB days.

The proposed Eccles-Tyldesley-Wigan line also signalled a new phase of mining development by the Bridgewater Trustees, part of which was the sinking of the first shafts at Mosley Common in 1860, on a site previously mined for the Worsley Four Foot outcrop. Sinking of the shafts were not completed until late 1868 with coal production beginning about twelve months later.

Mosley Common Colliery was situated south of the Eccles-Tyldesley-Wigan railway and eventually was to become the largest in Manchester Coalfield. A standard gauge branch line, replacing the earlier tramway, was constructed to run from the new colliery to the Bridgewater Canal at Booths Hall Bank where, in 1871, a new wharf was built. At the same period the colliery railway was extended northward from Mosley Common, passing beneath the London & North Western's lines, to the Ellesmere Pit at Walkden, the sinking of which had begun in 1865, and also to Ashtons Field Colliery, about a mile to the north west of Walkden. The Bridgewater Collieries standard gauge connection at Ellenbrook Sidings is contemporary with these works and probably opened in 1871.

The Bridgewater Trustees were, with these new colliery railways and mainline connections, able to get the best of both worlds. To the industrial heart of Manchester by canal, or export to America via the mainline railways and Liverpool Docks.

It is worth noting that the trackbed of the former colliery line at this point was part of Wigan Metro's draft development plan (1991) for the re-connection of Leigh and Tyldesley to the rail network. A connection would have been made with the former Lancashire & Yorkshire Railway line west of Walkden (high level) Station, thence following the colliery trackbed to Ellenbrook and on through to Tyldesley and Leigh following the original London & North Western route. However, BR publicly stated at the time that they had nothing in their next 10 year plan to this effect. Save for Hough Lane bridge all structures and most embankments on the route have been removed. The latest plan is for a link with the Walkden-Atherton line from a point near the sewage works, then to cross open ground, meeting with the old alignment at Parr Brow.

Plate 175. A 1969 photograph of a dilapidated looking Ellenbrook Signal Box, taken from an approaching Manchester bound Diesel Multiple Unit. Ellenbrook had been a 25 lever signal cabin, opening two shifts, 5am-10.05pm Mondays to Fridays *c.* 1960.

Photo, Authors collection.

Plate 176. With Ellenbrook Station in the background, Ex-London & North Western 0-6-2 "Coal Tank", LMS No. 7799, approaching bunker first working light engine towards Tyldesley in October 1947. A particularly long lived design of locomotive, lasting in BR ownership until 1957. Access to Ellenbrook Station was by a wooden staircase on the Up platform and by an inclined ramp for the Down, to Wigan, platform.

Photo, W.D.Cooper.

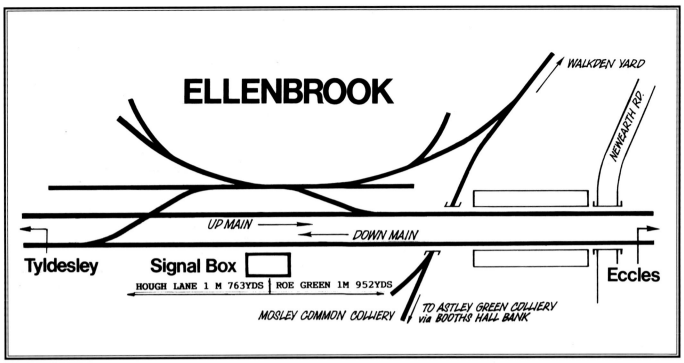

ELLENBROOK

WALKDEN YARD

NEWEARTH RD.

UP MAIN → ← DOWN MAIN

Tyldesley

Signal Box

HOUGH LANE 1 M 763YDS | ROE GREEN 1M 952YDS

Eccles

MOSLEY COMMON COLLIERY

TO ASTLEY GREEN COLLIERY
via BOOTHS HALL BANK

Plate 177. A trio of Stanier locomotives at Ellenbrook on 21st October 1963. On the right is 8F No. 48770, already mentioned on *Plate 149* at Tyldesley, waiting for the road in Ellenbrook Sidings with a coal train for Patricroft North Yard. Driver Jim Carter had gained an advantageous position in Ellenbrook Signal Box for the shot. Drawing slowly up towards the signal box are Class 5 No. 45413 and Jubilee Class No. 45657 *"Tyrwhitt"* also en-route to Patricroft having worked local trip freights in the area. Note the brake van sandwiched between the locomotives, an unusual and possibly illegal working as the power of the locomotives could literally pull the van apart if they were not working in unison.

Plate 178. Ellenbrook Station *c.* 1950 as viewed in the Tyldesley direction with, on the right Ellenbrook Sidings and on the left, Mosley Common Colliery. The station closed on 2nd January, 1961. *Photo, Stations U.K.*

Plate 179. Hughes/Fowler design of 1926 in the shape of "*Crab*" 2-6-0 No. 2862 on the approach to Ellenbrook Station working a Manchester Exchange to Tyldesley train on 12th May 1945 with Ellenbrooks outer distant signal visible to the rear of the train. The bridge in the background is known locally as "Ladybridge" whilst the pleasant open aspect to the left now houses the Broadway Estate. *Photo, W. D. Cooper.*

ROE GREEN JUNCTION

FURTHER London & North Western Acts of 1865-9 authorised a new branch to leave the Eccles-Tyldesley line at Roe Green near Worsley, to Bolton Great Moor Street, where a new station was to be built on an adjacent site to the original Great Moor Street Station opened in 1831, which had been demolished by a runaway goods train in 1858. Stations would also be provided at Walkden, Little Hulton and Plodder Lane. The line from Roe Green Junction to collieries at Little Hulton, as authorised in the 1865 Act, opened for freight Traffic on 1st July 1870. The 1869 Act authorised the extension of the Roe Green Branch to its junction with the Bolton & Leigh line at Fletcher Street and this opened on 16th November 1874. The new station at Great Moor Street had opened on 28th September 1874 with the passenger service to Hunts Bank (Manchester Victoria) via Roe Green beginning on 1st April 1875. Manchester Exchange sited west of Victoria was opened by the London & North Western in June 1884. Walkden became Walkden Low Level on 2nd June 1924, to distinguish it from the Lancashire & Yorkshire station. The Manchester Exchange-Great Moor Street passenger service was withdrawn on 29th March 1954 and the stations closed. (The same date as those on the Great Moor Street-Kenyon Junction line) Goods facilities remained at Plodder Lane until 30th January 1965.

Plodder Lane's four road engine shed was authorised in 1874 but soon became overcrowded, enlargements taking place in the 1890's. As a sub-shed of Patricroft, Plodder Lane worked the local passenger services to Manchester, Bolton and Kenyon along with freights from the local collieries on the Roe Green Branch. Before closure of the shed took place in 1954 many of the turns on the Bolton & Leigh line were worked by Plodder Lane crews.

In the mid 1930's plans were drawn up by the LMS for a station at Roe Green Junction with platforms serving both the Bolton and Wigan lines. It is probable that the outbreak of W.W.II curtailed this scheme and consequently the station was never built.

Plate 180. May 1948, a short distance west of Roe Green Junction is Patriot Class 4-6-0 No. 5536 *"Private W Wood V.C."* with the 3.55 pm Manchester Exchange to Windermere & Barrow train composed of LMS brake third, four LMS corridor composites with another LMS brake third at the rear. Calling at Tyldesley at 4.16 pm, Wigan North Western at 4.33 pm and Preston at 5.03 pm, with additional through coaches from Morecambe being attached at Lancaster. The train has just passed under Greenleach Lane bridge, the diverging point for the branch to Great Moor Street, Bolton, the signals of which are visible over the leading coach. *Photo, W. D. Cooper.*

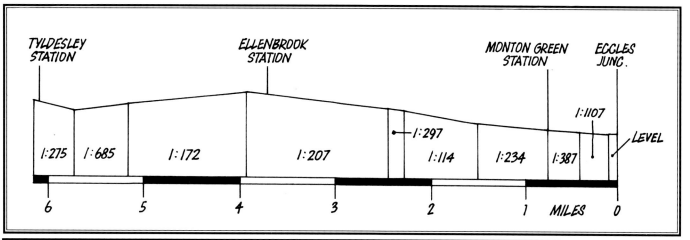

TYLDESLEY STATION   ELLENBROOK STATION   MONTON GREEN STATION   ECCLES JUNC.

1:275   1:685   1:172   1:207   1:297   1:114   1:234   1:387   1:1107   LEVEL

6   5   4   3   2   1   MILES   0

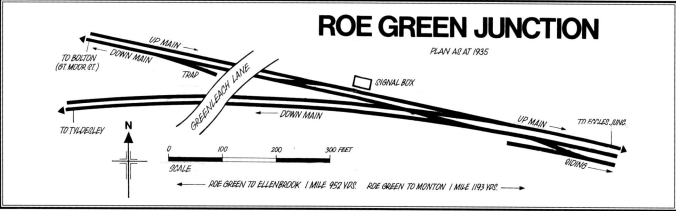

ROE GREEN JUNCTION

PLAN AS AT 1935

UP MAIN

TO BOLTON
(GT. MOOR ST.)   DOWN MAIN

TRAP   GREENLEACH LANE   SIGNAL BOX

TO TYLDESLEY   DOWN MAIN   UP MAIN   TO ECCLES JUNC.

N   SIDING

SCALE   0   100   200   300 FEET

ROE GREEN TO ELLENBROOK 1 MILE 952 YDS.   ROE GREEN TO MONTON 1 MILE 1193 YDS.

Plate 181. Today the trackbed at the former Roe Green Junction forms a useful and scenic footpath and like its railway predecessor diverging for, on the left as viewed, Little Hulton or on the right Ellenbrook. Take a seat for a while and ponder. Close your eyes and you might just hear wheels squealing or steam blowing, and in your imagination see it . . . .as it was.

Photo, Author.

145

Plate 182. Can you see it yet, well here it is, in the summer of 1947. The Signalman has his cabin well ventilated as one of F. W. Webbs 0-6-2 Coal Tanks No. 27586 of 1882 vintage takes the Bolton line with the service from Manchester Exchange.

Plate 183. Taking the route to Tyldesley with a Wigan N.W. train is Stanier designed 2-6-4T No. 2561 with a mixture of LMS and L&NW stock on 10th June 1947.

Photos, W. D. Cooper.

Plate 184. Track maintenance and re-laying was a far more labour intensive task than is the case today. This view at Roe Green Junction on 21st April 1950 shows the number of men engaged thereon. The line curving left out of sight is for Tyldesley and Wigan, straight on under Greenleach Lane Bridge for Bolton Great Moor St.   *Photo, W. D. Cooper.*

Plate 185. Drifting down the gradient from Roe Green with a Chester via Kenyon, Leigh and Tyldesley to Manchester Exchange train on 24th April 1948, is an example of the post-grouping development of Johnson three cylinder compound 4-4-0 locomotives No. 925.   *Photo, W. D. Cooper.*

Plate 186. At the same location as **Plate 187** but photographed from the opposite direction, another of the L&NW Coal Tanks approaches with a Manchester Exchange to Bolton Great Moor Street service, push-pull operated with No. 7789 providing the power on 10th June 1947. *Photo, W. D. Cooper.*

Plate 187. Royal Scot Class 4-6-0 No. 46116 *"Irish Guardsman"* works an afternoon Fleetwood-Crewe fish train past the same spot in1961 having been diverted over this route from Wigan Springs Branch because of an accident on the main lines at Dallam, Warrington involving Jubilee Class No. 45630 *"Swaziland"* and Class 5 No. 45401, which blocked the WCML for about 24 hours. *Photo, J. R. Carter.*

SANDERSONS SIDINGS

SANDERSONS Sidings, situated between Roe Green and Worsley, was another of the despatch points for coal traffic from the Bridgewater Collieries rail system.

The name comes from Sandersons Pit which had been sunk about 1835 on a site approximately ½ mile to the north of the later London & North Western line. A horse drawn tramway, contemporary with Sandersons Pit had been built to connect the colliery with the Bridgewater Canal at Worsley.

The 1847 proposal for the Manchester & Southport Railway which, had it been built, would have passed to the north of Sandersons Pit, had the effect of persuading the Bridgewater Trustees to convert their Sandersons tramway to standard gauge and this was completed in 1852.

Further mining developments were to take place in the area in the 1860's when Bridgewater Colliery was sunk to the north of Sandersons Pits and the standard gauge colliery railway extended to it. Eventually the colliery railway would join with the Ellenbrook branch at Ashtons Field.

Connections between the Colliery Railway and the London & North Western Railway at Sandersons Sidings date from the opening of the main Eccles-Wigan lines and were effected by a short north to west curve, involving reversal by colliery locomotives when descending from Sandhole, (the later name for Bridgewater Colliery). The main London & North Western lines passed beneath the colliery lines at this location.

Sandhole Colliery had closed in 1962 but the washery remained open to receive coal traffic from other collieries, which included slack from Bedford Colliery, Leigh, worked to Sandersons by British Railways from Speakmans Sidings. The re-opening of Nook washery in 1966 made this arrangement redundant and as a consequence the connection at Sandersons Sidings with British Railways was out of use by late 1966.

Plate 188. A young boy keeps his eye on the tracklaying gang at Sandersons Sidings from the steps of the signal box on 21st April 1950, perhaps dreaming of one day being a train driver, or even a signalman. Sandersons cabin had 25 levers and worked only one shift, 11 am to 7 pm Mondays to Fridays. *Photo, W. D. Cooper.*

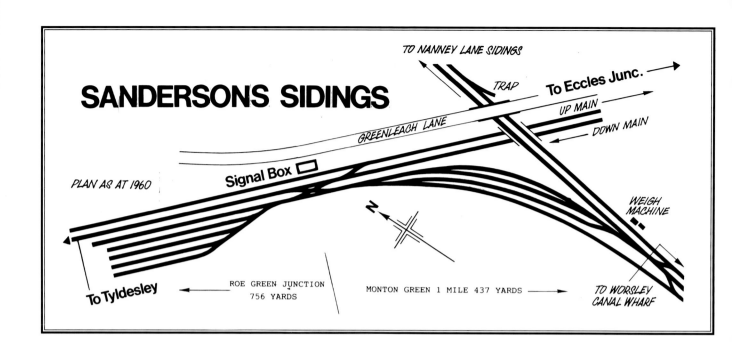

SANDERSONS SIDINGS

TO NANNEY LANE SIDINGS

TRAP

To Eccles Junc.

UP MAIN

DOWN MAIN

GREENLEACH LANE

Signal Box

PLAN AS AT 1960

N

WEIGH MACHINE

To Tyldesley

ROE GREEN JUNCTION 756 YARDS

MONTON GREEN 1 MILE 437 YARDS

TO WORSLEY CANAL WHARF

Plate 189. In April 1948, still bearing LMS insignia Ex-L&NW 0-8-0 No. 9134 had arrived at Sandersons to collect loaded wagons, whilst leaving the rest of the train on the Up Main. Shunting operations now complete 9134 re-starts from Sandersons Sidings with what is now a fifty-six wagon train. The bridge under which the train is passing carries the mineral line from Sandhole Colliery and points North on the Manchester Collieries system, to the Bridgewater Canal at Worsley, or by reversal into Sandersons Sidings for mainline despatch. *Photo, W. D. Cooper.*

Plate 190. The Eccles-Tyldesley-Wigan line was also a useful diversionary route for WCML traffic. Still carrying LMS livery, 4-6-2 Pacific No. 6233 *"Duchess of Sutherland"* is seen here passing Sandersons Sidings having been diverted via Manchester London Road, Castlefield and Eccles Junction on 25th April 1948 because of a serious accident at Winsford that had occurred on 17th April involving LMS Pacific locomotives Nos. 6207 & 6251. The working is the Royal Scot, Euston to Glasgow with at least sixteen on, timed to depart Euston at 10 am.

Photo, W. D. Cooper.

Plate 191. Also on 25th April 1948, another re-routed express at Sandersons, headed by one of Sir William Staniers Class 5's in experimental lined green livery, No. 4764. This time the letter "M" has been applied over the cabside number as opposed to under it with the new owners name on the tender. The working is a Birmingham-Blackpool train and like 6233 would re-join the WCML at Springs Branch, Manchester Lines Junction, to continue the journey North.

Photo, W. D. Cooper.

Plate 192. 8F's Nos. 48720 & 48181 wait to reverse into Sandersons Sidings with a coal train from Speakmans Sidings on a spring day in April 1965. The train would be split into manageable loads for the NCB engines and taken by them to Sandhole for washing.

Photo, J. R. Carter.

WORSLEY

OF all the stations on the Eccles-Wigan route, Worsley, in its early years, must have resembled a gleaming talisman, surrounded in rural tranquillity, a shining jewel in the crown of the London & North Western Railway.

The station buildings were of white brick, arched over the windows and doorways in alternate white, red, and black brick. There were two First Class and two Second Class Waiting Rooms and a Booking Office. On the Up platform a seven ridged canopy, with the ridges at right angles to the station buildings, gave shelter from the elements. A less elaborate canopy projected, at eaves level in cantilevered fashion, from the Down platform waiting rooms.

The platforms themselves were some 300 ft in length with red and blue tiles edged with stone. At the western end of the Up platform was a horse dock, used on occasions to transport stock to and from the Earl of Ellesmere's Estate.

Roads to the station were quickly opened out and house building in the area increased as those who were able to afford to commute settled in the vicinity.

Worsley had been the venue for the inaugural sod cutting ceremony on "Old Factory" site, about half a mile from Worsley Village, in September 1861. The invited guests had assembled at the Grapes Inn, worsley, which occupied the present M63 junction adjacent to Worsley Court House, before proceeding, in procession, to the appointed place.

In cutting the first sod the Earl of Ellesmere had been assisted by a railway "Navvie", a name in years past used to describe that stalwart band of men who cut the first canals, and here Worsley had been in the forefront of technology with Brindley's engineering feats in the eighteenth century.

The development of canals in the area provided a much needed transport system for the movement of coal, from the Bridgewater Estates, to Manchester. Consequently the success of the canals led to an increase in mining which, by the early nineteenth century, was causing congestion, particularly on the underground sections.

A hundred years after Brindley, the arrival of the railways had spurred on the deep mining activity around Worsley and for the next century the steam locomotive provided the power required to move the vast tonnages of coal produced.

The one hundred year cycle continued with the arrival at Worsley of the motorway network in the 1960's, the construction of which has swallowed up vast tracts of land and in its wake removed many traces of Worsley's historic past. Brindley's canal survived and today provides recreation. Unfortunately the railway was seen as expendable. What value today would be attached to Worsley Station for the commuter were it still open!

Plate 193. An early BR view at Worsley as Ivatt 2-6-2T No. 41214, a class of locomotive frst introduced in 1946, gets away with a Bolton Great Moor Street to Manhester Exchange train. *Photo, W. D. Cooper.*

Plate 194. A very early, undated view at Worsley Station of the Up platform for Manchester trains. Admire the quality of construction reflecting the Victorian values of the time and perhaps also the influence of those who were to use it. As neat a little station as you would have found anywhere on the London & North Western, approached by a cobbled lane from Worsley Road and the only station on the line to be of brick construction. Is the chap on the corner the station master? if so he looks a rough diamond. Note also the porters "tools" and the wheelchair against the gable end.

Photo, T Gray collection.

Plate 195. An Edwardian view of Worsley Station looking in the Down direction, that is towards Wigan. Note the loading gauge on the little shunting neck and also the addition of a footbridge over the lines. There is a cross-over this side of Worsley Road bridge for working onto the horse dock and also a short head shunt. Note also the low level signal box behind the footbridge steps. *Photo, Stations U.K.*

Plate 196. The railway has gone, but the air of tranquility surrounding the remains of Worsley Station still remains today. This is a May 1996 view, in the Down direction towards Ellenbrook. Note the new arched bridge carrying Worsley Road over the railway trackbed in the background. *Photo, Author.*

MONTON GREEN

MONTON GREEN Station had opened in November 1887, to cater for the increasing suburban commuter traffic into Manchester at a time when the railways were consolidating their transport monopoly by expanding their services and improving line capacity generally, much of it connected with the invention of one Alexander Graham Bell.

The station was an all timber construction, including the platforms, built on an embankment and supported by cross braced wooden piles. The platforms themselves spanned Parrin Lane, but were reached by enclosed stairways from the adjacent Green Lane, at the Manchester end of the station.

Monton Green Signal Cabin was sited alongside the Up line again at the Manchester end, having 18 levers and worked three turns, opening at 5am Monday until 1.45pm Sunday in the LMS period.

The beginning of the scenic footpath, westward along the route of the railway trackbed, already referred to at Worsley and Roe Green, begins at Monton Green, where canal and railway ran side by side.

Suggestions have been made for the possible re-use of the railway route here as part of the Metrolink Tramway. However, it has to be said that the M602 Motorway and nearby developments at the former Eccles Junction site, would seem to preclude any such use in the foreseeable future.

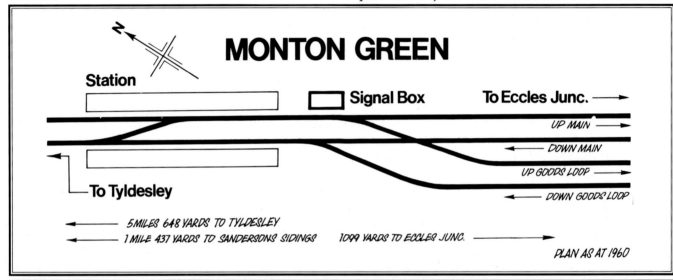

Plate 197. Monton Green Station, an undated view towards Eccles Junction. This photograph is one of a number taken by Horatio (Harry) Grundy of Eccles, a well known photographer of scenes in and around the Salford and Eccles areas up to the 1920's. *Photo, T Gray collection.*

Plate 198. The view towards Worsley from Monton Green *c.* 1916 as a Manchester Exchange train approaches with a number of smartly turned out passengers ready to board. *Photo, T. Gray collection.*

Plate 199. In late LMS days, Stanier Class 5 No. 4794 departs from Monton Green with a Manchester Exchange to Wigan North Western local train. *Photo, W. D. Cooper.*

Plate 200. Monton Green as viewed from Parrin Lane shortly after closure. Salford Corporation Bus No. 286 approaches with the No. 15 service to Manchester Piccadilly on 7th August, 1969. *Photo, T. Gray.*

Plate 201. Over a quarter of a century later, the site of Monton Green Station from the same viewpoint, Spring 1995. *Photo, Author.*

Plate 202. Stanier Class 5 No. 45375 about to depart from Monton Green Down Loop with a special, Summer Saturday evening empty stock working to Morecambe in 1961 as the crew pose for the camera.   *Photo, J. R. Carter.*

Plate 203. On the last day of service, 3rd May, 1969, a view of Monton Green Station from an approaching D.M.U., ex 15.50, Leigh to Manchester Exchange. *Photo, A. Yates.*

Plate 204. With Monton Green Station to the rear, Jubilee Class No. 45676 "*Codrington*" enters Monton Green Loop with a trip freight from local yards and is passing over Landsdowne Road Bridge. The engine at the time was an Edge Hill locomotive and would have arrived on shed at Patricroft after working a morning Lime Street-Manchester Exchange train. It was not uncommon for the locomotive to remain on shed for quite a few hours without turning a wheel. However, when the opportunity occurred, as in the case here, it was put to use on these local trip workings. Note also the letter "C" between the Up Loop and Main running lines, this signifies the commencement of a speed restriction, perhaps because of re-ballasting which has recently taken place and the necessity to allow the track to settle firmly. The end of the restriction would be signified by the letter "T".

Photo, J. R. Carter.

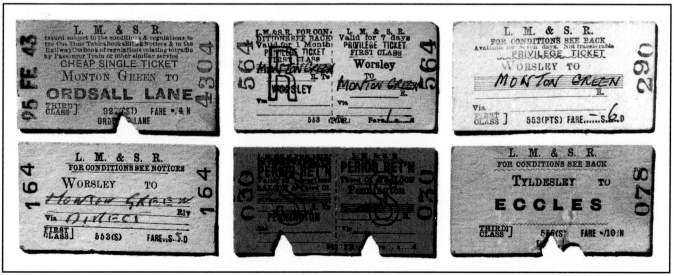

Plate 205. Rebuilt Patriot Class No. 45526 *"Morecambe and Heysham"* passing the Monton Loop lines with the 7.05pm Liverpool Road-Carlisle goods train on 19th May 1964. The locomotive had worked into Manchester Exchange with a fish train from Aberdeen and after various shunt movements between Exchange, Millgate Signal Box on Miles Platting Bank and Manchester Victoria would work light engine to Patricroft Shed for service before this return working north. Liverpool Road had of course been one of the original passenger stations on the Manchester-Liverpool line, becoming a goods only station on the opening of Hunts Bank (Victoria) in 1844 and continuing as such until closure by BR in 1971.

Photo, J. R. Carter.

Plate 206. Stanier Class 5 No. 45411 arrives in the Monton Loop with a late afternoon pick-up freight from Leigh about 1962. The locomotive would have worked coal empties to Jacksons Sidings then worked light engine to Leigh Goods Yard, engaging in a spot of shunting to marshall the train and if necessary wait for farm machinery from David Browns, examples of which can be seen behind the locomotive. This would have been the last trip working of the day from Leigh, arriving between 6&7pm at Monton. In summer the loop lines here would be completely filled with coaching stock for holiday specials.

Photo, J. R. Carter.

Plate 207. Royal Scot Class 4-6-0 No. 46105 *"Cameron Highlander"* passing Patricroft North Yard in the summer of 1963 with the 4.15pm Manchester Exchange to Glasgow train. St. Andrews Parish Church is prominent left of centre with Wellington Road and the Engineers Sidings of the same name also in view. To the rear of train is Patricroft North Sidings signal box. The photograph is taken from the "Black Harry" line overbridge, more of which in the next photo and the signal is the distant for Monton Green.

Photo, J. R. Carter.

Plate 208. BR Standard 2-6-2T No. 82009 is engaged on shunting duties in Patricroft North Sidings in late 1967. A number of these locomotives had been transferred to Patricroft on the closure of Machynlleth shed and unfortunately were not very popular with Patricroft crews, as often they were thirsty little engines. An example being when rostered to work the Manchester Exchange to Preston trains and although departing from Exchange with a full tank having to fill again at Wigan North Western. Running across the picture in the background is the former Clifton Branch from Patricroft Junction to Clifton and known locally as the "Black Harry" line. This branch achieved notoriety in 1953 when the 1299 yard long Clifton Hall Tunnel collapsed taking with it a number of houses above killing three people. The line closed completely in 1961.

This bridge had been constructed under the same 1880 Acts that authorised the Bolton & Leigh deviations, to replace the original flat crossing here. The bridge was probably completed in 1882, following which the Monton Green Loop lines were built and are shown on the revised 1883 line plan.

At or about the same period an Eccles Junction-Clifton Branch curve was installed which seems to have been short lived, closing in May 1891. The remnants came to be used as engineers sidings and the earthworks can be seen on the extreme right hand.

Photo, J. R. Carter.

163

ECCLES JUNCTION

THROUGH workings from Manchester to Carlisle and Glasgow via Eccles Junction and Tyldesley, operated from the opening of this route. The fastest train to Glasgow being the 2.35 pm departure from Hunts Bank, calling at Worsley at 2.48, Tyldesley 2.55, Wigan 3.08 and Preston 3.37, to arrive Glasgow at 9.30pm, a journey time of 6 hours 55 minutes, quite a creditable time in the 1864-70 period. The Up working took some twenty minutes longer, departing Glasgow at 9.45am, reaching Tyldesley at 4.35pm and arriving in Manchester on the hour at 5.00pm.

During the 1880's a departure at 2.00 pm from Manchester stopped only at Tyldesley, 2.17 pm, before reaching Wigan where connections were made with the 1.45 pm departure from Liverpool to depart Wigan at 2.38 pm, reaching Preston at 3.00 pm and Glasgow at 8.00 pm, giving an even 6 hours journey. This in fact was five minutes faster than the "Scotch Mail" which left Manchester at 1.00 am, ran non-stop to Wigan arriving at 1.30 am and reached Glasgow at 7.05 am. A fast return train left Glasgow at 10.00 am, stopped at Wigan, 3.46 pm, Tyldesley, 3.59 pm, reaching Manchester at 4.20 pm, again twenty minutes longer on the return.

In the early 1890's a direct Manchester Exchange to Windermere service departed Exchange at 4.15 pm, stopped at Tyldesley at 4.31 pm and arrived in Wigan North Western at 4.43 pm to combine with the 3.55 pm from Liverpool which reached Wigan at 4.37 pm. Departure from Wigan was at 4.49 pm, arriving Preston at 5.10 pm and Windermere at 6.50 pm. Additionally, on Tuesdays only, this train called at Cross Lane, 4.19 pm, to pick up passengers for the north of Preston only. The return working departed Windermere at 8.10 am, arrived Wigan, 10.00 am, Tyldesley, 10.14 am and Manchester Exchange at 10.31am.

The late 19th century was a period of change regarding passenger services from Manchester to the north, many ceased to operate or were superseded by improved or new services and facilities to cater for increasing demand, including the opening of Manchester Exchange Station in 1884 and in the 1890's the first of the exclusive "Club" trains made their appearance, available for use by season ticket holders only.

Early in the 20th century the 4.15 pm to Windermere also called at Hindley Green on Tuesdays and Thursdays, giving a three minutes later arrival in Windermere.

Plate 209. In July 1957 un-named Patriot No. 45542 is in charge of the 7.05pm Carlisle goods and is seen west of Eccles Junction, passing the Engineers Sidings prominent on the left. Note the position of St. Andrews Church in relation to the previous photo of 46105 on *Plate 207*, giving some idea of the curvature of tracks here. The footbridge in the background is the location of the next shot.   *Photo, W. D. Cooper.*

Plate 210. Jubilee Class No. 45635 "*Tobago*" passing Caprotti fitted Class 5 No. 44738 and Ex-L&Y Class 25, Barton Wright 0-6-0 2F of 1887 vintage bearing its LMS No. 12045. The photo though undated is early BR with the first two coaches behind the Jubilee in carmine & cream livery and the working is the 4.15pm Manchester Exchange to Glasgow. The footbridge is known locally as "Four Bridges" and gave access across the lines or to Patricroft Yard.

Photo, W. D. Cooper.

Plate 211. Eccles Junction as Ex-WD No. 90157 runs into the engineers sidings on 28th April 1964, only three months from withdrawal, its last shed being Springs Branch. This locomotive was built in June 1943 by North British at Glasgow as WD No. 77171 and immediately went on loan to the LNER before being re-called to WD service in December of 1944, entering BR service in May 1949.

Photo, W. D. Cooper.

Plate 212. Also at Eccles Junction in July 1956, the doyen of the BR Standard "*Clan*" Class 4-6-2 Pacifics No. 72000 "*Clan Buchanan*". Again the working is the 4.15 pm Manchester Exchange to Glasgow. Basically these locomotives were a Britannia chassis with a smaller boiler with a 6P5F power rating and originally intended for the Highland Lines. As things worked out they were regarded as unsuitable for such use and as a consequence spent much of their time working the Manchester or Liverpool to Glasgow trains, their shed allocation being split between 12A, Carlisle Kingmoor and 66A, Glasgow Polmadie. *Photo, W. D. Cooper.*

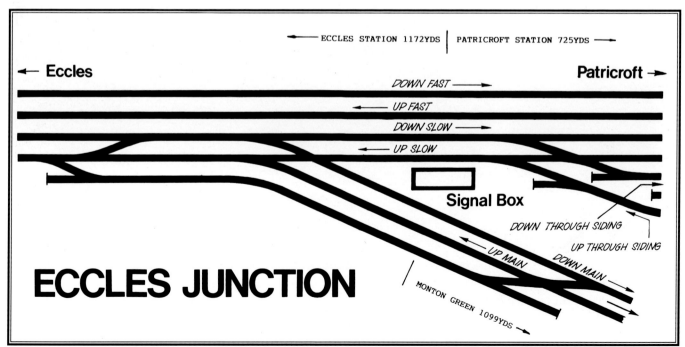

ECCLES STATION 1172YDS | PATRICROFT STATION 725YDS →

← **Eccles**   **Patricroft** →

DOWN FAST →
← *UP FAST*
DOWN SLOW →
← *UP SLOW*

Signal Box

DOWN THROUGH SIDING

UP THROUGH SIDING

UP MAIN

DOWN MAIN

ECCLES JUNCTION

MONTON GREEN 1099YDS →

The Fridays only express "Club" train for Windermere departed Manchester Exchange at 5.07 pm and working via Bickershaw and Amberswood East Junctions traversed the former Lancashire Union Railways Whelley route, to arrive in Preston at 5.58 pm and Windermere at 7.12 pm. The Mondays only return train departed Windermere at 8.30 am but worked via Wigan North Western arriving at 10.00 am, thence running non-stop via Tyldesley to arrive Manchester Exchange at 10.26 am.

In the same period a "Corridor Express" left Manchester Exchange at 5.45 pm, running non-stop to arrive in Preston at 6.31 pm and connected with the 5.50 pm from Liverpool Exchange which contained a through dining car. Departure from Preston was at 6.40 pm, arriving in Glasgow Central at 11.00 pm, thereby reducing the fastest journey time to five hours fifteen minutes. The timing of this train, 46 minutes to Preston from Manchester, suggest it also worked via the Whelley route. However, the return working which had left Glasgow at 4.30 pm went via Wigan, 9.26 pm, to arrive in Manchester Exchange at 9.55 pm.

From 1911 the 5.07 pm to Windermere worked daily, Saturdays and Sundays excepted, with the same timing, 51 minutes to Preston with the Down service. The Up train from Windermere again went via Wigan North Western, arriving at 10.00 am with an additional stop being made at Tyldesley upon notification being given to the guard before leaving Oxenholme.

Timing of the 5.45 pm to Glasgow remained the same for the Down train but an additional 12 minutes had been added to the Up working, arrival in Manchester at 10.07 pm.

Slight timing changes affected the 4.15 pm to Windermere from Manchester Exchange. An additional stop at Eccles was made, if, on booking, passengers gave notification at the station. Arrival at Tyldesley was now at 4.34 pm, Wigan 4.49 pm, Preston 5.17 pm and Windermere 6.56 pm, six minutes later than the 1890's timing.

Between the two world wars the principal p.m. departures from Manchester Exchange were firstly the 4.10 to Windermere & Barrow, calling at Eccles, 4.18, Tyldesley 4.29, Wigan 4.43. and Preston at 5.10 to arrive in Windermere at 6.45 pm. A Direct Up express departed Windermere at 4.05 pm, reaching Preston at 5.57, Wigan 6.20, Tyldesley 6.32, Eccles 6.45 and Manchester Exchange at 6.54 pm. This train also carried through coaches to/from Morecambe which were detached/attached at Lancaster.

Next away was the 5.00. "Restaurant Car Express" to Glasgow running non-stop to arrive

Plate 213. The evening sun glints off the smokebox of Jubilee No. 45581 *"Bihar and Orissa"* at Eccles Junction with a short parcels train routed over the Tyldesley line on 18th June 1960. St. Andrews Church stands on the corner of Cromwell Road and Wellington Road. Note that the L&NW gantry, seen in *Plate 214*, has now been replaced by LMS pattern Upper Quadrant signals, mounted on an overhead lattice gantry at the far side of the bridge.

Photo, W. D. Cooper.

Plate 214. Royal Scot Class No. 46136 *"The Border Regiment"* slows for Eccles Junction and the Tyldesley route on 30th July 1957, with the 7.05 pm Manchester Liverpool Road-Carlisle Goods. Note the L&NW Lower Quadrant gantry on the left. A more recent view from the bridge in the background can be seen on *Plate 215*. *Photo, W. D. Cooper.*

Wigan at 5.30 and Preston at 6.05. In the late 1930's the timing of this train had been brought forward to 4.45pm, but an additional departure from Exchange at 5.05 pm also contained through coaches for Glasgow and Edinburgh. The 4.45 taking 5hrs 10minutes to reach Glasgow and the 5.05 taking 5hrs 36 minutes. An equivalent Up working made an extra stop at Tyldesley at 7.10 pm, to arrive in Manchester at 7.31 pm. As established in London & North Western days these workings combined and split at Wigan or Preston with Ex-Liverpool workings.

Finally from Exchange the 5.10pm "Club" train to Windermere, which from London & North Western days included exclusive saloons for the commuting businessman. This train ran non-stop via Tyldesley, Bickershaw Junction and Hindley & Platt Bridge to join the Whelley route at Amberswood East Junction, taking 44 minutes to reach Preston at 5.54 and arriving in Windermere at 7.07 pm. This was now the only regular, Ex Manchester Exchange passenger train, diagrammed to work over the Great Central Railway. The morning "Club" train departed Windermere at 8.30am, reached Preston at 9.40am and here again worked via Wigan North Western to arrive there at 10.03am and then ran non-stop to Manchester Exchange in 27 minutes.

Post W.W.II. the Windermere & Barrow train

consistently departed from Manchester Exchange at 3.55 pm, calling at Eccles, Tyldesley and Wigan, arrived Preston at 5.03 pm to reach Barrow at 7.05 pm. and Windermere at 7.11 pm. The 4.15 pm to Glasgow, complete with through restaurant car, ran non-stop to Preston arriving at 5.14 pm, only 11 minutes behind the Barrow train. Connections

Plate 215. On 23rd October 1993, Type 4 diesel No. 47 211 passes the site of the former Eccles Junction with a Trans-Pennine freight from Warrington, Arpley. The once extensive sidings, yards and locomotive depot that occupied acres of land on the right now extinct, colonised by industrial units and the M602 motorway. A visible reminder that it is the same location is the remaining span of "Four Bridges" to the rear of the train. *Photo, Author.*

were made with the 4.25 pm from Liverpool Exchange departing Preston at 5.30 pm. A much later arrival in Glasgow was at 10.40 pm as the railways struggled with the effects of a run down and neglected system in post war Britain.

Throughout the intervening years the successor of the 1880's "Scotch Mail" continued to run from Manchester Exchange, including sleeping coaches and in the 1950's a through coach from York, which had departed at 9.50 pm, was attached at Manchester. Departure for Glasgow was at 1.10am and arrival at 7.45 am.

The former Club train, departing still at 5.10 pm from Manchester Exchange, continued to use the Whelley route, but now worked over Ex Lancashire & Yorkshire metals via the Walkden High Level lines, Hindley No. 2 and De Trafford Junctions, arriving Preston at 6.02 pm and Windermere at 7.32 pm. It is probable that this change of route was instituted slightly before W.W.II, after the introduction of new power boxes at Deal Street and Victoria West, Manchester, along with track modifications completed in March 1929 which provided new connections from the "A" Slow, or Ordsall Lane Lines, to the "B" Slow, or Pendleton Lines. Departing from Windermere at 8.10 am, the corresponding Up train reached Preston at 9.29 am and Wigan at 9.56 am, then ran non-stop via Tyldesley to Eccles, arriving at 10.24 am and Exchange at 10.33 am, some 20 minutes longer than the pre-war working.

By 1955 the Barrow train departed Exchange at 3.53 pm, stopped at Tyldesley at 4.17 pm, Wigan at 4.36 pm and Preston at 5.03 pm, arriving in Barrow at 7.11 pm. Coaches to/from Morecambe continued to be attached/detached at Lancaster.

It appears considerable effort had been made to improve the timing of the 4.15 pm Manchester Exchange to Glasgow train which now arrived at its destination at 10.10 pm. An improvement of 30 minutes over the immediate post-war timing.

A two minute later arrival in Windermere was the only timing change to 5.10 pm departure from Manchester Exchange and this train continued using Walkden high level lines, Hindley No. 2 and De Trafford Junctions to gain access to the Whelley line.

In the early 1960's timetable, departure time from Manchester for the Glasgow train was the same at 4.15 pm. It again stopped at Wigan North Western, departing at 4.53 pm to arrive Preston at 5.20 pm connecting with the 4.35 pm from Liverpool Exchange which contained through coaches for Glasgow and Edinburgh. Arrival time in Glasgow had been improved by a further half hour to 9.40 pm.

The Barrow train now departed from Manchester Victoria at 4.03 pm and travelled via the former Lancashire & Yorkshire lines to Preston, arriving at 5.10 pm, and Barrow at 7.00 pm.

The 5.10 pm Manchester Exchange-Windermere had continued to use the Walkden high level-Whelley route running non-stop to reach Preston at 6.02 pm, and as it had throughout the post war years, making connections with the Ex 5.00 pm Liverpool Exchange-Windermere, arriving in Windermere at 7.35 pm. The Whelley route ceased to be used by regular passenger diagrams from September 1965.

Plate 216. One reason for the demise of the Eccles-Tyldesley-Wigan route was the land requirement for the M602 Motorway, removal of the railway here saving on expensive bridge construction. This narrow minded view of the roads *v.* rail scenario had only one winner, the road lobbying fraternity with its vested interests. Twenty years on this short sighted approach has left us all so much the poorer. The motorway did not offer "freedom of choice" as is so often quoted by the road lobby, for at a stroke it removed the alternative and left no choice at all.

In this view the trackbed of the Black Harry line tapers away on the extreme right and in the centre earth moving equipment has been busy removing the Eccles-Tyldesley trackbed. *Photo, Tom Yates.*

The first timetables for the Eccles-Tyldesley-Wigan and Tyldesley-Pennington branches are re-printed in the format of the original, as advertised in the Leigh Chronical, on 17th September, 1864. In particular note the headings "OLD LINE" and "NEW LINE".

LEIGH CHRONICLE RAILWAY TIME TABLES
17th SEPTEMBER, 1864

OBSERVE.—*Passengers for Bolton, Bedford, Leigh, Bradshaw Leach, Kenyon, and Stations on the Bolton Branch change Carriages at Tyldesley.*

NEW LINE

The class of trains refers to the Manchester, Eccles, Leigh, and Wigan line only.

From Manchester, Tyldesley, Leigh to Wigan, Preston, and the North.
WEEK DAYS ONLY.

	1, 2, 3.	1, 2, 3.	1 & 2.	1, 2, 3.	1 & 2.	1, 2, 3.	1 & 2.	1 & 2.	1, 2, 3.	1, 2, 3.	1 & 2.	1, 2, 3.	1, 2, 3.	1 & 2.
..Manchester	7 40	6 5	8 0	9 30	10 0	11 20	1 05	1 30	2 35	3 40	4 30	5 15	5 50	7 20
Cross Lane		6 13	8 8	... ...	10 8	... ...	1 13	... ...	... ...	3 48	... ...	... ...	5 58	7 28	... ...
Eccles...........		6 20	8 15	... ...	10 15	... ...	1 20	... ...	... ...	3 55	4 42	... ...	6 5	7 37	... ...
Worsley		6 25	8 20	9 45	10 20	... ...	1 25	... ...	2 48	4 0	4 46	... ...	6 10	7 45	7 55
Ellenbrook		6 30	8 25	... ...	10 25	... ...	1 30	... ...	... ...	4 5	4 50	... ...	6 15	7 47	8 0
Tyldesley... arr.		6 35	8 30	9 55	10 30	11 40	1 35	1 50	2 55	4 10	4 55	5 33	6 20	7 53	8 5
Tyldesley ..lves .		7 10	8 40	10 15	... ...	11 50	... ...	1 55	3 0	... ...	5 10	... ...	6 25	... ...	8 5
Bedford, Leigh, arr.		7 15	8 45	10 20	... ...	11 55	... ...	2 0	3 5	... ...	5 15	... ...	6 30	... ...	8 10
Bedford, Leigh . lv		... ...	8 5	9 15	10 0	11 15	... ...	1 28	2 35	... ...	4 20	... ...	... ...	... ...	7 25
Tyldesley, ... arr.		... ...	8 10	9 20	10 5	11 20	... ...	1 33	2 45	... ...	4 20	... ...	... ...	... ...	7 30
Tyldesley.. dep.		6 35	8 30	9 55	10 30	11 45	... ...	1 50	2 55	... ...	4 55	5 33	... ...	... ...	8 5
Chowbent		6 39	8 34	9 59	10 34	... ...	... ...	1 54	... ...	... ...	...4 59	... ...	... ...	... ...	8 9
Hindley Green		6 43	8 38	... ...	10 38	... ...	... ...	... ...	... ...	... ...	5 3	... ...	... ...	... ...	8 13
Platt Bridge		6 48	8 43	... ...	10 43	... ...	... ...	... ...	... ...	... ...	5 8	... ...	... ...	... ...	8 19
Wigan		6 55	8 50	10 10	10 50	11 58	... ...	2 7	3 8	... ...	5 15	5 45	... ...	... ...	8 25
Preston		7 55	... ...	10 48	... ...	12 30	... ...	2 40	3 37	... ...	5 50	6 28	... ...	... ...	9 5
Fleetwood		9 4	... ...	12 0	... ...	1 40	... ...	4 35	4 35	... ...	7 18	... ...	... ...	... ...	... ...
Lancaster		9 0	... ...	11 32	... ...	1 40	... ...	3 18	... ...	... ...	6 42	... ...	... ...	... ...	10 5
Carlisle		2 15	... ...	1 55	... ...	4 40	... ...	5 45	6 10	... ...	9 10	... ...	... ...	... ...	... ...
Edinburgh		5 40	... ...	5 40	... ...	... ...	... ...	... ...	9 10	... ...	12 25	... ...	... ...	... ...	... ...

From Preston, Wigan, the North, and Tyldesley and Leigh, to Manchester.
WEEK DAYS ONLY.

	1, 2, 3.	1, 2, 3.	1 & 2.	1, 2, 3.	1 & 2.	1, 2, 3.	1 & 2.	1 & 2.	1, 2, 3.	1, 2, 3.	1 & 2.	1, 2, 3.	1, 2, 3.	1 & 2.
Glasgow									9 45		7 30			1 0
Edinburgh									10 0		7 45			1 0
Carlisle		... ...		8 10	7 45				1 5		1 45			5 0
Lancaster		... ...	7 15	9 7	10 26	11 12			3 9		5 0			7 23
Fleetwood		... ...	7 5	8 5	10 0	11 30			2 55		5 15			7 0
Preston		6 15	8 20	10 0	11 15	12 25			3 50		6 20			8 15
Wigan		7 5	9 5	11 0	11 50	1 15		2 35	4 20	5 50	7 15			8 50
Platt Bridge		7 10	9 10	11 5	... ...	1 20		2 40		5 55	7 20			
Hindley Green		7 15	9 15	11 10	... ...	1 25		2 45		6 0	7 25			
Chowbent		7 19	9 19	11 14	12 0	1 29		2 49		6 5	7 29			
Tyldesley		7 23	9 23	11 18	12 5	1 33		2 56	4 35	6 10	7 33			9 5
Tyldesley ..leaves		8 40	9 25	11 50	... ...	1 55		3 0		5 10	6 25		8 5	
Bedford, Leigh, arr.		8 45	9 30	11 55	... ...	2 0		3 5		5 15	6 30		8 10	
Bedford, Leigh . lv		... ...	9 15	11 15	... ...	1 28		2 40		4 20	6 2		7 25	8 50
Tyldesley, ... arr.		... ...	9 20	11 20	... ...	1 33		2 45		4 25	6 7		7 30	8 55
Tyldesley		7 23	9 23	11 22	12 5	1 33	1 50	2 55	4 20	4 35	6 10	6 45	7 33	8 46	9 5
Ellenbrook		7 28	9 28	11 27	... ...	... ...	1 55	2 58	4 25	... ...	6 15	6 50	7 38	8 50	
Worsley		7 33	9 33	11 32	12 15	... ...	2 0	3 3	4 30	4 45	6 20	6 55	7 43	8 56	9 13
Eccles		7 38	9 38	... ...	... ...	... ...	2 5	3 8	4 35	... ...	6 25	7 0	7 48	8 58	
Cross Lane		7 45	9 45	... ...	... ...	... ...	... ...	3 15	... ...	... ...	... ...	7 7	... ...	... ...	
Manchester ..		7 55	9 55	11 50	12 30	1 55	2 22	3 25	4 50	5 0	6 40	7 15	8 0	9 15	9 25

Manchester, Tyldesley, Leigh, to Wigan, Preston, and the North.
SUNDAYS ONLY.

	1, 2, 3.	1 & 2..	1, 2, 3.	1, 2, 3.	1, 2, 3.
Manchester ..	8 40	9 10	2 0	3 0	6 30
Cross Lane	8 48	... ...	2 8	3 38	6 38
Eccles...........	8 55		2 15	3 45	6 45
Worsley	9 0	9 25	2 20	3 50	6 50
Ellenbrook	9 5	9 30	2 25	3 55	6 55
Tyldesley, .arr.	9 10	9 35	2 30	4 0	7 0
Tyldesley, ..leaves	9 10	9 36	... ...	... ...	7 80
Bedford, Leigh arr.	9 15	9 40	... ...	... ...	7 35
Bedford, Leigh, lvs.	... ...	9 43			6 45
Tyldesley, .arrives	... ...	9 48			6 50
Tyldesley, .dep.	9 10	9 56			7 0
Chowbent	9 14	9 59			7 4
Hindley Green	9 18	... ...			7 8
Platt Bridge	9 23	... ...			7 13
Wigan	9 30	... ...			7 20
Preston	10 35	... ...			8 40
Fleetwood	... ...				... ...
Lancaster	... ...				... ...
Carlisle	... ...				... ...
Edinburgh	... ...				... ...
Glasgow	... ...				... ...

Preston, Wigan, and the North, and from Tyldesley and Leigh, to Manchester.
SUNDAYS ONLY.

	1, 2, 3.	1, 2, 3..	1, 2, 3.	1, 2, 3.	1, 2, 3.
Glasgow					
Edinburgh					
Carlisle					
Lancaster					
Fleetwood					
Preston	8 30				
Wigan	10 0				
Platt Bridge	10 5				
Hindley Green	10 10				
Chowbent	10 14				
Tyldesley	10 18				
Tyldesley, ..leaves	10 25				
Bedford, Leigh, ..	10 30				
Bedford, Leigh, lvs.	10 10			6 45	8 5
Tyldesley	10 15			6 50	8 10
Tyldesley	10 18	2 40	5 0	7 0	8 20
Ellenbrook	10 23	2 45	5 5	7 5	8 25
Worsley	10 28	2 50	5 10	7 10	8 30
Eccles	10 33	2 55	5 13	7 13	8 35
Cross Lane	10 40	3 3	5 22	7 22	8 42
Manchester ..	10 50	3 12	5 30	7 39	8 50

From Tyldesley and Leigh, to Liverpool and the South.

	WEEK DAYS.										SUNDAYS.				
Manchester ..	6 5	8 0	... ...	9 30	11 20	1 30	2 35	4 30	5 50	7 40	8 40	9 10	... ...	... ...	6 30
Tyldesley	7 10	8 40	9 25	10 15	11 50	1 55	3 0	5 10	6 25	8 5	9 10	9 36	10 25	6 30	7 30
Bedford, Lgh.	7 15	8 45	9 30	10 20	11 55	2 0	3 5	5 15	6 30	8 10	9 15	9 40	10 30	6 35	7 35
Bradshaw Leach ..	7 20	8 50	9 35	... ...	12 0	2 5	3 10	5 20	6 35	8 15	9 20	9 45	10 35	6 40	7 40
Kenyon	7 36	9 6	9 40	10 35	1 10	2 10	3 28	5 55	7 24	8 17	9 25	10 0	10 40	6 51	7 45
Newton	7 50	9 16	... ...	10 42	1 18	... ...	3 35	6 0	7 31	8 22	... ...	10 7	... ...	7 5	... ...
St. Helens	7 35	9 15	... ...	11 15	... ...	... ...	3 30	6 0	8 0	... ...	... ...	9 40	... ...	7 0	... ...
Liverpool	8 55	10 0	... ...	11 25	... ...	... ...	4 20	6 40	8 20	9 10	10 0	10 45	... ...	7 50	... ...
Warrington	8 20	9 37	... ...	10 50	1 34	... ...	... ...	6 45	... ...	9 20	... ...	... ...	... ...	7 50	... ...
Chester	... ...	10 15	... ...	11 45	2 10	... ...	... ...	7 50	... ...	10 0	... ...	... ...	... ...	8 45	... ...

From Liverpool and the South, to Leigh and Tyldesley.

	WEEK DAYS.										SUNDAYS.			
Chester	... ...	... ...	8 15	... ...	... ...	... ...	2 40	4 25	... ...	... ...	... ...	... ...	... ...	5 50
Warrington	... ...	... ...	9 6	... ...	... ...	... ...	3 30	5 15	... ...	... ...	... ...	... ...	... ...	6 40
Liverpool............	6 30	... ...	9 5	10 0	12 0	... ...	3 0	4 40	... ...	7 30	... ...	8 40	... ...	7 10
St. Helens	7 5	... ...	9 15	10 15	12 30	... ...	3 30	5 0	... ...	8 0	... ...	9 10	... ...	7 0
Newton................	7 32	... ...	9 40	10 39	12 52	... ...	3 55	5 23	... ...	8 23	... ...	9 33	... ...	7 40
Kenyon	7 55	9 5	9 50	11 5	1 10	2 30	4 10	5 55	7 15	8 40	9 35	10 0	6 5	7 55
Bradshaw Leach..........	8 0	9 10	9 55	11 10	... ...	2 35	4 15	... ...	7 20	8 45	9 38	10 5	6 10	8 0
Bedford, Lgh........	8 5	9 15	10 0	11 15	1 28	2 40	4 20	6 2	7 25	8 50	9 43	10 10	6 15	8 5
Tyldesley.............	8 10	9 20	10 5	11 20	1 33	2 45	4 25	6 7	7 30	8 55	9 48	10 15	6 20	8 10
Manchester	... ...	9 55	... ...	11 50	1 5	3 25	5 0	6 40	8 5	9 20	... ...	10 50	7 50	8 50

From Bolton, to Manchester, *via* Tyldesley.

	WEEK DAYS.								SUNDAYS.		
	1, 2, 3.	1, 2, 3.	1, 2, 3.	1, 2, 3.	1, 2, 3.	1, 2, 3.	1, 2, 3.	1, 2, 3.	1, 2, 3.	1, 2, 3.	1, 2, 3.
Bolton	7 45	9 20	10 50	1 0	2 25	4 0	7 5	8 40	6 0	7 0
Daubhill	7 49	9 24	10 54	1 4	2 29	4 4	7 9	8 44	6 4	7 4
Chequerbent	7 55	9 30	11 0	1 10	2 35	4 10	7 15	8 50	6 10	7 10
Atherton..........................	8 1	9 36	11 6	1 16	2 41	4 16	7 21	8 56	6 16	7 16
Chowbent..........................	8 5	9 40	11 10	1 21	2 45	4 21	7 26	9 1	6 21	7 21
Tyldesley.........................	8 10	9 45	11 15	1 25	2 50	4 25	7 30	9 5	6 25	7 25
Bedford, Leigh, arr........	8 45	10 20	11 55	2 0	3 5	5 15	8 10	9 15	6 35	7 35
Manchester........................	9 55	... ...	11 50	1 55	3 25	5 0	8 0	10 50	7 30	8 50

From Manchester, to Bolton, *via* Tyldesley.

	WEEK DAYS.								SUNDAYS.		
	1, 2, 3.	1, 2, 3.	1, 2, 3.	1, 2, 3.	1, 2, 3.	1, 2, 3.	1, 2, 3.	1, 2, 3.	1, 2, 3.	1, 2, 3.
Manchester, depart	8 0	9 30	11 20	*1 30	2 35	5 15	7 40	9 10	6 30
Bedford, Leigh, depart............	8 5	10 0	11 15	1 18	2 40	... ...	7 25	9 43	8 5
Tyldesley.........................	8 35	10 10	11 50	1 50	3 0	5 40	8 10	9 56	8 15
Chowbent..........................	8 40	10 14	11 54	1 55	3 4	5 44	8 14	9 58	8 19
Atherton..........................	8 45	10 19	11 59	2 0	3 9	5 49	8 19	10 4	8 24
Chequerbent.......................	8 55	10 25	12 3	2 6	3 13	5 53	8 23	10 8	8 8
Daubhill..........................	9 0	10 32	12 10	2 12	3 20	6 0	8 30	10 15	8 35
Bolton	9 5	10 30	12 15	2 17	3 26	6 6	8 36	10 20	8 40

* Passengers to and from Bolton, change at Chowbent by this train. All other change at Tyldesley.

OLD LINE

From Bolton, Atherton, and Leigh, to Manchester, Liverpool, and London.

	WEEK DAYS.								SUNDAYS.			
	1,2,3.	1 & 2*	1 & 2.	1 & 2.†	1 & 2.‡	1 & 2.§	1 & 2.||	1,2,3**	1,2,3.	1,2,3.¶	1,2,3.¶	1,2,3.¶
Bolton..............	7 0	8 35	... ...	10 0	12 40	3 30	4 30	6 50	8 15	8 40	6 0	7 0
Daubhill............	7 4	8 39	... ...	10 3	12 44	3 34	4 34	6 54	8 19	8 44	6 4	7 4
Chequerbent	7 10	8 44	... ...	10 8	12 49	3 40	4 40	7 0	8 25	8 50	6 10	7 10
Atherton............	7 16	8 49	9 23	10 13	12 54	3 46	4 45	7 5	8 31	8 56	6 16	7 16
Leigh...............	7 22	8 54	9 28	10 19	12 59	3 52	4 50	7 12	8 37	... ...	... ...	... ...
Bradshaw Leach	7 26	8 58	9 31	... ...	1 3	3 56	4 53	7 17	8 40	9 20	6 40	7 40
Kenyon..............	7 30	9 4	9 35	10 25	1 7	4 0	4 56	7 22	8 45	9 25	6 45	7 45
Manchester, arr.......	8 30	10 15	10 15	11 30	1 45	4 45	5 20	8 29	9 35	10 25	... ...	8 32
Newton..............	7 50	9 5	... ...	10 44	1 45	4 15	6 0	7 35	... ...	9 40	7 5	... ...
St. Helens, arr..........	8 20	10 0	... ...	... ...	2 55	4 45	6 30	8 42	... ...	10 20	7 40	... ...
Liverpool	8 55	10 0	... ...	11 25	2 55	5 3	6 40	8 20	... ...	10 55	7 50	... ...
Wigan	... ...	10 13	... ...	12 0	2 11	5 20	... ...	9 29	... ...	9 53	7 30	... ...
Preston.............	... ...	10 43	... ...	12 30	2 40	5 50	... ...	9 5	... ...	10 35	8 40	... ...
Warrington	8 20	9 37	... ...	11 31	1 34	4 48	6 42	8 0	... ...	10 20	7 40	... ...
Chester.............	... ...	10 45	10 45	11 45	2 10	5 20	7 50	... ...	... ...	10 50	8 35	... ...
Birmingham	1 30	12 30	... ...	3 0	5 45	7 20	10 55	... ...	... ...	1 40	... ...	... ...
London..............	5 55	2 30	... ...	5 45	9 15	9 50	... ...	5 50a.m.	... ...	... ...	5 0	... ...

* 3rd to Wigan. † 3rd to Manchester, Liverpool, Birmingham, Wigan, Chester, and London, arriving at 7-5 p.m.
‡ 3rd to St. Helens and Wigan. § 3rd to Manchester and Wigan. || 3rd to Birmingham and Chester. ** 1,2, 3 to all except London. ¶ By Tyldesley.

From London, Liverpool and Manchester, to Leigh, Atherton, and Bolton.

London	9 0 p.m.	... ...	... ...	... 0	6 15	10 0	... ...	11 20	... ...	... ...	... ...	... ...	10 0
Birmingham	10 30 ,,	... ...	... ...	6 0	8 45	11 15	... ...	12 20	... ...	... ...	... ...	... ...	1 5
Chester	... ...	... ...	8 15	9 0	12 5	1 50	... ...	4 25	... ...	7 10	... ...	... ...	5 50
Warrington...........	7 1	8 30	9 6	9 20	12 50	2 28	... ...	5 15	7 0	8 0	... ...	... ...	6 40
Preston.............	6 15	... ...	8 20	... ...	11 10	... ...	3 5	6 20	... ...	... ...	... ...	... ...	6 5
Wigan	7 0	... ...	8 54	... ...	11 45	... ...	3 40	7 4	... ...	... ...	... ...	... ...	6 42
Liverpool...........	6 30	7 40	9 5	10 0	12 0	3 0	4 20	4 40	6 45	7 45	... ...	... ...	7 0
St. Helens	7 5	... ...	9 15	10 15	12 30	3 30	4 10	5 0	7 5	8 15	... ...	... ...	7 0
Newton	7 32	8 45	9 40	10 39	12 52	3 55	4 50	5 23	... ...	8 38	... ...	... ...	7 40
Manchester	7 0	... ...	9 10	10 10	12 40	3 30	... ...	A	6 45	... ...	8 40	6 15	... ...
Kenyon..............	7 45	9 10	9 55	11 0	1 15	4 15	5 15	5 48	7 40	8 55	9 30	6 33	7 53
Bradshaw Leach..........	7 48	... ...	9 58	11 3	1 18	4 18	5 18	... ...	7 43	8 58	9 38	6 56	8 0
Leigh...............	7 51	9 16	10 1	11 6	1 21	4 21	5 21	5 54	... ...	9 1	... ...	6 59	... ...
Atherton............	7 57	9 22	10 10	11 12	1 27	4 27	5 27	6 1	7 53	9 7	10 4	7 5	8 24
Chequerbent..........	8 3	9 28	10 20	11 18	1 33	4 33	5 33	6 15	8 0	9 17	10 8	7 11	8 29
Daubhill	8 9	9 34	10 26	11 24	1 39	4 45	5 39	6 23	8 7	9 23	10 15	7 17	8 35
Bolton, arr...........	8 15	9 40	10 30	11 30	1 45	4 50	5 45	6 30	8 15	9 30	10 20	7 25	8 40

1st & 2nd Class train from Manchester to Bury Lane every night at 10.45, reaching Bury Lane at 11.10.
A 1st and 2nd class only from Leigh to Bolton. All others Third class.

Elimination of the Barrow service via Tyldesley is countered by a stop at Tyldesley, from June 1964 of the 4.15pm to Glasgow, this the first stoppage of a direct Glasgow train here since the 1880's but is merely a prelude to the withdrawal of local passenger services from Manchester Exchange via Tyldesley to Wigan North Western in November 1964. Consequently the Glasgow service departed from Victoria, working to Preston via Lancashire & Yorkshire metals and an era of exactly 100 years of fast passenger express trains to the North via Tyldesley had come to an end.

Plates 217 and 218. On more than one occasion Eccles Junction Cabin was the victim of runaway locomotives or erratic shunting. In these November 1963 views Stanier 8F No. 48213 extracates Class 5 No. 45252 from the demolished end of the box after the Class 5 had run amok.

Photos, D. W. Cooper.

ON SHED AT PATRICROFT

CONSTRUCTION of an engine shed at Patricroft began in April 1884 on a greenfield site to the west of Manchester, situated in the triangle between the Liverpool & Manchester, the Eccles Junction to Tyldesley lines and the Clifton Branch. It was built originally to accommodate locomotives from the overcrowded shed at Ordsall Lane and had eight roads. In 1905 Patricroft "New" shed, as it came to be known, was opened. This had ten roads and was approached from the east, that is from Manchester as opposed to the 1884 shed which was approached from the opposite direction. During the mid 1930's the LMS carried out improvements, including a 70ft turntable to replace the earlier L&NW installation. "New" shed also received a new pitched roof replacing the original northlight pattern, but the 1884 shed had to wait until the BR era for attention, being almost completely re-built with the corrugated sheet style roof favoured by the new owners.

From an allocation of some thirty locomotives in 1885, rising to one hundred and twenty plus in the 1920's the figure dropped to around seventy in the 1950's and early 1960's.

Patricroft shed closed at the end of the steam era and in fact provided many of the locomotives for the end of steam specials.

Plate 219. A rare visitor to Patricroft Shed in the form of Ex-LMS Princess Royal Class No. 46206 *"Princess Marie Louise"*. The date is 1960, during the period London Road Station was being re-built when some services were being diverted into Manchester Exchange & Victoria Stations. The locomotive had arrived on a West of England train, a footplate crew sent from Patricroft had relieved the wrong engine at platform 11 and worked the empty stock to Ordsall Lane Sidings, then working light engine to Patricroft shed. At the time this class of locomotive were banned from working over the viaducts at Ordsall Lane, due to the axle load being to great. I am assured by former BR Staff that there was hell to play when 46206 un-expectedly arrived on shed. Since that time engines of the same class have worked the route with official blessing, i.e. the Liverpool & Manchester 150 Celebrations.

Note also the running lines, between the wagons and coaching stock, of the "Black Harry" branch and in the distance Monton Green signal box on the Eccles Junction-Tyldesley line. *Photo, J. R. Carter.*

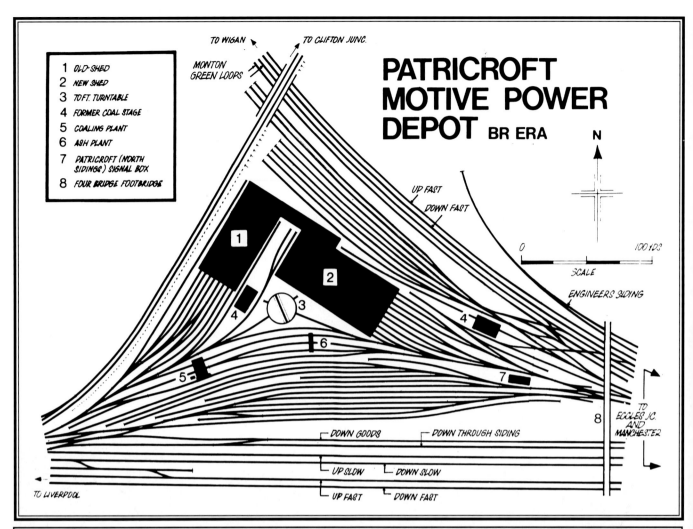

PATRICROFT MOTIVE POWER DEPOT BR ERA

1 OLD SHED
2 NEW SHED
3 70 FT. TURNTABLE
4 FORMER COAL STAGE
5 COALING PLANT
6 ASH PLANT
7 PATRICROFT (NORTH SIDINGS) SIGNAL BOX
8 FOUR BRIDGE FOOTBRIDGE

TO WIGAN
TO CLIFTON JUNC.
MONTON GREEN LOOPS

UP FAST
DOWN FAST

N

0   100 YDS
SCALE

ENGINEERS SIDING

TO EGGLES JC. AND MANCHESTER

DOWN GOODS   DOWN THROUGH SIDING

UP SLOW   DOWN SLOW

TO LIVERPOOL   UP FAST   DOWN FAST

Plate 220. Accidents will happen, Ex-L&NW 0-8-0 No. 49249 in the process of being re-railed with the assistance of Newton Heath crane and crew. The footbridge from which the shed view was taken provides a convenient spectators stand in June 1958.

Photo, W. D. Cooper.

Plate 221. An elevated view of Patricroft "Old" shed, taken from the coal shute. Prominent is Stanier Class 5 No. 45156 *"Ayrshire Yeomanry"* which had been spruced up to work an enthusiasts special from Liverpool Lime Street on 20th April 1968 and was transferred to Patricroft from Edge Hill on the following Monday and is seen shortly after arrival on shed. The trackbed of the former "Black Harry" line is clearly visible as is Landsdowne Road bridge carrying the Tyldesley branch.   *Photo, J. R. Carter.*

Plate 222. Patricroft shed as viewed from the footbridge seen in **Plate 220** as on 7th August 1965, looking towards North Yard. *Photo, W. D. Cooper.*

Plate 223. Post W.W.II, in a period of full employment, and when better paid, less arduous jobs were available, the railways often found it difficult to recruit labour in a labour intensive industry. This view at Patricroft on 31st May 1957, shows no less than ten railway staff preparing Royal Scot Class 4-6-0 No. 46101 *"Royal Scots Grey"* to work the 4.15pm Manchester Exchange-Glasgow Central train which, from my recollections, I observed at Chester Road, Tyldesley, later that day. *Photo, W. D. Cooper.*

Plate 224. Pictured outside "Old Shed" at Patricroft on 30th July 1957, is Patriot Class 4-6-0 No. 45500 *"Patriot"*, coaled and watered rady to work one of the late afternoon passenger trains from Manchester Exchange. This locomotive and another of its Class No. 45501 *"St. Dunstans"* were re-builds of Claughton Class 4-6-0's of 1912, retaining original wheels and other details, but in truth little of the Claughton design remained. A further fifty new locomotives constituted the rest of the Class and were to a Fowler design, first introduced in 1933. From 1946 onwards, eighteen of the Fowler designed locomotives were re-built to the design of H. G. Ivatt with taper boiler, new cylinders and double chimney (as, for example, in **Plate 205**). *Photo, W. D. Cooper.*

Plate 225. On 21st September 1965, BR Standard 2-10-0 No. 92027 makes its way through Patricroft Yard to join the main running lines with the 08.10 Stott Lane (Eccles) to St Helens through freight. J. O. Williamson is the Driver and photographer J. R. Carter is the Fireman.

This locomotive was one of a batch of ten Class 9F's built in 1955 with Italian designed Franco-Crosti boilers supposedly to achieve greater steam efficiency. However, much to the chagrin of the designer, BR deemed this experiment a failure and converted these locomotives to operate in a conventional manner, as can be ascertained in this example.

Photos, J. R.Carter.

Plate 226. Class 5 No. 45260 on the turntable alongside Patricroft "New" Shed with, on the left, one of the 2-6-2T Class 3 engines on duty as shed pilot next to the water tower. Again this photograph is taken from a precarious position up the coal shute in the mid 1960's.

Plate 227. Ex-War Department 2-8-0 No. 77362 seen at Patricroft shortly after arrival and photographed on 16th April 1949. This locomotive was one of a batch of three hundred, to Lot 943, and built by North British at Glasgow, emerging from their works in September 1943. It immediately went on loan to the LNER, returning to the WD in December 1944. After seeing service in France during 1945-46 the locomotive returned to England and again went to the LNER in March 1947 and finally taken into BR at nationalisation on 1st January 1948. By December 1950 it had been re-numbered by BR as 90258 and was shedded at Rose Grove, Burnley. In 1954 No. 90258 was at Lostock Hall Shed and finally at Langwith Junction from where it was withdrawn in January 1966. *Photo, W. D.Cooper.*

Plate 228. A typical view inside a signal box, this particular one being Patricroft Station box having 81 levers with, on the left, Fred Cooper and on the right Fred Davies. Note the telephone concentrator box towards the gable end of the cabin, issued when a particular signal box had more than three or four telephones, thus saving space.

Photo, W.D.Cooper.

Plate 229. The "Royal Scot" hauled by Type 4 locomotive No. D321 later to become Class 40 No. 40121, seen on the Up Slow east of Eccles Junction, having been diverted via Springs Branch, Manchester Lines Junction and Tyldesley and will work via Ordsall Lane and Manchester London Road to Crewe. The passing three car D.M.U on the Down Slow is signalled to take the Tyldesley route at Eccles Junction and working left to right across the gantry are signals for the Monton Green Loop, Patricroft Sidings and slow lines to Patricroft Station and Barton Moss, and lastly Tyldesley. All the properties seen alongside the railway at this location were demolished to make way for the M602 motorway. D321 was withdrawn from service in March 1983 and cut up at Crewe in December 1983.   *Photo, J. R. Carter.*

Plate 230. Pictured midway between Eccles Station and Eccles Junction is Jubilee Class No. 45555 *"Quebec"* with coal empties working from Manchester Ship Canal Sidings to Astley Green Colliery in the early 1960's.

Photo, J. R. Carter.

ECCLES TO MANCHESTER

ECCLES Station was the scene of a serious accident at 8.18am on 30th December 1941, in which 23 persons were killed and a further 56 seriously injured.

Two passenger tains were involved, the 6.53am Rochdale-Pennington with 2-6-4T No. 2406 in charge, and the 6.53am Kenyon–Manchester Exchange (via Leigh and Tyldesley) hauled by 2-6-2T No. 207. Each train consisted of eight non-corridor coaches.

The accident occurred in dense fog which had persisted for over 21 hours previously, with visibility down to ten yards in places and when fogsignalling arrangements were in operation. It was still dark and some 37 minutes before the end of blackout regulations. The tempeature was 0° C (32° F).

Traffic patterns had been disrupted by the prolonged period of fog and both trains were running late. The Pennington bound train by 27 minutes and the Manchester train by 49 minutes.

Arrival of the Manchester train at Eccles Station, on the Up Slow, was at 8.15am. Because of congestion ahead, the train was crossed, by the Signalman at Eccles Station Cabin having received acceptance from the next cabin at Cross Lane Junction, from the Up Slow to the Up Fast. This manoeuvre necessiatated crossing the Down Slow, upon which the Pennington train was travelling at approximately 35mph, having passed the Eccles Outer Home Signal at "Danger".

The engine of the Pennington train struck the first coach of the crossing Manchester train amidships and was de-railed. Slewing to the right, the locomotive ripped through the second and third coaches completely demolishing them and came to rest 70 yards from the initial impact, embedded in the fourth coach and resting in the Up Slow Line cess. The leading coach of the Pennington train was also completely destroyed and the second and third coaches partially crushed.

All lines were blocked by the debris except the Down Fast and this, together with the Up Fast, were utilised to clear the wreckage with the assistance of the breakdown cranes. Normal working was not resumed until 37 hours later.

At the subsequent inquiry, the reporting Inspector, Major G. R. S. Wilson, held that the Signalman at Eccles Station was "primarily responsible", but also that the Driver of the Pennington

Plate 231. Traffic movements from fast to slow lines for trains working via Tyldesley were instituted at Eccles Station. In August 1956 Stanier Class 5 No. 44891 makes the necessary manoeuvre with the 4.15 pm Manchester Exchange-Glasgow train, composed of BR Mk. I and Stanier stock in carmine and cream livery. *Photo, W. D. Cooper.*

train "must accept a considerable share of the responsibility". However, the real culprit was undeniably the fog and the implications for the working of the railway in cuch circumstances.

Many local people still recall this terrible accident, although it happened over fifty years ago. Some were on the Manchester bound train at the time, having boarded at local stations. Others had near misses, fate on that particular day showing its guiding hand. In the latter class was Mr. W. D. Cooper, one of the photographic contributors to these volumes, who had walked to Worsley Station that morning, a few minutes earlier than he normally would have done in clearer weather. Because of the fog, trains were running out of sequence and as he arrived at Worsley, a train pulled into the station. This was probably a late running Ex-Bolton Great Moor Street-Manchester local, which Mr. Cooper duly boarded. Here we are talking about just a few seconds, and yet, those few moments which, in a lifetime are immeasurable, did on this occasion, make all the difference between life and death.

Having stopped at Monton Green and Eccles, the Bolton-Manchester train continued on the Up Slow towards Weaste at a sedate pace as a train flashed by in the opposite direction. The memory of it is still with Mr. Cooper to this day, for this was non other than the ill fated Rochdale-Pennington, which in a couple of minutes would collide with the Kenyon-Manchester train that had called at Worsley shortly after the Ex-Bolton.

Enjoy Mr. Coopers photographs. But for the Grace of God there may never have been many!

Plate 232. A train of coal empties from Manchester Ship Canal Sidings with Class 5 No. 45271 in charge, signal checked at Stott Lane Sidings and the opportunity taken to climb the signal ladder for the shot. *Photo, J. R. Carter.*

Plate 233. Another of the Jubilee Class locomotives No. 45563 *"Australia"* propelling a mixed freight from Adswood down the falling gradient to Manchester Ship Canal Sidings, again a view from the early 1960's.   *Photo, J. R. Carter.*

Plate 234. A panorama of Ordsall Lane Junction, Salford with No. 1 signal box centre, late 1960's. The main lines to Manchester Victoria Station via Ordsall Lane Viaduct trail off to the left with a Class 08 shunter in Liverpool Road Goods Yard, the former terminus of the Liverpool & Manchester Railway which is now part of the Greater Manchester Museum of Science and Industry. Behind the signal box, the small cabin is said to be the first signal box on the Liverpool & Manchester Railway. To the right of Ordsall Lane No. 1 is the route to Castlefield Junction, used by diverted traffic to and from Manchester, London Road, which worked via Tyldesley and Springs Branch, Manchester Lines Junction. There had, in years previous, been a locomotive turntable in the bottom left hand corner, used by locomotives coming off Ex-Yorkshire-Manchester workings prior to their return trip and others off North Wales turns, eliminating the need to go to Patricroft for turning.
                                                                                                    Photo, Tom Yates.

Plate 235. Stanier Class 5 No. 44887 seen coming off platform 3 at Manchester Exchange Station with an express for Chester and North Wales about 1962. Deal Street Signal Box is on the left, with the passing 2-6-4, two cylinder, Stanier designed taper boilered tank No. 42444, working bunker first to Agecroft Shed. Note the Salford Corporation bus and also the CIS building under construction. Smoke problems within Manchester Exchange had resulted in the removal of glazing panels from the ends of the station canopy as seen here, in an attempt to assist nature in clearing the smoke.

Photo, J. R. Carter.

Plate 236. Class 5 No. 44986, paired with a self weighing tender, departs Manchester Exchange on a summers afternoon with the 5.07pm to North Wales. On the right is the Station Announcer's Office. Over on the left, ready for banking in Horse Dock Siding, is one of the 4-4-0- Class 2P engines, No. 40671, built by the LMS in 1928 which were a development of an earlier Midland design. Railwayman Jim Carter had been rostered for the day on this banking turn and had again taken the opportunity to record for posterity this and many other scenes of railway activity at this long closed station.

Photo, J. R. Carter.

A thin line between the hour and minute figures indicates p.m.

MANCHESTER (EXCHANGE), TYLDESLEY, MANCHESTER (EXCHANGE)
(For Kenyon and Bolton (Great)

LEIGH, AND WIGAN (NORTH WESTERN), AND BOLTON (GT. MOOR ST.),—
Moor Street) service, see page 22.

WEEK DAYS—continued.

Manchester (Ex.) dep.	
Ordsall L. (for Salford)	
Cross Lane	
Seedley	
Weaste	
Eccles	
Monton Green	
Worsley	
Walkden (Low Level)	
Little Hulton	
Plodder Lane (for Farnworth)	
Bolton (Gt. Moor St.) ...arr.	
Ellenbrook for Boothstown ...arr.	
Tyldesley ...arr.	
Tyldesley ...dep. for Leigh	
Leigh ...arr.	
Tyldesley ...dep. for Wigan	
Howe Bridge	
Hindley Green	
Platt Bridge	
Wigan (North Western) ...arr.	
Preston ...arr.	
Blackpool { Central / North }	
Morecambe (Euston Road)	
Kendal	
Windermere	

WEEK DAYS.

Manchester (Ex.) dep.	
Ordsall L. (for Salford)	
Cross Lane	
Seedley	
Weaste	
Eccles	
Monton Green	
Worsley	
Walkden (Low Level)	
Little Hulton	
Plodder Lane (for Farnworth)	
Bolton (Gt. Moor St.) ...arr.	
Ellenbrook for Boothstown ...arr.	
Tyldesley ...arr.	
Tyldesley ...dep. for Leigh	
Leigh ...arr.	
Tyldesley ...dep. for Wigan	
Howe Bridge	
Hindley Green	
Platt Bridge	
Wigan (North Western) ...arr.	
Preston ...arr.	
Blackpool { Central / North }	
Morecambe (Euston Road)	
Kendal	
Windermere	

SUNDAYS.

A—Calls at Eccles to pick up trip only.
B—On Saturdays Leigh depart 11.9 p.m., Wigan arrive 11.43 p.m.
B—On December 22nd, 1934, arrive Preston 8.17 p.m.
C—Morecambe (Promenade Station).
c—On Mondays and Saturdays to October 20th, 1934, inclusive, arrives Blackpool (N.) 11.40 a.m.
D—Applies on October 6th, 13th and 20th only.

For train service between Manchester (Vic.) and Wigan (Wallgate), and Manchester (Victoria) and Bolton (Trinity Street), see pages 4 to 9.

E—Thursday, Friday and Sunday mornings only.
f—On Saturdays leaves Leigh 4.38 p.m.
F—West Leigh Station.
F—On Fridays arrives Preston 2.35 p.m., Kendal 4.57 a.m.
H—On Saturdays arrives Blackpool (Cen.) 6.54, Blackpool (N.) 7.21, Morecambe (E. i.d.) 7.28 p.m.
h—On December 21st, 1934 and April 18th, 1935, arr. Preston 5.16 p.m. Kendal 6.38 p.m. and Windermere 7.5 p.m.
J—Morecambe (Prom. Station).

J—Fridays only ... also arrive Blackpool (C.) 4.12 p.m. on Thursday, April 18th, 1935.
P—On Fridays arrives Morecambe (E. Rd.) 4.38 p.m.
r—On Sats. leaves Tyldesley 10.5 p.m. and arrive Leigh 10.10 p.m.
SO—Saturdays excepted.
S—Saturdays only.
Suo—Sunday mornings only.
T—Morecambe (Promenade Station).
Passengers cross from Castle to Green Ayre station, Lancaster at their own expense.

16   17

184

Timetable *c.* 1934

A thin line between the hour and minute figures indicates p.m.

WIGAN (NORTH WESTERN), LEIGH, TYLDESLEY, AND MANCHESTER (EXCHANGE)—BOLTON (GT. MOOR ST.) AND MANCHESTER (EXCHANGE).

(For Bolton (Great Moor Street) and Kenyon service see page 23.)

WEEK DAYS.

Station	Mondays excepted. First and Third Class Sleeping accommodation and Through Carriage from Glasgow.		From Bolton.	Via Kenyon.					
Windermere dep.									
Kendal "									
Morecambe (E. Rd.) "									
Blackpool North "									
Blackpool Central "									
Preston "	4 43							5 35	
Wigan (North Western) dep.	5 25							7 38	
Platt Bridge								7 43	
Hindley Green								7 49	
Howe Bridge			6 15					7 56	
Tyldesley arr. from Wigan			6 20					8 1	
Leigh arr.			6 27					8 15	
Leigh dep.		6 5	Stop	6 28	7 5		7 37	7 50	
Tyldesley arr. from Leigh		6 10			7 10		7 42	7 55	
Tyldesley dep.		6 11			7 12		7 44	8 6	
Ellenbrook for Boothstown		6 15			7 17		7 49	8 11	
Bolton (Gt. M. St.) dep.			6 30			7 25			8 10
Plodder Lane (for F'worth)			6 35			7 30			8 16
Little Hulton			6 39			7 34			8 20
Walkden (Low Level)			6 43			7 37			8 24
Worsley		6 20	6 47		7 22	7 41	7 55	8 17	8 29
Monton Green		6 23	6 50		7 25	7 44	7 59	8 20	8 33
Eccles (For complete service see page 241.)		6 28	6 54	7 6	7 29	7 48		8 24	
Weaste			6 58			7 51			
Seedley			7 0			7 53			
Cross Lane		6 34	7 2	7 11	7 35	7 56		8 30	
Ordsall Lane (for Salf'rd)		6 37	7 5	7 15	7 38	8 0	8 8	8 33	8 43
Manchester (Ex.) arr.	5 53	6 42	7 9	7 19	7 43	8 5	8 13	8 38	8 47

Station	Via Kenyon.						From Bolton.		
Windermere dep.									
Kendal "									7 15
Morecambe (E. Rd.) "						6 55			7 57
Blackpool North "						7 0			7 28
Blackpool Central "						7 28			7 51
Preston "						8 12			8 55
Wigan (North Western) dep.						9 10			9 40
Platt Bridge						9 14			9 45
Hindley Green						9 19			
Howe Bridge						9 23	9 40		
Tyldesley arr. from Wigan						9 27	9 45		
Leigh arr.						9G40	10 5		9 56
Leigh dep.	8 18		8 44	9 10				9 43	9 58
Tyldesley arr. from Leigh			8 49	9 15				9 48	10 3
Tyldesley dep.			8 50	9 16		9 32		9 49	
Ellenbrook for Boothstown			8 54			9 37			
Bolton (Gt. M. St.) dep.		8 25			9 15				
Plodder Lane (for F'worth)		8 30			9 20				
Little Hulton		8 34			9 24				
Walkden (Low Level)		8 37			9 28				
Worsley		8 41	8 59	9 23	9 33	9 42		9 56	
Monton Green		8 44	9 2	9 26	9 36	9 45		9 59	
Eccles		8 47	9 7	9 30	9 39	9 50		10 4	
Weaste		8 51			9 43				
Seedley		8 53			9 45				
Cross Lane	8 44	8 56			9 47			H	
Ordsall Lane (for Salf'rd)		8 58	9 14		9 51				
Manchester (Ex.) arr.	8 50	9 3	9 20	9 39	9 55	9 59		10 14	

Station	Express—Windermere to Manchester (Exchange).	Via Kenyon.	S		S	SO	S		SO
Windermere dep.	8 30						9 30		9 20
Kendal "	8 43						9 50		9 50
Morecambe (E. Rd.) "	8 30						10 5		10 5
Blackpool North "	8 28						9 47		9 47
Blackpool Central "	8 32						10 10		10 20
Preston "	9 40						11 18		11 18
Wigan (North Western) dep.	10 3						11 56		11 56
Platt Bridge									
Hindley Green									
Howe Bridge									
Tyldesley arr. from Wigan									
Leigh arr.							12 11		12 11
Leigh dep.		10F24	10 27	11 5			12 13		12 20
Tyldesley arr. from Leigh			10 32	11 10			12 18		12 25
Tyldesley dep.			10 33	11 11			12 19		12 30
Ellenbrook for Boothstown									12 36
Bolton (Gt. M. St.) dep.					11 30			12 15	
Plodder Lane (for F'worth)					11 35			12 20	
Little Hulton					11 39			12 24	
Walkden (Low Level)					11 42			12 27	
Worsley			10 40	11 18	11 46		12 26	12 31	12 41
Monton Green			10 43	11 21	11 49	12 15	12 29	12 35	12 44
Eccles		10 55	10 47	11 25	11 54	12 18			12 48
Weaste		10 58			11 57	12 21			
Seedley		11 0			11 58	12 23			
Cross Lane					12 0	12 25			
Ordsall Lane (for Salf'rd)					12 4	12 29			
Manchester (Ex.) arr.	10 30	11 7	10 56	11 34	12 9	12 34	12 39		12 56

Station	S	SO	S From Bolton.		SO From Bolton.	SO		S	SO
Windermere dep.									
Kendal "									
Morecambe (E. Rd.) "									
Blackpool North "				11K15					
Blackpool Central "				10 55					
Preston "				12K15					
Wigan (North Western) dep.	12 10	12 20		12 55					
Platt Bridge	12 14	12 24		1 0					
Hindley Green	12 19	12 29		1 6					
Howe Bridge	12 23	12 33	12 50	1 11	1 22				
Tyldesley arr. from Wigan	12 27	12 37	12 55	1 16	1 27				
Leigh arr.	12 40	12 54	Stop.	1 23	2 2				
Leigh dep.			1 7		Stop		1 55		
Tyldesley arr. from Leigh			1 12				2 0		
Tyldesley dep.	12 28	12 38	1 13	1 22			2 1		
Ellenbrook for Boothstown	12 32	12 42		1 27	S		A		
Bolton (Gt. M. St.) dep.					1 25	1 40		2 20	2 20
Plodder Lane (for F'worth)					1 30	1 45		2 25	2 25
Little Hulton					1 34	1 49		2 29	2 29
Walkden (Low Level)					1 37	1 52		2 32	2 32
Worsley	12 38	12 48		1 33	1 41	1 56	2 9	2 36	2 36
Monton Green	12 41	12 51		1 36	1 44	2 0	2 12	2 39	2 39
Eccles	12 46	12 55		1 40	1 49	2 4	2 16	2 44	2 44
Weaste		12 58			1 53	2 9		2 48	
Seedley		1 0			1 55	2 11		2 50	
Cross Lane		1 2			1 57	2 13		2 52	
Ordsall Lane (for Salf'rd)		1 6			2 1	2 16	2S22	2 56	
Manchester (Ex.) arr.	12 55	1 11	1 30	1 49	2 5	2 20	2 27	3 0	

Station		From Bolton.		SO	Through Train—Blackpool (Cen.) to Manchester (Victoria).	SO
Windermere dep.	11 25				12S05	
Kendal "	11 49				12S025	
Morecambe (E. Rd.) "	12 0			12D22	1 48	
Blackpool North "	12 30				1 38	
Blackpool Central "	12f 8			12 50	2 5	
Preston "	1J 9			2 5	2 57	
Wigan (North Western) dep.	2 25			3 12	3 22	
Platt Bridge	2 29			3 16		
Hindley Green	2 34					
Howe Bridge	2 38	3 6				
Tyldesley arr. from Wigan	2 42	3 11				
Leigh arr.	2 51	3a25		3 28		
Leigh dep.	2 28		3 15	3 33		
Tyldesley arr. from Leigh	2 33		3 20	3 38		
Tyldesley dep.	2 43		3 21			
Ellenbrook for Boothstown	2 47		B			
Bolton (Gt. M. St.) dep.						3 27
Plodder Lane (for F'worth)						3 32
Little Hulton						3 36
Walkden (Low Level)						3 39
Worsley	2 52		3 29			3 43
Monton Green	2 55		3 32			3 46
Eccles	2 59		3 36			3 51
Weaste						
Seedley						
Cross Lane						
Ordsall Lane (for Salf'rd)						
Manchester (Ex.) arr.	3 9		3 44		3R50	4 0

WEEKDAYS—continued.

Station	S	SO		SO From Bolton.	SO Via Kenyon.	S	SO Via Kenyon.	SO	
Windermere dep								2 18	
Kendal "								2 37	
Morecambe (E. Rd.) "								3 15	
Blackpool North "								2 50	
Blackpool Central "									
Preston "								4 10	
Wigan (North Western) dep.			4 7					4 55	
Platt Bridge			4 12					4 59	
Hindley Green			4 18					5 4	
Howe Bridge			4 24	4 45				5 8	
Tyldesley arr. from Wigan			4 29	4 50				5 12	
Leigh arr.			4 38	5 13				5 50	
Leigh dep.			4 5	Stop	4 22	4 40	4 46		5 25
Tyldesley arr. from Leigh			4 10			4 45			5 30
Tyldesley dep.			4 31			4 47			5 31
Ellenbrook for Boothstown			4 37	S					5 37
Bolton (Gt. M. St.) dep.	3 32	4 15		4 30					
Plodder Lane for F'worth	3 37	4 20		4 35					
Little Hulton	3 41	4 24		4 39					
Walkden (Low Level)	3 44	4 27		4 42					
Worsley	3 48	4 31	4 42	4 46		4 55			5 42
Monton Green	3 51	4 34	4 45	4 50		4 58			5 45
Eccles (For complete service see page 241.)	3 56	4 39	4 48		5 9	5 2	5 24		5 48
Weaste	4 0		4 52						
Seedley	4 2		4 54						
Cross Lane	4 4		4 57						
Ordsall Lane (for Salford)	4 7		5 1						5 55
Manchester (Ex.) arr.	4 14		5 8		5 20	5 12	5 33		6 1

Station				Express Windermere to Manchester.	SO From Bolton.		Restaurant Car Express from Glasgow & Edinburgh.	SO
Windermere dep		2 18		4 5			5 0	
Kendal "		2 37		4 25			5 19	
Morecambe (E. Rd.) "		3 15		5D5			5 34	
Blackpool North "		2 50		5 10			5S30	
Blackpool Central "		3 10	4S 5				5 27	
Preston "		4 20	5S10	5 57			6 31	
Wigan (North Western) dep.		5 15	5 58	6 20			6 58	7 15
Platt Bridge		5 20	6 2					7 19
Hindley Green			6 7					7 24
Howe Bridge			6 11		6 45			7 28
Tyldesley arr. from Wigan			6 15	6 32	6 50		7 10	7 32
Leigh arr.		5 31		6 46	Stop		7 28	
Leigh dep.		5b40	5 50	6S021		6 49		7 22
Tyldesley arr. from Leigh		5b45	5 57	6S026		6 54		7 27
Tyldesley dep.			6 17	6 34		6 57	7 12	7 35
Ellenbrook for Boothstown			6 21			7 2		7 39
Bolton (Gt. M. St.) dep.	5 45				6 40			
Plodder Lane for F'worth	5 51				6 45			
Little Hulton	5 55				6 49			
Walkden (Low Level)	5 58				6 52			
Worsley	6 3		6 26		6 56	7 7		7 44
Monton Green	6 6		6 29		6 59	7 10		7 47
Eccles	6 10		6 33	6 45	7 3	7 14	7 22	7 51
Weaste	6 13		6S36		7 6	7S017		7 54
Seedley	6 15		6S38		7 8	7S019		7 56
Cross Lane	6 17		6S40					7 58
Ordsall Lane (for Salford)	6 20		6m43		7 12	7d21		8 1
Manchester (Ex.) arr.	6 25		6 48	6 54	7 17	7d26	7 31	8 6

Station	Via Kenyon.		SO	SO		Express from Glasgow and Edinburgh.	SO From Bolton.	
Windermere dep						6X25		
Kendal "						6X47		
Morecambe (E. Rd.) "						7 35		
Blackpool North "						7 45		
Blackpool Central "						7X35		
Preston "		6 50				8 55		
Wigan (North Western) dep.		7 55		8 45		9 20		9 25
Platt Bridge		7 59		8 49				9 30
Hindley Green		8 4		8 54				9 35
Howe Bridge		8 8		8 58			9 21	9 40
Tyldesley arr. from Wigan		8 12		9 2			9 26	9 45
Leigh arr.		8t49		9 20			Stop	10l 2
Leigh dep.	7 30	8 2		Stop	9 10			
Tyldesley arr. from Leigh		8 7			9 15			
Tyldesley dep.		8 13			9 16			9 46
Ellenbrook for Boothstown		8 17			9 20		SO	9 50
Bolton (Gt. M. St.) dep.			8 20	8 55			9 13	
Plodder Lane for F'worth			8 25	9 0			9 18	
Little Hulton			8 29	9 4			9 22	
Walkden (Low Level)			8 32	9 7			9 25	
Worsley		8 22		9 11	9 25		9 29	9 55
Monton Green		8 25		9 14	9 28		9 32	9 58
Eccles	8 0	8 30		9 19	9 33			10 3
Weaste		8 33		9 22				10 6
Seedley		8 35		9 24				
Cross Lane		8 37		9 26				10 9
Ordsall Lane (for Salford)		8 41		9 30				
Manchester (Ex.) arr.	8 10	8 46		9 35	9 42	9 47		10 15

Station	SO	S		SO From Bolton.		SO From Liverpool.	SO
Windermere dep			7 55				
Kendal "			8 12				
Morecambe (E. Rd.) "			8D30				
Blackpool North "			8 40				
Blackpool Central "							
Preston "			9Y30				
Wigan (North Western) dep.			10 22		10 53		11 0
Platt Bridge			10 27		10 58		11 5
Hindley Green					11 4		
Howe Bridge				11 2	11 10		
Tyldesley arr. from Wigan				11 7	11 18		
Leigh arr.			10 40	11 18	11 33		11 16
Leigh dep.			10 43	Stop	Stop	11 9	11 18
Tyldesley arr. from Leigh			10 48			11 14	11 25
Tyldesley dep.			10 49			11 15	
Ellenbrook for Boothstown			10S053	S	SO		
Bolton (Gt. M. St.) dep.	10 0	10 15		11 0	11 0		
Plodder Lane for F'worth	10 5	10 20		11 5	11 5		
Little Hulton	10 9	10 24		11 9	11 9		
Walkden (Low Level)	10 12	10 27		11 12	11 12		
Worsley	10 16	10 31	10 56	11 16	11 16		
Monton Green	10 19	10 34	10 59	11 19	11 19	11 25	
Eccles	10 24	10 38	11 3	11 24		11 30	
Weaste							
Seedley							
Cross Lane							
Ordsall Lane (for Salford)							
Manchester (Ex.) arr.	10 33		11 12	11 33		11 39	

SUNDAYS.

Station	First and Third Class Sleeping accommodation and Through Carriage from Glasgow.	From Liverpool.			From Liverpool		From Liverpool.	Runs on April 19th & 21st, 1935, only. From Liverpool.	From Liverpool.
Windermere dep									
Kendal "									
Morecambe (E. Rd.) "			7D58	1 10					
Blackpool North "			7 10	1 10		5 10			
Blackpool Central "			6 58	12 50		5 20			
Preston "	4 43		8 50	2 15		6 15			
Wigan (North Western) dep.	5 25		9 55	3 0		7 10			
Platt Bridge			9 59	3 4		7 14			
Hindley Green			10 4	3 9		7 19			
Howe Bridge			10 8	3 13		7 23			
Tyldesley arr. from Wigan			10 12	3 17		7 27			
Leigh arr.									
Leigh dep.		8 45			3 55		7 38	9 27	9 56
Tyldesley arr. from Leigh		8 50			4 0		7 43	9 32	10 1
Tyldesley dep.		8 51	10 15	3 19	4 1	7 28	7 44	9 33	10 2
Ellenbrook for Boothstown									
Bolton (Gt. M. St.) dep.									
Plodder Lane for F'worth									
Little Hulton									
Walkden (Low Level)									
Worsley		8 58	10 22	3 26	4 8	7 35	7 51		10 9
Monton Green		9 1	10 25	3 29	4 11	7 38	7 54		10 11
Eccles		9 6	10 30	3 33	4 16	7 43	7 59	9 43	10 16
Weaste									
Seedley									
Cross Lane									
Ordsall Lane (for Salford)									
Manchester (Ex.) arr.	5 53	9 15	10 39	3 42	4 25	7 52	8 8	9 52	10 25

For train service between Wigan (Wallgate) and Manchester (Victoria), and Bolton (Trinity Street) and Manchester (Victoria), see pages 10 to 15.

A—On Saturdays only calls at Ellenbrook at 2.5 p.m.
a—On Saturdays arrives Leigh 4.6 p.m.
B—On Saturdays only calls at Ellenbrook at 3.25 p.m.
b—On Sats. leaves Leigh 5.32 and arrives Tyldesley 5.41 p.m.
D—Morecambe (Prom. Stn.). d—Leaves Ordsall Lane 7.23 p.m. and arrives Manchester 7.28 p.m. on Saturdays.
E—On Saturdays leaves Blackpool (Cen.) 8.0 p.m.
F—West Leigh Station. FO—Fridays only.
f—On Sats. leaves Blackpool (C.) 12.5 p.m.
G—On Sats. arr. Leigh 9.42 a.m.
H—Calls at Cross Lane on Tuesdays to set down, on notice being given to the guard.
J—On Mondays and Saturdays leaves Preston 1.15 p.m.
K—On Saturdays leaves Blackpool (North) 10.45 a.m., Preston 12.5 p.m. l—Arrives Leigh 10.10 p.m. on Sats.
m—On Saturdays leaves Ordsall Lane 6.40 p.m.
R—Manchester (V.). S—Sats. excepted. SO—Sats. only.
T—Calls to set down only. t—Leigh arr. 8.20 p.m. on Sats.
X—On Saturdays leaves Windermere 7.0 p.m., Kendal 7.17 p.m., Blackpool (Cen.) 8.0 p.m.
Y—On Saturdays leaves Preston 9.40 p.m.

18 19

PRINCIPAL OPENING DATES

Bolton & Leigh Railway:
    Opened for goods on 1.8.1828.
    Opened for passengers on 11.6.1831
Liverpool & Manchester Railway:
    Opened for passengers and goods on 15.9.1830.
Kenyon & Leigh Junction Railway:
    Opened for goods on 3.1.1831.
    Opened for passengers on 11.6.1931.
Wigan Branch Railway:
    Opened on 3.9.1832.
London & North Western Railway:
    Eccles-Tyldesley-Wigan (Springs Branch) and Tyldesley-Bedford Leigh-Pennington
    Opened on 1.9.1864.
Pennington South Junction-Bickershaw Junction.
    Opened for goods on 9.3.1885.
Pennington East Junction-Pennington West Junction.
    Opened for goods on 2.6.1903.
Pennington East Junction-Bickershaw Junction.
    Opened for passengers on 1.10.1903.

The Bolton & Leigh, Kenyon & Leigh and Liverpool & Manchester Railways were absorbed by the Grand Junction Railway on 1.7.1845.

The London & North Western Railway was formed on 16.7.1846 with the amalgamation of The Grand Junction, Manchester & Birmingham and London & Birmingham Railways.

The Wigan Branch Railway amalgamated with the Wigan & Preston Railway to become the North Union Railway on 22.5.1834, becoming London & North Western Railway on 26.7.1889.

Whelley Lines, originally Lancashire Union Railway:
    Ince Moss to Haigh Junction.
    Opened for goods on 1.11.1869.
    Ince Moss to Whelley.
    Opened for passengers on 1.1.1872.
    Whelley Junction to Standish Junction.
    Opened on 5.6.1882.
    Amberswood West Junction to Bamfurlong.
    Opened on 25.10.1886.

The Lancashire Union Railway was fully absorbed by the London & North Western Railway on 1.10.1883.

The London & North Western amalgamated with the Lancashire & Yorkshire Railway on 1.1.1922, becoming The London Midland & Scottish Railway on 1.1.1923 and British Railways on 1.1.1948.

Finally, under the Governments 1993 Railways Act the nationalised railway system is in the process of, in a series of franchises, being sold to private enterprise and instead of having one operating authority, British Rail, there are to be twenty-five Train Operating Companies (TOC's). The first of these, "Stagecoach" commenced operations at 02.00 hrs on Sunday 5th February 1996, with services mainly in the South West of England.

British Rail freight companies, namely Loadhaul, Transrail, and Mainline Freight, passed into the hands of American operator Wisconsin Central on the morning of 24th February 1996. Wisconsin had already bought out Rail Express Systems (RES) in 1995.

Freightliner, BR's deep-sea container service was purchased by a management buy-out team in May 1996 leaving Railfreight Distribution as the sole remaining freight business in BR ownership. It is expected to be sold early in 1997.

The infrastructure of the railways, track, signalling and stations under the banner of Railtrack was floated on the London Stock Exchange on 20th May, 1996.

Passenger rolling stock is leased by three Rolling Stock Operating Companies (ROSCO's), namely Eversholt Train Leasing, Porterbrook Leasing and Angel Trains Company, to the TOC's.

Almost as printing began, Stagecoach purchased ROSCO operator Porterbrook in August 1996. Undoubtedly this is a pointer to the future and further takeovers or mergers are certain to follow. Perhaps we will again see the emergence of something akin to the "Big Four" of pre-war years as the wheel again begins to turn full circle.

BIBLIOGRAPHY

A Regional History of the Railways of Great Britain. Vol. X, G. Golt, 1978.
Collieries in the Manchester Coalfields. G. Hayes.
Clinkers Register of Closed Passenger Stations and Goods Depots, 1830-1980.
The Histories of Leigh, Tyldesley and Atherton. Dr. Lunn.
Colliery Railways of Worsley and Salford. F. Walsh, 1978.
Locomotives Illustrated No. 61, The Hunslet Austerity 0-6-0ST. D. Townsley, 1978.
The Industrial Railways of the Wigan Coalfields, Vol. II. Townley, Peden & Smith, 1992.
The History of the Bolton & Leigh Railway 1824-1828. L. Basnett, 1950.
Carbon Magazine, various issues, Leigh Library.
The Leigh Chronicle, various issues, Leigh Library.
The Leigh, Tyldesley & Atherton Journal, various issues, Leigh Library.
The Bolton Chronicle, various issues, Bolton Library.
The Manchester Courier, various issues, Manchester Central Library.
The Industrial Railways of Bolton, Bury and the Manchester Coalfields, Vols. I & II. Townley,
    Peden, Smith & Appleton, 1994-95.

ABBREVIATIONS

BICC	British Insulated Callenders Cables
B&L	Bolton & Leigh Railway
BR	British Railways
CWS	Co-operative Wholesale Society
DMU	Diesel Multiple Unit
FCB	Fireman's Call Box
GC	Great Central Railway
HL	Hawthorn Leslie
HP	Horse Power
K&WVR	Keighley & Worth Valley Railway
K&LJ	Kenyon & Leigh Junction Railway
L&Y	Lancashire & Yorkshire Railway
LUR	Lancashire Union Railway
LDC	Leigh District Council
LLC	Leigh Local Board
LC	Level Crossing
L&M	Liverpool & Manchester Railway
LMS	London Midland & Scottish Railway
LNER	London & North Eastern Railway
L&NW	London & North Western Railway
MSC	Manchester Ship Canal
MGR	Merry-Go-Round
NCB	National Coal Board
NUR	North Union Railway
PW	Permanent Way
ROSCO	Rolling Stock Operating Company
ROF	Royal Ordnance Factory
ST	Saddle Tank
SB	Signal Box
S&T	Signal & Telegraph
TOC	Train Operating Company
WD	War Department
WCML	West Coast Main Line
WJR	Wigan Junction Railway
WW	World War

Plate 237. Ex-Works Class 5 No. 45093 at Exchange with a through freight for Ordsall Lane, from Yorkshire. This is a 1960 shot taken during there building of London Road Station. Un-named Britannia No. 70047, is about to depart from platform 3 with empy stock for Ordsall Lane that had arrived at Exchange on a diverted West of England train. *Photo, J. R. Carter.*